INTRODUCTION
TO
TYPOLOGY

For Ida Mae Heemstra
I tried not to split too many infinitives.

INTRODUCTION TO
TYPOLOGY

THE UNITY AND DIVERSITY OF LANGUAGE

LINDSAY J. WHALEY

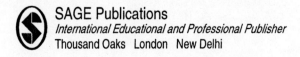

SAGE Publications
International Educational and Professional Publisher
Thousand Oaks London New Delhi

For information address:

 SAGE Publications, Inc.
2455 Teller Road
Thousand Oaks, California 91320
E-mail: order@sagepub.com

SAGE Publications Ltd.
6 Bonhill Street
London EC2A 4PU
United Kingdom

SAGE Publications India Pvt. Ltd.
M-32 Market
Greater Kailash I
New Delhi 110 048 India

Printed in the United States of America

Library of Congress Cataloging-in-Publication Data

Whaley, Lindsay J.
    Introduction to typology: The unity and diversity of language /
    Lindsay J. Whaley.
        p.   cm.
    Includes bibliographical references and index.
    ISBN 0-8039-5962-1 (alk. Paper). — ISBN 0-8039-5963-X (pbk. :
alk. paper)
        1. Typology (Linguistics)   2. Universals (Linguistics)   I. Title.
    P204.W48   1997
    410—dc20   96-35642

97   98   99   00   01   02   03   10   9   8   7   6   5   4   3   2   1

Acquiring Editor: Catherine Rossbach
Editorial Assistant: Kathleen Derby
Production Editor: Astrid Virding
Production Assistant: Karen Wiley
Typesetter/Designer: Christina Hill
Cover Designer: Candice Harman
Indexer: Teri Greenberg

CONTENTS

PART II: Word Order Typology

PART III: Morphological Typology

PART IV: Encoding Relational and Semantic Properties of Nominals

PART V: Verbal Categories

PART VI: Complex Clauses

PREFACE

The idea for this book arose in 1990 when I was coteaching a course titled "Grammar II" at the University of North Dakota. That course was taught to a mixed class of undergraduate and graduate students and was designed to cover the basics of typology, the basics of discourse, and the basics of Relational Grammar, all in the span of 10 weeks. My responsibility lay in the typology portion of the course, for which I was allotted 17 course hours. Needless to say, the constraints on time raised a pedagogical dilemma of a familiar sort: What aspects of the field of typology should be covered and in what depth? Minimally, it seemed to me, a student who is learning about typology should be exposed to the basic goals of the discipline, issues of methodology that have been, and continue to be, debated, and those areas of language that historically have received the greatest amount of attention within typology—holistic typologies based on constituent order and on morphology. Of course, in the hands of a prolix academic, even a cursory introduction to this limited set of topics could easily fill an entire semester, let alone 17 classroom hours, but I felt that to restrict attention to just these subjects would be to fall far short of conveying what typology is all about. In the modern era, at least, typologists have been among the most progressive members of the linguistic community in their desire to explore seemingly exotic aspects of language to discover the linguistic patterns that might be lurking there. Part and parcel to this spirit of discovery has been a desire to present a vision of language that is fully representative of both the unity and the diversity of the world's languages. To capture these aspects of typology, I determined that the course would also need to introduce many of the kinds of constructions that one runs across in human languages, especially those that might exist outside the awareness of the average college student or beginning graduate student.

The introduction to typology that I presented in North Dakota was embedded within a course that also presented a formal grammatical framework, so I felt it important to stress what typology has in common with the sort of syntactic theorizing that has come to dominate the linguistic world, particularly in the United States. I took this tack happily, for I have always found that typology has much to offer to formal grammatical frameworks and vice versa. Unfortunately, the relationship between formal theorists and typologists has been anything but symbiotic through the years.

The problem then became finding a textbook that would reflect the aims of such a course. I discovered that there were none. This fact was certainly not due to a lack of excellent introductory literature on typology. There were, and there remain, three outstanding resources in print for use in a typology class: Comrie (1989), the Shopen (1985) three-volume series, and Croft (1990). The authors of these works have all skillfully detailed certain aspects of typology; none of them, however, cover the full range of topics that I desired to address. As a consequence, I wrote the initial draft of this book, which was used at North Dakota the following year. Still, anyone familiar with these (and other) works on language typology will immediately recognize that I have drawn generous amounts of material from them.

Over the past several years, I have expanded the content of the book considerably so that it is appropriate for use in quarter- or semester-length classes. The end result is an introduction to grammar in a typological perspective that is aimed at undergraduate and beginning graduate students. In the first part, I orient the reader to the basic subject matter of typology: its basic aims, its history, its methods of analysis, and its core assumptions. Then, in Parts II and III, I examine some ways in which languages can be grouped into types in terms of their overall constituent order characteristics and the kinds of morphology that they employ. The final three parts focus on the comparison and classification of particular grammatical constructions rather than languages as wholes.

Although I intend the book to have an overarching unity, I have written individual sections and chapters so that they are largely self-contained. My rationale in doing this was to leave the book in a form in which individual parts could be extracted from the whole or used in a different sequence than they appear in the book. To this end, I have also kept the chapters to a limited length. By doing so, I believe the book is versatile enough to be utilized in a number of different classroom settings and is highly accessible to those using it as a general reference to typology.

With this same attention to ease of use, I have included several typographical and organizational aids in the chapters. In the first occurrence of key terms, they are placed in bold print and generally accompanied by a definition or description. Within each chapter, there is frequent use of section headers; this offers a convenient mechanism for instructors to refer to material in the book, and it assists students in locating material rapidly when reviewing for assignments or exams. Finally, each chapter concludes with a list of new terminology and concepts.

As with any book, many people have contributed significantly to the final form of this textbook. Perhaps more than anyone, Stephen Levinsohn deserves credit for its strengths. I borrowed heavily from a set of notes that he had used in teaching a typology course at the University of North Dakota. He also "field tested" the first draft of the book and provided me with invaluable feedback. Bob Dooley is another Summer Institute of Linguistics linguist who generously contributed his time, data, and ideas to this book.

I count myself as fortunate to have studied with some of the premier typologists and typologically sensitive grammarians in the United States: Joan Bybee, Matthew Dryer, Donna Gerdts, Len Talmy, and Bob Van Valin. Although they may not all be aware of it, their insights fill the pages that follow. In this regard, I should also mention my profound debt of gratitude to Bernard Comrie. The range of his knowledge about language has always amazed me. I cite his work often, not only because the standards of scholarship demand it but because his ideas have influenced me greatly. Martin Haspelmath kindly agreed to read a draft of the book, knowing full well that it was still sketchy in spots and incomplete in others. He caught many inconsistencies, oversights, and a few embarrassing errors. His labors have clearly led to a much better finished project. Finally, three anonymous reviewers provided extensive and helpful critiques on the material in this book. I have incorporated their suggestions where space limitations have allowed it.

Alex Schwartz at Sage Publications has been a pleasure to work with. He has a knack for promoting his vision for linguistic work that is specifically created for classroom use.

Closer to home, my colleagues at Dartmouth, Lenore Grenoble and Bill Scott, created time in their packed schedules to read the chapters that follow.

Whether they were at airports, on trains, in the office, or at home, they somehow managed to peruse the sections of the book I passed on to them. They are consummate teachers, and their criticisms were crucial in improving the style, organization, and content of the book so that it was clearer and better suited to the needs of the reader. Caren Whaley deserves special recognition for her part in assisting in the preparation of the book. She took over even more family responsibilities than usual so that I could dedicate additional time to writing and revising. She also willingly read through the final drafts of the chapters, making substantial suggestions for how the discussion might be made clearer.

Despite all the assistance granted to me by the individuals mentioned above, I am sure that the finished product still falls short of their full approval. They are in no way responsible for any remaining shortcomings.

THE WORLD'S LANGUAGES IN OVERVIEW

The bread and butter of typology is cross-linguistic comparison, so it should come as no surprise that this book contains information and data on a great many languages. No doubt, there will be some languages that are familiar, but probably far more that most readers have never encountered before. For this reason, I offer some basic facts about the languages of the world and the relationships among them. Readers who have had little or no exposure to language classification are encouraged to read this prefatory material. It may provide them with enough of a grounding in the topic to feel more comfortable with my continual reference to lesser-known languages.

Perhaps one of the most common questions that linguists are asked is, how many languages are there? The answer is that no one really knows. This is partly due to the fact that some areas of the globe have not yet been surveyed in a systematic manner to determine the various dialects and languages that are spoken in them. An even bigger obstacle to answering the question about how many languages exist is that there is no consensus on when two varieties of speech are best analyzed as dialects of one another and when they should be taken as separate languages. From a linguistic standpoint, the choice of how to label two speech types has much to do with the degree of intelligibility between them. Thus, it seems patently obvious that the variety of English spoken in Manchester, New Hampshire, and that spoken in Manchester, England, are dialects of a single language. After all, a speaker of one of these dialects can understand nearly everything that the other one says. Likewise, everyone agrees that English and Japanese are not dialects of a single language, but rather two distinct languages, because the degree of mutual intelligibility between them is about zero. These cases are relatively straightforward, but what about those instances in which speakers grasp about 95% of the content of another speech variety? How about 80% or 70%? Where does one draw the line? Situations in which there is imperfect comprehension between members of two speech communities pose an intractable problem for any simple counting of the number of languages in the world.

With these difficulties in mind, it is possible only to provide an estimate of roughly 4,000 to 6,000 languages that are currently in use. There is, of course, no way to know how many additional languages may have been spoken previously but have disappeared without leaving any trace.

Because no individual, no matter how strong their expertise in linguistics, knows about each of these languages, it has become a common practice in Linguistics to provide a genetic identification of a language when it is being described for those who may not be familiar with it. The genetic identity of a language is the language family to which it belongs. A language family is a group of languages or dialects that have arisen from a common ancestor. For example, at some point in the distant past (prior to 1,000 BC), Danish, English, German, Gothic, and Swedish (as well as several others) were not distinct tongues, but rather formed a single language that is commonly referred to as Proto-Germanic. We do not possess any written material from Proto-Germanic. We know a great deal, however, about the sounds of the language and the rules of its grammar because historical linguists have meticulously developed a reconstruction of what the language would have been like. Over time, dialects of Proto-Germanic formed, just as they do with any language. These dialects became more and more differentiated until they were no longer mutually intelligible—that is, they became distinct languages.

The evolution of languages from a shared ancestor is commonly depicted by a family tree. Figure A, for instance, is a family tree for Germanic languages.

The family tree in Figure A captures the genetic affinity between all the languages that are listed by having them all ultimately branch from the node

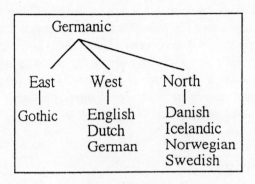

Figure A. The Germanic Languages

labeled "Germanic." The tree also reflects that certain members of the Germanic family are more closely related than others through subgroupings, called branches, such as West Germanic, East Germanic, and North Germanic.

The entire Germanic family is itself nested in a larger family named Indo-European, which includes branches such as Italic (French, Spanish, Portuguese, etc.), Balto-Slavic (Russian, Polish, etc.), and Indic (Hindi, Bengali, etc.) as well as many others. Consequently, one can classify English as West Germanic, Germanic, or Indo-European. All are accurate labels; they simply reflect different degrees of association.

When languages are introduced in this book, I will use labels of genetic relatedness that are roughly equivalent to the level of Germanic. These groupings are largely, although not completely, uncontroversial and can be established quite easily using the conventional tools of historical linguistics. They reflect a time depth (the point at which languages start branching off from the common ancestor) of about 2,500 to 4,000 years. Where my sources for language data did not provide sufficient information to determine an appropriate label of family membership, I relied on Ruhlen (1987).

In addition to furnishing the genetic affilation of a language, I also give the geographic area with which the language is most commonly associated—for example, French (Italic: France). For languages that are no longer spoken, the genetic affiliation is furnished, but there is no geographic data. The identificational information is only provided the first time a language is discussed in a chapter. I have also only included it in cases in which some linguistic feature of the language is exemplified or discussed.

I end this brief overview with a list of the languages that appear in the book. To provide a sense for how the various language families cluster together into larger groups, I have organized this list by language phyla (also called macrofamilies). Some of these phyla are generally accepted (e.g., Indo-European), whereas others are highly controversial (e.g., Altaic and Amerind). The phyla names are in all capital letters, the family names are in italics, and individual language names are in regular type.

INDO-EUROPEAN
   Albanian:
      Albanian
   Armenian:
      Armenian
   Balto-Slavic:
      Bulgarian, Lithuanian, Polish, Rumanian, Russian, Serbian
   Celtic:
      Welsh
   Germanic:
      Danish, German, Swedish
   Hellenic:
      Greek
   Indo-Iranian:
      Bengali, Hindi, Persian, Punjabi
   Italic:
      French, Latin, Spanish
URALIC
   Finno-Ugric:
      Finnish, Hungarian, Komi
NIGER-KORDOFANIAN
   Niger-Congo:
      Akan, Awutu, Bambara, Bamileke, Beembe, Dewoin, Ewe, Kinyarwanda,
      Kirundi, KiVunjo-Chaga, Lobala, Mende, Sesotho, Swahili, Wolof, Yoruba
NILO-SAHARAN
   Nilotic:
      Maasai
   Saharan:
      Kanuri

KHOISAN
  Nama
AFRO-ASIATIC
  Chadic:
  Hausa, Ngizim
  Cushitic:
  Somali
  Semitic:
  Akkadian, Arabic, Hebrew, Tigre, Tigrinya
CAUCASIAN
  South:
  Georgian
  Northwest:
  Abaza, Abkhaz
  Northeast:
  Avar, Tabassaran
ALTAIC
  Japanese-Ryukyuan:
  Japanese
  Korean:
  Korean
  Manchu-Tungusic:
  Even, Evenki, Oroqen
  Mongolian:
  Mongolian
  Turkic:
  Turkish
ESKIMO-ALEUT
  Aleut:
  Aleut
  Eskimo:
  Greenlandic Eskimo, Iñupiaq
ELAMO-DRAVIDIAN
  Dravidian:
  Malayalam, Tamil, Telegu
SINO-TIBETAN
  Sinitic:
  Mandarin Chinese

Tibeto-Burman:
  Burmese, Gurung, Lisu, Manipuri, Tamang, Tangut
AUSTRIC
Miao-Yao:
  Yao
Mon-Khmer:
  Khmer
Munda:
  Mundari
Daic:
  Thai, Yay
Austronesian:
  Achenese, Agutaynen, Chamorro, Enga, Fijian, Futunu-Aniwa, Hawaiian,
  Indonesian, Malagasy, Paamese, Palauan, Tagalog
INDO-PACIFIC
New Guinea:
  Barai, Daga, Dani, Kobon, Taoripi
AUSTRALIAN
Burarran:
  Burera
Kalkatungic:
  Kalkatungu
Karnic:
  Diyari
Pama-Nyungen:
  Dyirbal, Mparntwe Arrernte, Wangkumara, Warlpiri, Yidiny
NA-DENE
Athabaskan:
  Navaho
Tlingit:
  Tlingit
AMERIND
Almosan-Keresiouan:
  Blackfoot, Cayuga, Halkomalem, Kutenai, Lakhota, Nootka, Oneida
Carib:
  Carib, Hixkaryana, Makusi
Chibchan:
  Guaymi

Equatorial-Tucanoan:

Bare, Guarani, Inga, Kaiowa-Guarani, Quechua, Tuyuca, Urubú, Yagua

Ge-Pano:

Cashibo

Hokan:

Atsugewi, Eastern Pomo, Mohave, Seri, Yuma

Oto-Manguean:

Isthmus Zapotec, Otomi, Mixtec

Penutian:

Choctaw, K'ekchi, Miwok, Mixe, Sierra Popoluca, Tepehua, Yokuts

Tanoan:

Southern Tiwa

Uto-Aztecan:

Comanche, Hopi, Kawaiisu, Michoacan Nahuatl, 'O'odham, Shoshone

ISOLATES/UNKNOWN

Burushaski

Illyrian (unclassified)

CREOLES/PIDGINS

Melanesian Pidgin, Papiamentu

ABBREVIATIONS

Abbreviation	Explanation	Abbreviation	Explanation
1	First person	AUX	Auxiliary
1D	First-person dual	BEN	Benefactive
1P	First-person plural	C1, C2	Noun Class 1, Class 2,
1S	First-person singular		and so on
2	Second person	CAUS	Causative
2D	Second-person dual	CLASS	Classifier
2P	Second-person plural	CM	Case marker
2S	Second-person singular	CMPLT	Completive
3	Third person	COM	Comitative
3P	Third-person plural	COMP	Complementizer
3S	Third-person singular	CONTR	Contrastive
ABL	Ablative	D	Dual
ABS	Absolutive	DAT	Dative
ACC	Accusative	DECL	Declarative
ACT	Active	DEF	Definite
ADJ	Adjective	DEM	Demonstrative
AFFIRM	Affirmative	DET	Determiner
AGR	Agreement	DIR	Directional
AGT	Agent	DO	Direct object
ANIM	Animate	DPST	Distant past
ANT	Anterior	DS	Different subject
AOR	Aorist	ERG	Ergative
APPL	Applicative	EXCL	Exclusive
ART	Article	FACT	Factive
ASP	Aspect	FEM	Feminine
ATTN	Attention	FOC	Focus

Abbreviation	Explanation	Abbreviation	Explanation
FUT	Future	PART	Participle
GEN	Genitive	PASS	Passive
HAB	Habitual	PAT	Patient
HUM	Human	PERF	Perfect(ive)
HYP	Hypothetical	PFV	Perfective
IMPF	Imperfect	PNoun	Proper noun
INCH	Inchoative	POSS	Possessive
INCL	Inclusive	POT	Potential
IND	Indicative	PRES	Present
INF	Infinitive	PROG	Progressive
INST	Instrument(al)	PROHIB	Prohibitive
INTER	Interrogative	PROP	Propriative
INV	Inverse	PST	Past
IRR	Irrealis	PTL	Particle
LOC	Locative	QUES	Question word
MOD	Modalis case	RCP	Reciprocal
MSC	Masculine	REAL	Realis
NEG	Negative	REL	Relativizer/relative pronoun
NEUT	Neuter	S-O REV	Subject-object reversal
NOM	Nominative	SBJV	Subjunctive
NOML	Nominalizer	SEQ	Sequential
nonFUT	Nonfuture	SS	Same subject
nonPST	Nonpast	STAT	Stative
NPOSSD	Nonpossessed	SUB	Subject
OBJ	Object	TM	Tense marker
OBL	Oblique	TNS	Tense
OBV	Obviative	TOP	Topic
OH	Object higher	TRANS	Transitive
OPT	Optative	VOL	Volitional
P	Plural		

Basics of Language Typology

1

Introduction to Typology and Universals

What is language? On the face of it, the question seems simple. After all, language is so much a part of our everyday experience, so effortlessly employed to meet our impulses to communicate with one another, that it cannot be too intricate a task to figure out how it works. Hidden below the surface of the "what is language" question, however, is a web of mysteries that have taxed great minds from the beginning of recorded history. Plato, Lucretius, Descartes, Rousseau, Darwin, Wittgenstein, and Skinner, to name just a few, have all probed into some aspect of the human capacity for speech, yet none of them were able to explain the origin of language, why languages differ, how they are learned, how they relay meaning, or why they are the way they are and not some other way. Language largely remains an enigma that awaits further exploration.

This is not to say that we have learned nothing or know nothing about our ability to utter meaningful sequences of sound. Centuries of careful observation and experimentation on language have revealed some extraordinary insights into its fundamental properties, some of them quite surprising. Perhaps most significant, language has no analogs in the animal kingdom. Nothing remotely similar to language has been discovered in the vast array of communication systems utilized by the fauna of our planet. Language, it seems, is uniquely human, a fact summarized well by Bertrand Russell (1948) when he exclaimed, "A dog cannot relate his autobiography; however eloquently he may bark, he cannot tell you that his parents were honest though poor."

In addition to the species-specific quality of language, a second basic notion about language might be highlighted that has become foundational for modern linguistics: There is a basic unity that underlies the awesome diversity of the world's languages. Whether it be Apache or Zulu or Hindi or Hebrew, there are certain core properties that languages have in common. These properties, often referred to as **language universals,** allow us to say that all languages are, in some sense, the same.

This is, in many ways, an astonishing claim, especially when confronted by the immense variety in the structures of the world's languages. Consider the following sentences, the first from Lobala (Niger-Congo: Zaire) and the second from Hixkaryana (Carib: Brazil).[1]

(1) a. moto   me   t-a-iká   mo-phé   ná   baphalnágá   ná   ntóma
        man   DEM   NEG-3S-PST   C1-give and money   and food
        The man didn't give him either money or food.

                                                        (Data from Morgan 1994, 133)

     b. apaytara   y-ari-hira   nexe-ye   wekoko
        chicken   3S/3S-take-NEG   be-DPST   hawk
        The hawk didn't take the chicken.

                                                    (Data from Derbyshire 1985, 138)

Despite the fact that the two sentences in (1) are both simple negative clauses, they appear to have little in common with each other or with the equivalent

English sentences. For instance, the order of words varies: The subject of the Lobala example, *moto me* ("the man") occurs at the beginning of the sentence, whereas the Hixkaryana subject *wekoko* ("hawk") is located at the end. The negation in Lobala is indicated by an auxiliary verb *t-*, but in Hixkaryana there is a negative suffix (*-hira*) on the main verb, *-ari-* ("take"). Both languages exhibit verb agreement, but in Lobala the agreement suffix (*-a*) is found on the negative auxiliary, and it only reveals information about the subject (namely, that the subject is third-person singular). In Hixkaryana, the agreement marker is a prefix (*y-*) rather than a suffix. Furthermore, it is located on the main verb, and it reveals information about both the subject and the object (namely, that both are third-person singular). With regard to these, and many other, differences, the concept of "language universals" may seem hard to accept. Nevertheless, most linguists would claim that there is an underlying homogeneity to language that is far more striking than differences like those just described. Discovering instances of this homogeneity and determining why it exists constitutes one of the major research goals of modern linguistics in general and typology specifically. It also represents the primary concern of this book.

The consensus in linguistics about the underlying unity of language is not paralleled by agreement over how the unity is to be explained or, even more fundamentally, what even constitutes an explanation for the unity. On this point, there are profound philosophical and methodological differences. For example, Noam Chomsky, perhaps the most significant figure in modern linguistics,[2] has argued that the unity is due to human biology. In his view, all humans are genetically endowed with a "language faculty," which is distinct from other cognitive capacities. As children are exposed to the particular language (or languages) of their speech communities, this language faculty directs them in the rapid acquisition of a complex and mature grammatical system. To accomplish this, the language faculty must contain enough information (called **Universal Grammar**) to ensure that the child can learn a language accurately and learn it in the space of just 4 or 5 years. On the other hand, the innate language faculty must be flexible enough to give rise to the diverse array of structures that we actually find in the world's languages.

Chomsky has appealed to an extraterrestrial authority on several occasions (e.g., Chomsky 1988, 1991) to drive this point home. Chomsky (1991) suggests that a Martian scientist who visited Earth would reach the following conclusion about a human's inborn capacity for language:

Surely if some Martian creature, endowed with our capacities for scientific
inquiry and theory construction but knowing nothing of humans, were to
observe what happens to a child in a particular language community, its initial
hypothesis would be that the language of that community is built-in, as a
genetically-determined property, in essentials . . . . And it seems that this
initial hypothesis may be very close to true. (26)

In contrast to Chomsky, other linguists have argued that the unity that
underlies languages is better explained in terms of how languages are actually
put to use. To be sure, languages are all employed for like purposes: asking
questions, scolding bad behavior, amusing friends, making comparisons,
uttering facts and falsehoods, and so on. Because languages exist to fulfill
these types of functions, it stands to reason that speakers will develop
grammars that are highly effective in carrying them out. Consequently, under
the pressure of the same communicative tasks, languages evolve such that
they exhibit grammatical similarities. Language universals, under this "functional" perspective, result from commonalities in the way language is put to
work. Closely allied with this view is the proposal that common experiences
among humans can account for certain universals in language structure. Lee
(1988) articulates this view well:

Despite the fact that I come into contact with quite a different set of objects
than a Kalahari bushman, the possible divergence between our experiences
in the world is circumscribed by a number of factors independent of us both,
and even of our speech communities as a whole. For example, we can both
feel the effects of gravity and enjoy the benefits of stereoscopic vision. These
shared experiences exert a force on the languages of all cultures, giving rise
to linguistic universals. (211-12)

Which explanation for the similarities between languages is right? In all
likelihood, the unity of language, and consequent language universals, arises
from a slate of interacting factors, some innate, others functional, and still
others cognitive, experiential, social, or historical. What this means in practical terms is that there are a number of legitimate ways to approach the
question, "What is language?" This book examines the nature of language
from a "typological" approach. In the following section, a better sense for
what this means is developed.

1.0. Defining "Typology"

What exactly is meant by typology in the context of linguistics? In its most general sense, **typology** is

(2) The classification of languages or components of languages based on shared formal characteristics.

As a point of departure, it is important to note that typology is not a theory of grammar.[3] Unlike Government and Binding Theory, Functional Grammar, Cognitive Grammar, Relational Grammar, or the many other frameworks that are designed to model how language works, typology has the goal of identifying cross-linguistic patterns and correlations between these patterns. For this reason, the methodology and results of typological research are in principle compatible with any grammatical theory. The relationship between typology and theories of grammar is further explored later in this chapter and in Chapter 3.

Having described something that typology is not, we now must come to understand what it is. There are three significant propositions packed into the dense definition in (2): (a) Typology utilizes cross-linguistic comparison, (b) typology classifies languages or aspects of languages, and (c) typology examines formal features of languages. These parts of the definition will be examined one at a time with an eye to better understanding what is involved in performing language typology.

Proposition 1: Typology involves cross-linguistic comparison.

Ultimately, all typological research is based on comparisons between languages. Consider the following data:

(3) a. I met *the man* **who taught you French.**
   b. *The dog* **which licked Cora** has become her friend.
   c. I sent the story to *the newspaper* **that your mother owns.**

From these sentences, we could form the generalization that English relative clauses (in bold type) follow the nouns that they modify (in italics). This description is of import to someone investigating English, but it is incomplete as a typological claim because it is not grounded in a cross-linguistic perspective. Instead, in a typological approach we expect to find a description such as "English is typical in placing relative clauses after the nouns which they modify." Note that to employ a term such as "typical" properly, one must first have gathered data on relative clauses from a representative sample of the world's languages. Compiling an adequate sample remains one of the central methodological issues in typological research, an issue to which we return in Chapter 3.

> *Proposition 2:* A typological approach involves classification of either (a)
> components of languages or (b) languages.

In the first case—classification of components of language—attention is directed toward a particular construction that arises in language—for example, reflexive verbs, oral stops, or discourse particles. Then, using cross-linguistic data, all the types of these specific phenomena are determined. The goal is to better comprehend how this facet of language operates by identifying the degrees of similarity and the degrees of variance that one finds among languages. There is also keen interest in determining whether there are correlations between the various patterns that one finds in a language.

For instance, we might do a typological investigation on oral plosive sounds.[4] These are sounds, also called "stops," that are produced when the airstream is completely impeded in the vocal tract, as in English [p] and [g]. If we were to examine the distribution of oral stops in the world's languages, we would immediately be struck by the fact that all languages have at least one plosive sound. Thus, we would have discovered a universal about sound systems in human language. It is important to realize that this fact is not a logical requisite for language because we can easily conceive of a language that does not have any oral plosives. Therefore, our empirical discovery that all languages have at least one stop leads to an ontological question: Why should language be structured in this way? I return to the problem of explanation presently, but first let us determine what other sorts of facts about stops we would learn from our typological investigation.

There are over 50 distinct oral stops that occur in language, but individual languages utilize only a small proportion of this universal set, with languages such as Punjabi (Indo-Iranian: India, Pakistan), which has 24 plosives, being highly exceptional in how many plosives it contains (Gill and Gleason 1963). As we continued our investigation, we would further discover that plosive sounds are not equally distributed in the languages of the world. Some are extremely common, such as [p], [t], and [k]. In fact, nearly all languages have at least one of them. In contrast, some plosives are relatively rare, such as the voiced uvular stop [G], which is found, for example, in Somali (Cushitic: Somalia). We now might notice certain intriguing facts about our emerging typology of plosives such as "unexpected" gaps. For instance, plosives created by bringing the lower teeth into contact with the upper lip are nonexistent, even though they are physically possible to articulate. Finally, we might identify certain stops as being "dominant"—for example, the voiceless alveolar stop [t] appears to be an especially dominant plosive sound because, if a language has only two voiceless stops, one of them is bound to be [t].

From this simple typological study we have learned a host of important facts about sound systems. Not all these facts are of the same sort. For example, some were absolute universals (e.g., all languages have at least one stop); some were universal tendencies (e.g., almost all languages have [p], [t], or [k]); and some were implicational universals (e.g., if a language has two voiceless stops, then one is a [t]). Implicational universals have played a particularly prominent role in typology because they commonly suggest connections between two or more aspects of language. We discuss the differences between these types of universals in Chapter 3.

Having ascertained some universals about stops, the next task is to provide an explanation for them. After all, the ultimate goal is to understand why language is the way it is. For present purposes, attention is restricted to one of the facts provided previously—that [p], [t], and [k] are extremely common in the languages of the world. In dealing with sounds, simple facts about human speech anatomy are generally a good place to begin when seeking an account for universals. Keating, Linker, and Huffman (1983) have proposed that [p], [t], and [k] are so widespread because they are aerodynamically efficient and they require less effort to produce than other stop sounds. Then, assuming that there is a tendency for "efficient" sounds to be incorporated into languages, we now have a reasonable account for the commonness of [p], [t], and [k].

The simplicity of our account thus far is a bit misleading. There are many further complexities that enter into a comprehensive explanation for the frequency of [p], [t], and [k] in language. First, note that the "efficiency" of sounds cannot be the sole factor involved in the evolution of sound systems. If it were, then the existence of sounds such as [G] in Somali, which are not particularly efficient aerodynamically, would be completely inexplicable.

Therefore, the assumption that efficient sounds tend to arise in language must be tempered with a proposal about how inefficient sounds get into phonological systems in the first place.

The explanation for common plosive sounds falls short in another way: We have not indicated how it is that efficient sounds are "incorporated" into languages. After all, a community of speakers does not consciously determine which sounds they will use in their language. Rather, new sounds gradually develop from existing sounds over time, the whole process being largely imperceptible to individual speakers. When we make a statement such as "efficient sounds tend to be incorporated into languages," we are using a sort of convenient shorthand. In a full exposition, we also want to indicate the set of mechanisms through which efficient sounds enter a language.

For simplicity's sake, I will not attempt to remedy the deficiencies with the original account of common plosive sounds. To do so would require a detailed discussion that does not directly relate to the purposes of this chapter. Nonetheless, it is important to keep in mind that simple statements that purport to explain language universals are usually intended as highly generalized accounts of the phenomena being investigated. As such, they are just the beginning of a satisfactory explanation.

The modest typological study just described focused on a single feature of language. The aim was not so much to classify languages as to understand some basic facts about phonology. A second kind of typological classification has the goal of classifying entire languages into categories based on shared properties. For instance, in the investigation of oral plosives we would instantly have found that different languages have different numbers of stops. We could take a sample of languages—for example, two languages from each of the major language families[5]—and divide them into types based on the number of oral stops that exist in their phonological inventories (Table 1.1).

The left-hand column of Table 1.1 indicates the number of oral stop sounds found in the language. The middle column furnishes the name(s) of the language(s) that possesses this number of stops. The right-hand column reflects the total number of languages that have a given stop inventory.

From Table 1.1, one can get a sense for the most common types of languages in terms of the number of oral stops (38% of our sample has between 6 and 8 oral stops) as well as the rarest (e.g., languages with over 14 stops). Furthermore, we begin to see the overall range of oral stop inventories in language (between 3 and 17).

TABLE 1.1 Number of Oral Stops in Languages[a]

Number of Stops	Language	Total
3	Taoripi (IP)	1
4	Burera (Australian), Nama (Khoisan)	2
5	Beembe (NK), Dani (IP)	2
6	Evenki (UA), Greek (IE), Hopi (NAm), Mandarin (ST), Tagalog (AT)	5
7	Carib (SAm), Hebrew (AfA), Kanuri (NS), Maasai (NS)	4
8	Diyari (Australian)	1
9	Finnish (UA), Khmer (AuA), Thai (AT)	3
10	Hausa (AfA), Wolof (NK)	2
11		
12	Quechua (SAm)	1
13	Tlingit (NAm), Yao (ST)	2
14		
15	Telegu (Dravidian)	1
16	Bengali (IE)	1
17	Mundari (AuA)	1

a. AfA, Afro-Asiatic; AT, Austro-Tai; AuA, Austro-Asiatic; IE, Indo-European; IP, Indo-Pacific; NAm, Northern Amerind; NK, Niger-Kordofanian; NS, Nilo-Saharan; SAm, Southern Amerind; ST, Sino-Tibetan; UA, Ural-Altaic.

To keep this example simple, it is necessary to ignore a host of potential problems surrounding the database of 26 languages. (The difficulties in developing an adequate database are described in Chapter 3). Therefore, the conclusions drawn from the study are purely impressionistic. We need to implement a much more rigorous study to confirm them.

Proposition 3: Typology is concerned with classification based on formal features of language.

There are many conceivable ways that one can talk about relationships between languages. For instance, languages can be placed into classes on the basis of their genetic relationships. Were this our concern, we would group together all languages that demonstrably have a common origin. In doing so, we would produce a set of "language families": Indo-European, Afro-Asiatic, Manchu-Tungus (as in Figure 1.1), and so on.

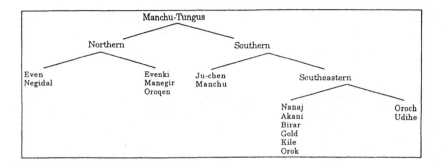

Figure 1.1. Manchu-Tungus Languages

In other circumstances we might choose to classify languages by their geographic location. We might then talk about Australian languages or the languages spoken in Northwestern Nigeria (Table 1.2).

In still other cases, we might classify languages in terms of demographic features—for example, languages with over 100 million speakers (Table 1.3).

Of course, all these methods of classification are useful devices for a particular goal. Their potential significance should be quite clear. They are not typology, however. Typologists, in contrast, classify languages in terms of the forms out of which a language is composed—its sounds, morphemes, syntax, or discourse structure.

This is not to say that these other kinds of classification are entirely unrelated to typology. The strong association between typological and genetic classification is most obvious. It is no surprise that Spanish (Italic: Spain and Latin America) and French (Italic: France) both have articles that reveal gender or that they both have subject agreement marked on verbs because we know that both languages have inherited these traits from Latin (Italic). The typological similarity of the two languages is a function of their genetic association.

The relationship between typology and areal classification is less well understood. To what extent the structure of one language can be affected by the languages around it is an area of intense current research. There is plenty of evidence, however, to demonstrate that grammars are flexible enough to adopt some features of other languages that are close to them spatially. One well-known instance of a group of languages that share grammatical features

TABLE 1.2 Languages of Northwestern Nigeria

Asu	Gurmana	Lela	Shama
Baangi	Gwamhi	Lopa	Shanga
Baatonun	Hausa	Madaka	Sorko
Basa	Hugworo	Nupe	Tiyal
Busa	Hun-Saare	Pongu	Wayam Rubu
Cinda	Kag	Regi	Zarma
Dendi	Kambari	Reshe	
Fungwa	Koromba	Sagamuk	
Gbagyi	Laru	Sambuga	

TABLE 1.3 Languages With Over 100 Million Speakers

Language	No. of Speakers (in Millions)
Mandarin	907
English	456
Hindi	383
Spanish	362
Russian	293
Arabic	208
Bengali	189
Portuguese	177
Indonesian	148
Japanese	126
French	123
German	119

because of their geographic proximity is found in the Balkans. In this region (often referred to as a **Sprachbund**), one encounters among other languages Albanian (Albanian: Albania), Bulgarian (Balto-Slavic: Bulgaria), and Rumanian (Balto-Slavic: Romania), all of which come from different subfamilies of Indo-European. Certain linguistic patterns permeate the languages in this area despite their different genetic affiliations. For example, many of them have definiteness marked by a suffix on the noun:

(4) Albanian   mik-u   "friend-the"

   Bulgarian   trup-at   "body-the"

   Rumanian   om-ul   "man-the"

(Data from Bynon 1977)

What is amazing about this particular example is that the use of suffixes to mark definiteness is not a trait of any of the language branches from which the languages come. Indeed, the origin of this formal trait is still somewhat of a mystery. What is crucial for present purposes, however, is that, from a genetic standpoint, none of these languages are expected to employ this morphological strategy. The fact that they share it can only be due to their geographical connection.

This type of linguistic similarity between languages of different genetic stock is particularly common in speech communities where two or more languages coexist and there is a high degree of multilingualism; in such cases, it is well attested that parts of the grammar of one language can be adopted by another (see Myers-Scotton 1993).

Therefore, although typological classification is a different sort of procedure than are genetic, geographic, and demographic classifications, it must be recognized that the typological characteristics of languages can be greatly influenced by these other factors.

One final point about typology's focus on the formal features of language requires comment. "Formal features" are the chunks of information that one finds in language, its phrases, sentences, and so on. These features are, of course, used to convey meaning. Consequently, typologists have always been concerned with semantic categories, such as "tense," "agent," or "gender," and how these categories are manifested by the formal units of language. Therefore, the emphasis on formal features in the definition of typology given previously should not be taken to exclude semantic considerations.

2.0. Summary

Breaking down the definition of typology into three parts has helped to clarify what is involved in exploring language from a typological perspective. Before we move on to the next chapters, one reminder is needed: Typology is more than mere taxonomy (listing)—what we find in a typological analysis should have implications for our question, "What is language?" To get to the heart of this question requires one to seek explanations for typological patterns. It is not enough to say "labiodental stops do not exist" or "relative clauses typically follow the noun which they modify." We must seek a plausible explanation for why these things are so. This type of "why" question, however, often forces us to go beyond grammar itself for an answer. We commonly must enter other "extragrammatical" domains: discourse, pragmatics, physiology, cognition, speech processing, language contact, social influences, and so on.

A reliance on extragrammatical explanation closely aligns typology with functional approaches to language, which are also based on the premise that language structure cannot be properly understood without reference to its communicative functions. Even so, formal linguistic theories which have traditionally eschewed explanations based on extragrammatical factors, are increasingly integrating typological research as well (Kayne 1994 and Fukui 1995 are representative examples). I return to this topic in Chapter 3.

Typology has also enjoyed some prominence in the area of historical linguistics. When linguists attempt to reconstruct languages that no longer exist and for which there is no written record, they are essentially involved in making a series of "educated guesses" about what these languages looked like. The principles and methods of historical linguistics provide the tools necessary to do reliable reconstructive work. Typological findings are one of these tools. Recalling the previous discussion on oral stops, any reconstruction of a phonological system that posited an inventory with only the two voiceless plosives [p] and [k] would immediately be suspect because it is a violation of the implicational universal, "if a language has two voiceless stops, then one of them is [t]."

Perhaps most important, typology is extremely useful as a tool in linguistic fieldwork. Most linguists never have the opportunity to organize large samples of languages to test for universals, nor do they ever propose completely new grammatical theories. All linguists, however, do research on individual languages. How is typology useful in this endeavor? First, it aides in learning about languages that previously have not been documented by making the linguist aware of what is "out there" and what is "typical." Many phenomena that might seem quite exotic in comparison to one's native language may actually be typologically common. Such phenomena are not likely to cause confusion or frustration for the field-worker familiar with typology. This is not only true for typological claims about language in general but also with analyses of typological characteristics of individual language groups. Today, the vast majority of fieldwork is carried out with languages in language families about which a fair amount is known. Becoming an expert on the typical characteristics of a given family before arriving on the field is vital.

In the same vein, if linguists know what is common in language, they will be quick to recognize unexpected patterns in the language(s) being examined. The recognition of these unusual data leads to the search for explanations, which in turn can reveal important details of the language history, contact with other people groups, or other features of the grammatical system. In an extreme case, the aberrant construction may ultimately prove to be something that typologists have thought not to exist. The linguist who knows the claims that have been made about language universals can grasp the significance of such a discovery and pass it on to the field as a whole. This is precisely what happened with Des Derbyshire's work with Amazonian languages. Languages that ordered direct objects before both verbs and subjects (see (1b)) were not thought to exist until Hixkaryana data proved otherwise (Derbyshire 1977; Derbyshire and Pullum 1981).

Finally, a knowledge of typology provides access to a major corpus of linguistic literature. To be able to use this research correctly, one must have a good background in the terminology and methodology of the discipline.

3.0. Key Terms

Language universals	Typology
Sprachbund	Universal Grammar

Notes

1. A key to the abbreviations used in the morpheme-by-morpheme glosses may be found at the beginning of the book. Because the data are drawn from a variety of traditions, all with their own terminology, I have taken the liberty of unifying the glosses in many instances and simplifying them in others. Throughout the book, language names are followed by an indication of genetic affiliation (i.e., the language family to which the language belongs) and the location of the largest concentration of native speakers or the area with which the language is commonly associated. The classification and geographic information appears only with the first mention of the language in a chapter. For details on the genetic affiliations I have ascribed to the languages see "The World's Languages in Overview".

2. This terse description does not do Chomsky's name full justice. In a very real sense, Chomsky has directed the course of linguistics, especially in North America, for the past 30 years.

In addition, he has had a major influence on political thinking, psychology, and the philosophy of language. See Lyons (1991) and Salkie (1990) for overviews of Chomsky's impact on the intellectual community.

3. Croft (1990, 2-3) points out that the term *typology* is often used to denote a perspective on language that is unique from that which undergirds grammatical frameworks such as Government and Binding Theory, and in this way typology might be considered a theory of grammar.

4. Data to support the generalizations about oral stops can be found in Maddieson (1984).

5. The seemingly innocuous decision to draw two languages from each of the major language families is, in fact, highly problematic because there is little consensus on how many major language families there are or on the internal constitution of these families. For convenience, I have employed the genetic classification used by Maddieson (1984) because the data are also taken from this source.

2

A (Brief) History of Typology

Broadly speaking, typology has a twofold purpose: to identify universals and to establish the potential range of variation among languages. These research aims first arose in linguistics back in the 1800s, particularly in the work of two German linguists, Friedrich von Schlegel and Wilhelm von Humboldt (Ramat 1995). Unlike contemporary typologists, they were interested almost exclusively in morphology. By examining the processes of word formation that occur in language, they developed a scheme to categorize languages on the basis of how much morphology was used in the construction of a word and how this morphology was used. Although contemporary linguistics still uses some of the terminology they developed in their investigations, modern typology has little in common with the research of these pioneers. The assumptions, methods, and focus of current typological research have all changed dramatically.

Understanding the transitions from early typology to the present day conveniently highlights certain central assumptions that underlie the analyses presented in this book and deepens our awareness of what typology is all about. Therefore, in this chapter, I investigate the changes that have occurred in typology during the past 100 years and have given rise to modern typological analysis.[1]

1.0. Early Typologists

No scholarly work occurs outside of a certain worldview. Today, for example, more and more research in linguistics begins with the belief that language (and all other mental activity) is explicable in purely physical terms. Under this view, which would have been incomprehensible for a good share of human history and laughable for most of the rest, the production and comprehension of sentences is ultimately nothing more than the firing of neurons. The neurons themselves are subject to the same physical laws that account for planetary motion, the properties of light, and reproduction.

The work of Schlegel, Humboldt, and their contemporaries was carried out under different presuppositions. Most significant for typology, they believed language to have an abstract organic unity. That is, the formal aspects of language (its sounds, morphemes, grammar, and the like) and the changes that happened to these forms over time were not random or arbitrary because they all were reflections of an inner character. Like any organism, a language could develop over time, but it would always have the same essence. They believed Chinese, English, Kiowa, and Yoruba, as well as any other language, differed because the inner character of the people, the fundamental spirit of their culture, which gave rise to the languages, was not the same.

Such a notion is difficult to grasp because it is far removed from the current conception of language, but it is not nearly as "strange" as one might think. If we move to a different sphere of human activity—for example, economics—we find that the dominant metaphors of today reflect a conception of an organic entity. Hence, certain behaviors such as fluctuations in the stock market indicate something about the "health" of our economy. It might be described as "shrinking" or "growing" (ideally the latter!). Not only do our metaphors depict the economy as a living being but we also treat it as a being that has power. It causes people to lose their jobs, to save or spend money, to invest, to go broke, etc. We, of course, must be careful not to push the analogy between the Humboldtian view of language and our view of the economy too far. The point is only to demonstrate that it is, in fact, not so "weird" to attribute coherence and life to abstract notions.

Perhaps because morphological differences between languages are so striking, it was this realm of grammar that was presumed to best mirror the organic essence behind languages. The basic distinction, due to Schlegel and his brother, was among **affixal** (1a), **inflectional** (1b), and **no structure** (1c) languages.

(1) a. *Affixal:* Kirundi (Niger-Congo: Burundi)
         Y-a-bi-gur-i-ye   abâna
         C1-PST-C8.them-buy-APPL-ASP   C2.children
         He bought them for the children.   (Adapted from Sabimana 1986)
     b. *Inflectional:* Attic Greek (Hellenic: Greece)
         hoi   stratiōtai   ēgoradz-on   ta   epitēdeia
         the   soldiers   buy-3P:IMPF:ACT:IND   the   provisions
         The soldiers were buying the provisions.   (Xenophon, *Anabasis* 1.5.10)
     c. *No structure:* Mandarin Chinese (Sinitic: China)
         wǒ   mǎi   le   shuǐguǒ   le
         I   buy   ASP   fruit   PTL
         I have bought the fruit.   (Adapted from Li and Thompson 1981)

Kirundi (1a) is representative of an affixal language in that it permits a series of morphemes to be affixed to a lexical head (i.e., a verb, noun, or adjective). Consider the verb, *yabiguriye*. There are three prefixes: *y-*, which indicates that the subject of the verb belongs to noun class 1; the past tense marker *a-*; and *bi-*, a morpheme that denotes a direct object belonging to noun class 8. In addition, there are two suffixes. The applicative morpheme, *-i,* being used here to identify the noun *abâna* (children) as the beneficiary of the act of buying, and *-ye,* which is an aspect marker (the concept of **aspect** is discussed in Chapter 8).

Inflectional languages, like Greek (1b), also evince affixation, but the affixes that are employed typically contain a great deal of semantic information. For example, the suffix *-on* reveals that the subject is third person (i.e., refers to someone other than the speaker or listener), that the subject is plural, that the verb is past tense and has a durative aspect, and that the sentence is a statement of fact rather than a command or a condition. In inflectional languages, all this meaning is fused into a single affix, unlike affixal languages which tend to employ affixes that provide one piece of information each.

In no structure languages, as the name suggests, little affixation is used at all. Note that Mandarin Chinese (1c), which is commonly used as the quintessential example of a no structure language, has no verb agreement with the subject and that aspect marking, when it occurs at all, arises as a separate particle rather than a verbal affix.

Because language was thought to be unified, morphological classification such as that discussed here was thought to serve as a handy means of categorizing languages in their entirety. An examination of the syntax, for instance, would ultimately reveal the same inner character of the language as the morphology and, consequently, there was little reason to study it. This assumption permitted a benign neglect of syntax in typology that was not corrected for roughly a century.[2]

Like linguists today, Humboldt assumed that language had an unseverable association with the human mind. In fact, he believed that universals of language were manifestations of universals present in human thought (Brown 1967). Unlike modern linguists, however, Humboldt (1971) also thought that differences among languages reflected basic differences in the mental life of various speech communities:

> Languages must have evolved along with the flourishing tribes from
> the respective intellectual peculiarities of the latter, which imposed
> numerous restrictions on them. . . . Languages are depicted as bound to,
> and dependent on, the nations to which they pertain. (2)

Even more removed from current perspectives on language, there was also a clear evaluative component to Humboldt's brand of typology. The quality of languages, he thought, could be determined by how closely they resembled an idealized linguistic system. Quite to the contrary, it is the consensus in modern linguistics that there is no qualitative difference between languages—no "better" or "worse."

Because Humboldt also held that language structure was revelatory of intellectual capacity, his linguistic philosophy could easily be manipulated into claims of cultural superiority using the following logic:[3] Because German more closely matches the structure of the perfect language than Chinese, it is superior to Chinese. Also, because language structure derives from intellectual prowess, it follows that German thought is superior to Chinese thought. Having rejected both the assumption that languages can be judged against an ideal and the claim that variations in language structure relate to differences in intellectual capacity, linguists in the present age find it absurd to make any judgments about the quality of a culture on the basis of how words are formed and sentences composed. Several other major shifts in thought have occurred that separate modern-day typology from its roots. This is the topic of the following section.

2.0. Revolutions in Typology

Even in Humboldt's era, linguistics was becoming dominated by an historical-comparative approach to language study. That is, the major goals of linguistics were seen as understanding the processes that gave rise to language change and determining the historical relationship among languages. For this reason, typology was marginal to linguistics in the first half of the 1900s.

Nevertheless, in the early twentieth century several important changes transpired in linguistics that radically altered the assumptions of the Humboldtian typology discussed in Section 1. Grounded in the pioneering work of Ferdinand de Saussure, linguists began to argue that, although language may be organic and therefore changing, at any given point in time it is a self-contained system. Thus, Leonard Bloomfield (1933, 19) wrote, "In order to describe a language one needs no historical knowledge whatever." This is a shift from a **diachronic** (historical) perspective to a **synchronic** perspective (looking at a language at a single stage in its development).

Although linguists like Bloomfield—cumulatively referred to as the American Structuralists—continued to emphasize morphology in their research on languages, they wholeheartedly rejected any belief that differences in morphological form revealed differences in the "inner form" of the language (or anything about the intellect of the people who spoke it). Discarding this assumption meant going beyond morphology in linguistic analysis. It was no longer proper to ignore the other aspects of language such as syntax. Moreover, the possibility of languages of mixed types arose. Although two languages might be similar with respect to their morphology, they might be radically diverse in terms of sentence structure. As a result, work in typology, when it arose, switched from a focus on languages as wholes (**holistic typology**) to features of languages (**partial typology**).

Across the Atlantic, another nucleus of linguistic thought, the Prague School, argued that certain characteristics of language are inherently linked.[4] Roman Jakobson (1929, 1963) pointed out that the vowel inventory and consonant inventory in languages are connected in predictable ways. For example, if a language has nasal vowels, it will also have nasal consonants. Statements like this capture facts about language that are always true. Later work by the Prague School, particularly by Skalička (1935, 1979), recognized that many language properties are associated in probabilistic rather than absolute fashion. In describing them, then, one can only propose a universal tendency—for example, if a language has only one fricative (i.e., a sound made by the airstream passing through a small aperture in the vocal tract), it is probably [s].[5] Although we can expect this "universal" to be true most of the time, there are languages that constitute counter-examples, such as Hawaiian (Austronesian: United States), which has the single fricative [h].

Although the American Structuralists and the Prague School furnished ideas that transformed typological thought, it was Joseph Greenberg who infused the field of linguistics with an optimism about typology's potential to deliver major discoveries about the nature of language. Although his impact on typology has been immense and varied, for present purposes I mention just a few of his more significant contributions. First, Greenberg (1954) sought to establish a quantificational basis for typological study. Until the time of Greenberg, typology was highly subjective—based almost entirely on the observations and intuitions of individual linguists.[6] The usefulness of such research to the burgeoning field of linguistics was limited, in part, because it did not meet the "scientific" standards that American linguists were trying so desperately to achieve in the 1940s and 1950s. Greenberg developed a strategy to measure numerically both the degree and the types of morphology present in a language. Although Greenberg's method is laudable in its own right, the lasting significance of his quantitative approach has been that it showed that languages did not fall into discrete morphological types (Croft 1990). That is, a language such as English cannot be said absolutely to be an inflecting or no structure language (to borrow terms from the nineteenth century). Rather, it is closer to being a no structure language than Greenlandic Eskimo (Eskimo-Aleut: Greenland) but more inflecting than Khmer (Mon-Khmer: Cambodia). In this early work of Greenberg, another equally important assumption was implicit—namely, that the proper task of typology is not comparing languages per se but instead comparing constructions. The point of typology is not to answer "What kinds of languages are there?" but to answer "What kinds of structures are in languages?" This assumption has become explicit in the work of many current typologists and also in several theories of grammar (e.g., Relational Grammar). There is ample opportunity to observe this fact in the chapters that follow.

Greenberg made full use of the Prague School notion that certain aspects of structure in language correlate and that implicational universals can be stated in terms of the correlation. These implicational universals have the form, "given X in a language, Y is also found." His seminal paper, "Some Universals of Grammar With Particular Reference to the Order of Meaningful Elements" (Greenberg 1966), laid out 45 implicational universals. Universal 2 provides an example:

(2) Universal 2 (Greenberg 1966): In languages with prepositions, the
     genitive almost always follows the governing noun, while in languages
     with postpositions, it almost always precedes.

Kinyarwanda (Niger-Congo: Rwanda) exemplifies the first type of language described by this universal:

(3) a. Umugore   y-oohere-je   umubooyi   **kw'**   iisoko
        C1.woman   C1-send-ASP   cook   to   market
        The woman sent the cook to market.
     b. umwaana   **w'**   *umugore*
        child   of   woman
        the woman's child

In accordance with Universal 2, Kinyarwanda is a language that uses prepositions (in bold type) and places the genitive (i.e., the possessor—in italics) after the noun that governs it (the possessee), as can be seen in (3b). Japanese (Japanese-Ryukyuan: Japan) demonstrates the opposite pattern. It employs postpositions, and genitives are placed before the nouns that they modify (4b).

(4) a. Yuuko   wa   Mitiko   **ni**   Koobe   **de**   dekuwasita
                      TOP   to   in   ran.into
        Yuko ran into Mitiko in Kobe.

b. *Tanaka*   *no*   hisyo

            POSS   secretary

  Tanaka's secretary   (Data from Dubinsky 1990)

Like the Prague School linguists, Greenberg (1966) made much use of probabilistic statements. In Universal 2, for example, he claims that "in languages with prepositions, the genitive almost always follows the governing noun." Languages such as Swedish (Germanic: Sweden) in (5) are atypical in terms of the universal statement, but they are not altogether unexpected.

(5) a. Han ramlade   i   sjön

        he   fell   into   water

        He fell into the water.

    b. *Eriks* mor

       Eric's mother   (Data from Björkhagen 1962)

Greenberg's Universal 2 is also indicative of his intent to incorporate syntax into typological study. In fact, over half of the 45 universal statements Greenberg provided in his 1966 paper dealt exclusively with word order, and many of the statements that made reference to morphology were concerned with the relationship between affix ordering and syntax. The move toward syntactic analysis, however, was not unique to Greenberg. As mentioned previously, it was also true of Prague School typology and the American Structuralists. In point of fact, however, the present-day dominance of syntactic phenomena in typology is probably not so much due to Greenberg and those before him as to another American linguist, Noam Chomsky, who is discussed later in this chapter.

    Another characteristic trait of modern typology that is represented well in Greenberg's work is a focus on the ways that language changes through time (see in particular Greenberg 1978). Greenberg's interest in diachrony was in many ways a throwback to the earlier days of typology in which historical-comparative linguistics predominated. The uniqueness of Greenberg's work, however, was in his use of language change as an explanation for language universals. The basic insight is the following: Because the form that a language takes at any given point in time results from alterations that have occurred to a previous stage of the language, one should expect to find some explanations for (or exceptions to) universals by examining the processes of language change. In other words, many currently existing properties of a language can be accounted for in terms of past properties of the language. Examples of typological explanations based on language change arise in many places throughout this book. I specifically return to this important topic in Section 4 of Chapter 3.

Finally, Greenberg helped to draw attention to the importance of a proper database in the search for language universals. He made at least some attempt to remove the genetic biases from his claims about universals by using what at the time was considered a large sample of languages (30 languages altogether) and including languages from many language families. Although his sampling techniques have ultimately been shown to be inadequate in that they clearly fail to avoid a genetic bias (Dryer 1989b, 1992; Hawkins 1983), they had the effect of drawing attention to the importance of solid methodology when making cross-linguistic claims. We examine many of the methodological issues that are still being debated today in Chapter 3.

The last development in linguistics that has had a shaping influence on typology is Noam Chomsky's model of linguistic competence (its evolution can be traced through Chomsky 1957, 1965, 1970, 1981, 1988, 1992). For those who are familiar with the field of linguistics, the inclusion of Chomsky as one of the major molders of typology may appear awkward or even objectionable. After all, Chomsky himself has never engaged in typological research and has seemed generally skeptical about typology's capacity to inform him in his own work on syntax. The fact remains, however, that the cornerstone concept of Chomsky's model, Universal Grammar, has greatly affected typology.

Chomsky's understanding of Universal Grammar (UG), which he originally outlined in 1965, has changed slightly over time. In general, however, UG is taken to be the linguistic structures that are shared by all languages and a limited set of **parameters** over which languages are permitted to vary. To get a clearer idea of how UG operates, consider a simple example. In the English question in (6), the question word *whom* is at the beginning of the sentence.

(6)   **Whom** did you see _____?

We recognize the placement of question words sentence initially to be a special feature of questions. Normally, the direct object in English is placed just after the verb, where the blank is found in (6). Thus, we might say that *whom* has moved from its typical position to the first position in the sentence. Compare this with Mandarin Chinese:

(7)   ni   kanjian-le   *shei*?
        you   see-ASP   who
        Who do you see?   (Data from Huang 1982)

In (7), the question word *shei* remains in the usual spot for direct objects. Unlike English, the question word does not need to move to a sentence-initial position. This raises an intriguing question: Why should languages differ with regard to where question words appear?

Under Chomsky's view of Universal Grammar, the question is answered in the following manner. At an abstract level, the English and Chinese sentences have precisely the same word order. Indeed, this order follows principles that hold true of all languages. English and Chinese, however, are different in terms of the parameter of verb agreement (Agr). English is +Agr as can be seen by the appearance of the agreement marker -*s* in the present tense (I run vs. He run*s*). Chinese, however, is -Agr. The language never displays agreement on the verb. It has been claimed that the variation along this parameter is what triggers the required fronting of question words. +Agr languages such as English require it, whereas -Agr languages do not (Huang 1982).

It should be fairly obvious how the notion of Universal Grammar relates to typology. Research on Universal Grammar is aimed at discovering what all languages hold in common and the boundaries of their differences, which is precisely the same goal as typology. By bringing the search for universals to the center of formal syntactic theory, Chomsky established a point of contact with typological study. Ideally, typology should inform the model of Universal Grammar, and Universal Grammar should inform typology on motivations for the patterns in language it unearths. Unfortunately, this ideal has not often been achieved (see Pullum 1979 and Newmeyer 1983, 67-72, for discussion) because of major disagreements about how universals are to be explained. Among other topics, we return to the issue of explanation in the next chapter.

3.0. Summary

In this chapter, some of the guiding assumptions of modern typology have been introduced by tracing developments in the field during the past century.

The starting point for all typology is the presupposition that there are recurrent structural patterns across languages that are not random or accidental. These patterns can be described in statements called *language universals*.

Once one grants this simple assumption, myriad questions arise. The first type of question is "What kinds of universals are there?" This is the topic of Section 1 in Chapter 3. The beginnings of the answer, however, were already hinted at previously; typologists explore both absolute properties of language and probabilistic properties. In addition, they are concerned with the connections between two or more properties.

A second key question about universals is "How are they determined?" I return to this question in Section 2 of Chapter 3. For now, it is sufficient to say that this question has become central to typology in the past few decades, and its answer has profound implications, particularly for universals that are based on statistical probability.

The final basic question that concerns modern typology is "How are universals explained?" A protracted debate over issues of explanation has been occurring since the 1950s. The most acrimonious elements of the debate have concerned the relationship between diachrony and synchrony (i.e., to what degree does an explanation require reference to past stages of a language?) and the need to go outside the language system itself in forming satisfying explanations (see Croft 1995 for a discussion on this latter topic). In Sections 3 and 4 of Chapter 3, I present some of the fundamental concepts involved in the debate.

4.0. Key Terms

Affixal languages	Parameters
Diachronic	Partial typology
Holistic typology	Synchronic
Inflectional languages	Universal Grammar
No structure languages	

Notes

———

1. See Greenberg (1974) for a more thorough treatment of the history of typology.

2. Martin Haspelmath (personal communication, 1995) rightly reminds me that the relative neglect of syntax at the time in favor of other aspects of language was also a function of the intense interest in Indo-European languages that were highly affixal.

3. Humboldt himself, however, explicitly denied that it was his intent to make claims about the ascendancy of one culture over another (see chapter 19 of Humboldt 1971).

4. Sgall (1995) surveys current and past contributions of Prague School linguistics to typology.

5. According to Maddieson (1984), this tendency holds true of 83.8% of the languages in his database that contain a single fricative.

6. Sapir (1921) sensed the dangers inherent in the overly subjective nature of the typology of his day: "It is dangerous to generalize from a small number of selected languages. To take as the sum total of our material Latin, Arabic, Turkish, Chinese, and perhaps Eskimo or Sioux as an afterthought, is to court disaster" (122).

3

Issues of Method
and Explanation

In 1995, a new pill arrived on the shelves of drugstores—the latest attempt to provide consumers with an easy way to trim off unwanted fat. The makers of the pill boldly asserted that their product sped up the body's metabolism so that fat was burned at an accelerated rate during exercise. It sounded too good to be true: lose more weight with less exercise. Best of all, proponents of the drug could provide test results to back up the efficacy of the drug. Additional research on the wonder pill, however, demonstrated that it actually had no effect on metabolism whatsoever and that it had no value as a weight loss measure. The desperate hopes for effortless weight loss were dashed yet again. What about all the research that initially had been put forth as evidence that the drug did what it was claimed to do? It turns out that the researchers had overlooked (or chosen to ignore) a simple fact: People who took the pill started to exercise more because they were told that it operated most effectively during periods of intense physical activity. It was this additional exercise, and not the pill, that led to weight loss.

This anecdote highlights a crucial point about any kind of empirical study. The method that one uses to research the phenomenon at hand has a profound impact on the results. If the methods are shoddy, the results will be also. For this reason, empirical scientists pay careful attention to how they go about their research. Typologists are no exception. There are key questions as to how universals are to be described, how they are to be determined, and how they are to be explained. In this chapter, each of these components of methodology is discussed.

1.0. Types of Universals

Language universals are statements of fundamental properties of language. They are empirical claims. To say that they are empirical is to say that they are descriptions of patterns found in observed language data. As such, their accuracy can be tested by applying them to previously unstudied languages.

It is crucial to recognize that descriptive statements like those reviewed in this section are not explanatory in any way. That is, they do not tell us why language is the way it is. Therefore, to get at the essential nature of language, statements of language universals must be supplemented by explanations for why they exist. I return to this issue in Section 3.0.

■ 1.1. Absolute Versus Nonabsolute Universals

In the previous chapters, I have alluded several times to a basic distinction in types of universal statements: absolute versus nonabsolute. When the word *universal* is used, most people generally take it to mean something that holds true in every instance. For all instances of X, Y, and Z, a universal statement is one that holds true only if it always holds true of X, Y, and Z. Thus, Ramat (1987) rightly points out that a term such as "nonabsolute universal" is, technically speaking, a logical contradiction. This terminology, however, has become common in typological research; therefore, it is used here and throughout the book.

Absolute universals hold true of all languages. The following are examples:

(1) a. All languages have consonants and vowels.
  b. All languages make a distinction between nouns and verbs.
  c. All languages have ways to form questions.

Notice that the universal properties listed in (1) are not logically necessary. That is, we can conceive easily enough of a language that lacked one or all of these properties. Consequently, although statements such as those in (1a-1c) might seem intuitively obvious to you, they are nonetheless quite exciting in that they reflect something about the essential nature of language. Absolute universals are assumed to be true of all languages at all times, even for the hundreds of languages for which there is no written description and for many hundreds of others that have become extinct without leaving behind any record. Theoretically, it is a simple thing to demonstrate that an absolute universal is inaccurate. One need only discover a single language for which it does not hold true. Most absolute universals, however, are sufficiently well established that it is a rare occurrence when they are shown to be false.

Nonabsolute universals admit exceptions. They are properties of languages that usually hold true. Although they cannot be regarded as reflecting properties that are essential to all languages, they represent significant tendencies. How significant the tendencies actually are depends on the number of exceptions to the universal. In (2), several nonabsolute universals are provided.

(2) a. Most languages have the vowel [i] (as in the English word *feet*).
  b. Most languages have adjectives.[1]
  c. Languages usually employ rising intonation to signal a yes or no question (i.e., a question that anticipates either a yes or a no answer such as "Did you have fun reading Chapter 2?").

All the statements in (2) have a high degree of probability. (2a), for example, is true of over 90% of languages (Maddieson 1984).[2]

■ **1.2. Implicational Universals**

Besides varying in whether they are absolute, statements of universals can be either implicational or nonimplicational. An **implicational universal** has a precondition. That is, it can be placed in an "if X then Y" form. Examples of implicational universals are given in (3).

(3) a. Greenberg's Universal 4: With overwhelmingly greater than chance frequency, languages with normal SOV order are postpositional.
     b. Greenberg's Universal 3: Languages with dominant VSO order are always prepositional.

In these universals, S is the subject, O is the object, and V is the verb. In (3a) and (3b), it is possible to rewrite the universals as a conditional statement—for example, if a language is SOV, then it is postpositional with overwhelmingly greater than chance frequency. This is an easy diagnostic for determining whether a universal is implicational.

There are several noteworthy properties of implicational universals. First, they can be absolute, as in (3b), or they can be nonabsolute, as in (3a). Second, the implications are unidirectional. This means we cannot take an implicational universal and switch around the precondition and the universal statement to derive another universal. For instance, taking (3b)—if a language is VSO, then it is prepositional—and reversing it—if a language is prepositional, then it is VSO—leads to an incorrect claim because there are many prepositional languages that are not VSO (e.g., English, which is SVO).

Finally, implicational universals are tetrachoric (from Greek *tetra* [four] and *choris* [separated], meaning *put into four parts*). That is, they introduce two independent variables (such as having VSO word order and being prepositional) that give rise to the following four logical possibilities:

(4)   *Prepositions*   *Postpositions*
          VSO   Yes   No
          –VSO   ?   ?

Remember that the implicational universal makes no claims about languages that are not VSO. These logical possibilities may or may not be attested. The implicational universal simply does not tell us. As Croft (1990) points out, the benefit of implicational absolute universals is that they eliminate one possible language type. In our example, for instance, the existence of a VSO language with postpositions is ruled out.

So far, the universals we have looked at have all been in a simple form. It is possible, however, to have **complex implicational universals** as well. In complex statements, there are two (or more) preconditions, as shown in the following:

(5) Greenberg's Universal 5: If a language has dominant SOV order and the genitive follows the governing noun, then the adjective likewise follows the noun.

The claim in (5) takes the form, "If X, then if Y, then Z."[3] At one and the same time, complex implicational statements are both more powerful and less powerful than simple ones. Complex implicational universals have the advantage of removing exceptions—frequently, then, they can be stated as absolutes. On the other hand, when they are absolute, they eliminate a smaller proportion of language types.

(6)

	Noun + Adjective	*Adjective + Noun*
SOV		
N + Gen	Yes	No
Gen + N	?	?
–SOV		
N + Gen	?	?
Gen + N	?	?

The three parameters of the complex implicational statement give rise to eight language types. The universal eliminates just one of the eight and affirms the possibility of the existence of one of the eight.

It is also relatively more difficult to account for complex implicational universals. Rather than trying to establish some kind of interrelationship between two variables as one would with a simple implicational universal, there must be a way to associate three. For the absolute universal given in (5), for instance, one must account for why the combination of an SOV constituent order and noun + genitive allows one to predict the order noun + adjective.

Because complex universals tend to eliminate exceptions, they make stronger predictions about the essential nature of language. They suggest properties that must hold true of any language. Therefore, locating a single counterexample is sufficient to refute the claim made by an absolute universal. For example, Campbell, Bubenik, and Saxon (1988) identify Tigre (Semitic: Eritrea) as a violation of the universal given in (5):[4]

(7) a. rabbí 'astar wāmədər faṭra
      God   heaven   and.earth   created
      God created heaven and the earth.

    b. 'ab   la-ḥəsān
      father ART-boy
      The boy's father

    c. la-gəndāb   'ənās
      ART-old   man
      The old man   (Data from Raz 1983, 32, 83, 94)

The data reveal that the language is SOV (7a) and has noun-genitive order (7b), yet also has the order adjective-noun (7c).

Although Tigre thus falsifies the absolute status of (5), this does not fully undermine the significance of the universal. It can be restated as a strong tendency.

> If a language has dominant SOV order and the genitive follows the
> governing noun, then the adjective almost always follows the noun.

Even in its reformulation as a nonabsolute universal, the claim still reflects an intriguing property of language—Why is it that languages usually behave in this manner?[5] For this reason, one must take care not to throw the proverbial baby out with the bathwater when exceptions to universals are encountered.

The fact is that the vast majority of universal statements about language are probabilistic rather than absolute. This prompts another issue, however. Claims about what "almost always" or "usually" occurs in language are only legitimate if they are based on a representative sample of human languages. For example, if I were to examine only English, French, Spanish, German, and Yuma (Hokan: United States), I could generate hundreds of "universals" such as in the following:

(8) Languages almost always have definite articles that precede the noun
    they modify.

Given my database of five languages, the statement in (8) is true because all the languages but Yuma (which has no definite articles) adhere to the generalization, but no linguist would give the universal much credence. After all, the claim is based on just 5 out of the 5,000+ languages of the world! Furthermore, the 4 languages that adhere to the universal are all closely related. English, French, Spanish, and German are Indo-European languages.

It is easy to see the problems with the method used to arrive at (8) because the example is extreme, but it begs the question, "what constitutes a representative sample of languages?" This is the topic of Section 2.0.

2.0. A Problem in Determining Universals—The Database

It has been my experience that people usually find discussions on methodology to be extremely dull. They are quick to remind me that the interesting aspect of data is what they reveal to us, not how data are collected or examined. However, the type of data that typologists use in formulating statements about language patterns is critical to their results. In fact, understanding the methodology used in typological research may be the single most important item one can learn about the field.

To see the significance of statistical techniques, compare the numbers in Table 3.1 that concern the relative order of S, O, and V.

The three studies depicted in Table 3.1 share certain results. One example is that they all reflect a statistical dominance of subject initial languages. There are, however, some troubling differences. For instance, Greenberg (1966) identifies SVO as the most common word order pattern, whereas the other two reveal SOV to be most common. Object initial languages only appear in Tomlin (1986). VSO languages range from constituting one-tenth of the world's language to one-fifth. Why do such differences appear? These discrepancies arise due to differences in the samples that the researchers used. The most glaring difference is the number of languages that were examined. The smallest sample is Greenberg's (30 languages) and the largest is Tomlin's (402 languages).

How many languages should a typologist examine in determining language universals? Your intuition might be that the only safe course of action is to look at all of them. For many reasons, however, a database consisting of all the languages of the world is impractical. First of all, many human languages are now extinct, and there is little or no record of them. Consider the case of Illyrian: The language is thought to be related to Albanian and to

TABLE 3.1 Relative Percentages of Basic Constituent Orders

	%		
Order	Greenberg (1966)	. Ohio State (1992)	Tomlin (1986)
SVO	43	35	42
SOV	37	44	45
VSO	20	19	9
VOS	0	2	3
OVS	0	0	1
OSV	0	0	0

have been spoken in southeastern Europe. No texts or inscriptions of the language survive, however, so the sum total of what is known about the language is a list of a few place names and a handful of words referred to in Greek texts. Consequently, although linguists know of Illyrian, they cannot include it in a typological study.

Even for languages that are currently spoken, and thus are accessible in principle, it is impossible in practice to gather information on all of them. Many of them are not documented adequately for the purposes of comparison, and many have no documentation at all.

It is also technically impossible to create a database of all human languages because many languages are yet to come into existence. Languages are constantly changing. As a result, different dialects of languages emerge. Over time, speakers of the different dialects cease to be able to understand one another very well. Eventually, if the dialects continue to diverge, the lack of intelligibility between them becomes so great that they must be considered separate languages. Because language is dynamic in this way, there is no possibility of ever comprising a sample of all human languages.

For all these reasons, one must choose a sample of languages when seeking to identify cross-linguistic patterns. Quite often, samples are constructed out of convenience. In such instances, the typologists examine languages that they are familiar with or have easy access to. This is what Greenberg did in compiling the 30 languages he used in his study of basic word order.

The shortcoming of this method is that the sample is not really representative of the distribution of human languages. Inevitably, it is biased toward certain language groups or geographical areas or both. In Greenberg's (1966) sample, almost a third of the languages are Indo-European (Greek, Hindi, Italian, Norwegian, Serbian, and Welsh) and almost a fourth are spoken in Africa. As a result, some of his conclusions are suspect because genetic traits of Indo-European have an inordinate influence on his statistics, as do any areal traits of Eurasian or African languages. For example, Greenberg suggested that languages with OV order also tend to place adjectives before nouns. This proposal, however, has been demonstrated to be false (Dryer 1988a, 1989b). In fact, it is only in the broad geographic region of Eurasia where this tendency holds true. Elsewhere in the world, it is far more common for OV languages to place adjectives after nouns—just the opposite of what Greenberg had proposed.

Despite the obvious problems with samples of convenience, they remain the most common form of database in typological literature (e.g., Foster and Hofling 1987; Hawkins 1983; Lehmann 1973; Nichols 1986; Venneman 1974a, 1974b). There is much of great value in each of these pieces of research. Indeed, their findings have been crucial to our current understanding of human language. One must recognize them, however, for what they are— not as accurate indications of the statistical distribution of language patterns but as suggestive guides to these distributions.

Three types of solutions to overcoming biases and constructing representative samples have been suggested within the field of typology. The first (outlined in Bell 1978 and developed in Tomlin 1986) is based on the frequency of language families. The idea is that each language family (e.g., Nilo-Saharan, Austronesian, Carib, etc.) is represented in the sample based on the number of languages in that family. If one decides to use 10% of the world's languages in a sample, then one would include 10% of known Nilo-Saharan languages, 10% of Austronesian languages, 10% of Carib languages, and so on. Using this method, language families with a greater number of members would receive greater representation in the sample than smaller language families. The strength of such an approach is that it provides a general idea as to the proportion of existing languages in the world that contain a particular linguistic trait. For example, Tomlin found 45% of languages are SOV, whereas 42% were SVO (see Table 3.1). Because of his methodology, these figures are probably good approximations of the percentages of SOV and SVO languages in the world. It is crucial to realize, however, that such numbers may not be indicative of the actual preferences that languages have for these word orders. On the basis of the percentages, it is illegitimate to assume that there is a slight tendency for languages to be SOV rather than SVO. Why? Because the actual frequency of different language families is due not only to purely linguistic factors but also to historical factors (see Dryer 1989b for a good discussion). The following example will help clarify this point.

Khoisan and Niger-Kordofanian are two language families in Africa. The Khoisan family has approximately 30 members, whereas Niger-Kordofanian has over 1,000. The reasons why Khoisan is so small and Niger-Kordofanian so large have little to do with the linguistic structures found in the languages. Rather, their relative sizes are due to the histories of their speakers and the sociological profiles of the communities that speak them. In general, Khoisan speakers were assimilated into or eliminated by Bantu groups expanding into their territory from the north and Europeans from the south. Attendant to these expansions was the elimination of many Khoisan languages and the containment of others. In contrast, Niger-Kordofanian groups, of which Bantu is a part, have been expansionists. Over time, as these languages have extended over most of Africa, they have fragmented into new dialects and languages. Thus, the Niger-Kordofanian family contains an unusually large number of languages. As can be seen, then, the relative sizes of these families is something of an historical accident.

Another proposal for constructing a representative sample of languages is to gather languages that bear only very distant or no genetic relationship and are not from the same culture area (Bybee 1985; Perkins 1980, 1989). In this way, a sample of **independent languages** is built that includes roughly 50 languages.[6] Unlike the previous approach to sampling, this method does not represent the frequency of languages within families. It makes no difference whether a family has 30 or 1,000 members; only 1 language will be selected from each for the sample. One strength of this method is that it more accurately reflects purely linguistic preferences than the previous approach. Another is that the required sample is manageable in size. In practical terms, a single researcher can easily construct a sample of 50 languages. This is not always the case with methods that entail larger numbers of languages.

One problem with this method, however, is that it may not be possible to construct a sample of 50 languages that are distinct enough in geographic terms. There are certain regions of the world where languages, regardless of their genetic affiliation, share linguistic features. As noted previously, the languages of Eurasia have a strong tendency toward noun-adjective ordering. These regions, called **linguistic areas,** arise due to sustained contact between languages for long periods of time. Because the linguistic areas can be extremely large, it may be impossible to construct a 50-language sample with no 2 languages from the same linguistic area.

Matthew Dryer (1992) has proposed a third sampling method that attempts to overcome some of the inherent shortcomings of the other two approaches. He employs a massive database (625 languages) but controls for genetic and areal biases by first grouping the languages into genera[7] (basically equivalent to language families that have been reconstructed to the same depth of time) and then grouping the genera into six large geographical areas. To determine whether a certain pattern is statistically significant (i.e., should be considered a universal), the pattern must be present in the genera of each of the six areas.

For a clearer idea of how this works, I will recount Dryer's (1989b) test of part of Greenberg's Universal 18, which states "If a language places the demonstrative after the noun, then it will place the adjective after the noun as well."[8] Fijian (Austronesian: Fiji) is a language that adheres to the claims of this universal:

(9)   a.   a   cauravou   *yai*
           ART   youth   this
           this youth
      b.   vanua   *suasua*
           place   wet
           wet place   (Data from Dixon 1988)

In (9a), the demonstrative *yai* follows the noun it modifies, as does the adjective *suasua* in (9b).

Using a sample of 542 languages, Dryer (1989b) presents the relevant data to test the reliability of the universal as in the following:

(10)	Afr	Eura	A-NG	NAm	SAm	Total
NDem and NAdj	28	14	8	8	5	63
NDem and AdjN	1	2	0	1	0	4

The five areal categories in (10) are Africa (Afr), Eurasia (Eura), Australia and New Guinea (A-NG), North America (NAm), and South America (SAm). By making a distinction between these areas in accumulating statistics, there is a control for broad areal biases. The numbers in the areal columns do not represent individual languages but rather language genera. Each genus is a group of genetically related languages, which tend to be quite similar typologically. By counting genera rather than individual languages, Dryer controls for any severe genetic bias in his sample. The top row of numbers in (10) represent the number of genera in each area that conform to Greenberg's universal. The second row is the number of genera that do not.

As can be seen in (10), the predictions of Greenberg's universal hold true in all five geographic areas. For this reason, the universal has statistical validity, and one can conclude with Dryer that "there is a linguistic preference for NDem languages to be NAdj" (1989b, 272). That is, the universal does in fact tell us something about the essential nature of language. If any of the five areas failed to show the expected preference, then Dryer would conclude that the pattern was not statistically significant, and he would not accept it as a linguistic universal. In this way, Dryer's method is extremely conservative. Because in all cases he requires all regions of the world to support a universal, it is likely that his method will lead to the rejection of certain universals that others would accept.

Dryer's approach is open to two criticisms. First, one is forced to decide to which genus a language belongs. This is not always a straightforward task because the genetic affiliation of many languages is controversial. Second, for the method to be effective one must accumulate information on an extremely large number of languages. This poses pragmatic difficulties for individual researchers.

All three of the approaches to databases that have been introduced require typologists to gather information on languages that they do not know firsthand. How is such information gleaned? The most common method is to use published sources such as reference grammars and journal articles (as I have done throughout this book). By doing so, abundant data on a diverse group of languages can be accessed quickly; there are problems, however, with reference materials that can also render them unsuitable for typological research. Most important, they only offer brief and incomplete coverage of most aspects of grammar. There is an unlimited amount of information that can be supplied about the structure of a language but a limited number of pages to furnish the information, so reference grammars necessarily present only what is felt by the authors to reflect the essence of how the language is structured. Consequently, a great number of details are omitted, often without any comment. As a result, the linguist who relies on these sources can easily draw erroneous conclusions about what does or does not actually occur in a language.

A second method for collecting data on a large number of languages is to create a questionnaire on the phenomenon under investigation and send it to specialists on the languages in the database (an excellent example is Dahl 1985). Because specialists will either be native speakers or be able to consult with native speakers, questionnaire data can be quite intricate. Consequently, the typologist can gather highly specific, yet accurate, details about constructions and how these constructions are used in particular languages. Moreover, the typologist frequently uncovers information about dialect variation of the sort one rarely finds in reference grammars.

Despite these obvious advantages, there are practical problems involved with questionnaires that make them difficult to use in many cases. First, their efficacy depends on the quality of the questionnaire. It must be designed carefully to elicit the appropriate information and not bias the result. For this reason, a great deal of preliminary research on a given topic must be carried out before the questionnaire can be properly constructed.

Second, questionnaires are time-consuming and potentially expensive. Even for a moderately sized database of 50 languages, the typologist using a questionnaire must contact linguists from around the globe who are willing to invest the time it takes to complete the questionnaire. Such linguists are not uncommonly working in remote areas that are not easily accessible. Interacting with them on a project can take months. If a follow-up on the original questionnaire is required, the time frame can easily turn into years.

Finally, questionnaires are nearly impossible to use for typological research that is closely tied to a particular grammatical theory. For example, syntactic theorists who operate within the grammatical framework called Government and Binding are constantly involved in developing statements about language universals (see the discussion on Noam Chomsky in Chapter 2, Section 2.0). In principle, one way to assess the accuracy of these claims would be to test them on several hundred languages of appropriate areal and genetic diversity. The universal claims made in Government and Binding, however, are highly abstract and rely on a specialized terminology and set of formalisms. Therefore, an effective questionnaire would almost certainly require all the specialists to whom it was sent to be quite familiar with the specifics of Government and Binding. This state of affairs is not likely, especially in the case of large-scale projects.

Despite certain shortcomings, both reference materials and questionnaires can be effectively employed to gather relevant data. They are perhaps most effective when used together. By doing so, the efficiency of published information can be combined with the detail and accuracy of information gathered through personal inquiry.

In this section, we have reviewed three approaches to determining and testing universals that serve to overcome some of the biases found in samples of convenience. The methods have slightly different functions, and none of them is without difficulties, not the least of which is determining the source of the data for the sample. Each of the sampling techniques, however, serves to produce generally reliable insights into the question "What is language?" Once one arrives at such insights about patterns in language, an even bigger task remains: to explain why these patterns hold true. It is to this issue that the following section is devoted.

3.0. Explaining Universals

In the previous two chapters, I have made several references to the issue of explanation in typological work. The issue has been a divisive one and one that has received much attention (e.g., Comrie 1984, 1989; Croft 1990; Givón 1979; Hyman 1984; Newmeyer 1983). At the heart of the controversy is a debate over whether explanations should be **internal** or **external**. Internal explanations are those that are based on the system of language itself, whereas external explanations draw on considerations outside of the language system. The following example will make this distinction clearer.

Many languages exhibit a contrast between active voice (11a) and passive voice constructions (11b).

(11) a. Barry took the book.

   b. The book was taken (by Barry).[9]

The English passive sentence in (11b) is typical of passive structures in a large number of languages in the following ways:[10]

1. The subject of the passive construction (*the book*) appears as an object in the active.

2. The verb in a passive construction occurs in a special form that marks it as
being passive (in English, an auxiliary verb, *was*, is used in conjunction with
a past participle, *taken*).

The question arises as to why these properties hold true for so many languages.
An internal explanation of these facts accounts for them in terms of a set of
rules or principles of syntax. For example, many grammatical theories view
passive as a special mapping between an abstract level of syntax and a surface
level of syntax. At the abstract level, passive and active sentences are structurally equivalent.

(12)	Level	Active	Passive
	Abstract	Barry took the book	_____ was taken the book
	Surface	Barry took the book	The book was taken

Notice that there is basic correspondence in meaning between actives and
passives. The semantic relationship between the verb *to take* and the noun
phrase *the book* remains constant. Whether in the active or passive, *the book*
is understood as the entity being removed. This semantic correlation is
captured in the model in (12) by virtue of actives and passives having the same
structure at the abstract level; in both sentences, *the book* is the abstract object
of *take*. The form of the verb, however, differs in the active and passive
sentences. Crucially, *was taken* is in an intransitive form. As an intransitive,
it is unable to take an object at the surface level and, as a consequence, *the
book* must become a subject. Under this analysis, there is an explanation for
both the properties of passives mentioned previously. The subject of a passive
corresponds to the object of an active because it is itself an object at an abstract
level. The motivation for the abstract object of a passive becoming a subject
at the surface level is that the verb arises in a special intransitive form.

The details of an internal account of passive are much more complex than
what I have outlined here. For present purposes, however, the important
feature of the analysis is that there is no reference made to anything other than
the system of language. Nothing is said about how passives assist the communicative process or how they are affected by it. This is, however, precisely
the kind of information one usually finds in an external account of passives.

Keenan (1985a), for example, describes passive as a "foregrounding
operation." By this he means that the passive construction is a device used to
highlight an element in a clause that normally would not be highlighted. To

understand this view, two of his assumptions must be made explicit. First, active sentences serve no specialized communicative function, and, consequently, they represent the default choice of a speaker. Conversely, passives are **pragmatically marked,** meaning that they are specifically designed to relate information in an atypical manner. The second assumption is that the subject of a sentence identifies the most topical element of that sentence. In other words, the subject is what the rest of the sentence is about. In active sentences, a subject is usually an agent—the entity that controls or initiates the event described in the sentence. In (11a), for instance, *Barry* is the agent because he carries out the action of taking.

When speakers are involved in communication, they make many choices about how to organize the information. Their choices influence how their listeners will interpret the message. The use of a passive is special in that a nonagent element appears as the subject—for example, *the book* in (11b). Because this packaging of information runs contrary to the default situation in which an agent is the topic, the subject of the passive is brought into the foreground of attention. Because there can be only one subject, the agent of a passive is either left unexpressed or it is backgrounded by putting it in a prepositional phrase (*by Barry*).

Each property of the passive is thus explained by the communicative function of the construction. A nonagent is the subject in order to foreground it. The agent is correspondingly backgrounded by appearing in a structure that is marginal to the clause, such as a prepositional phrase. The verb is in a special form to alert the listener to the fact that a pragmatically marked device is in use.[11]

This discussion on passives provides a sense for how different internal and external explanations can be; this does not, however, mean the two types of explanations are mutually exclusive, with either the internal explanation or the external explanation being the correct one. Rather, each type of explanation is designed to underscore a different truth about how language works (see Hyman 1984). On the one hand, internal explanations focus attention on the fact that language is a rule-governed system. The ways in which sounds are combined into meaningful elements and the ways meaningful elements are combined into words and phrases are conditioned by principles, which we call grammatical rules. Internal explanations appeal to these rules. On the other hand, external explanations focus attention on the fact that the grammatical rules do not generate words and phrases in a vacuum. The structures they produce are used with a particular intent and within a particular context and are affected by such things. Through time, these communicative pressures on language structure will bring about constructions such as the passive.

There have been many calls for explanations of language phenomena that bring together both an internal and an external perspective (e.g., Dooley 1993; Everett 1994; Hawkins 1988b; Hyman 1984), and this is the tack that is taken in this book. Historically, however, typological research has based explanations on external factors. Therefore, it is necessary to review some particularly common types of external conditioning to which typologists appeal. Five of the most common sorts of external accounts of typological patterns are described in Section 4.0: discourse explanations, processing explanations, accounts based on linguistic economy, accounts based on sensory perception, and accounts based on iconicity between language structure and semantics.

4.0. Types of External Explanations

As noted previously, external explanations are those that point to factors outside of the linguistic system to account for the form of the system. These factors (or perhaps a more fitting term is "forces") exert a steady pressure on the shape of a grammar so that over time the grammar becomes molded in particular predictable ways. As you read through this section, it is important to bear in mind that external forces do not directly determine the structures that appear in language. That is, they are not grammatical principles that dictate how an utterance must be constructed in a particular instance. Rather, they subtly influence the ways in which speakers use their language so that the grammar of the language eventually takes on a specific form.

■ 4.1. Discourse

When humans relay information through language, they have means at their disposal for combining utterances into coherent messages, grouping parts of the message more compactly than others, and highlighting certain aspects of the message. In other words, they structure their speech. The discourse-structure that they impose on their messages can have an effect on the form of phrases and clauses. An example of an external explanation based on discourse was provided in the discussion on passive. There, it is observed that three characteristic features of passive constructions arise to facilitate a communicative intent: encoding the patient nominal as the subject, placing the agent nominal in a prepositional phrase, and using a stative verb form.

This is not to say that each time a passive is used by an English speaker, for example, every part of the passive construction is selected anew to conform to the speaker's particular needs at that moment. Rather, the combination of treating the patient as a subject, putting the agent in a *by* phrase, and employing a sequence of *to be* + an auxiliary verb has become conventionalized in English. Significantly, speakers rarely stray very far from this convention. For this reason, the passive is readily formulated as a static "rule" of English.

The point of a discourse account of passive is to highlight that not just any static rule for the construction could have developed. Instead, the passive construction in English and those in all languages manifest universal features because only morphology and syntax that are well suited to carry out the discourse functions of passives ever become conventionalized.

■ 4.2. Processing

There are certain limitations on the kinds of language structures that humans can easily comprehend. For example, certain sentence types are difficult to process (and therefore are dispreferred) because they contain temporary ambiguities (13):

(13) The candidate hoped to win the election lost.

Although this sentence is well formed according to rules of English grammar, it is extremely difficult to understand at first. In fact, it is so hard to grasp that many speakers will simply reject it altogether. This is because at the point in the sentence when the word *hoped* is encountered, one expects it to serve as the main verb and not as a past participle. Therefore, when one reaches the word *lost,* the sentence seems to have a second main verb, which is not permitted. The sentence can then be reinterpreted as equivalent to "The candidate which we hoped would win lost the election." To do so, *hoped* must be reanalyzed as a modifying participle. It is easy to see why such structures are dispreferred in language: They constitute a serious obstacle to sentence comprehension and to the speed of the comprehension.

Processing constraints lead speakers to avoid structures that are hard to comprehend (or produce) and to favor structures that facilitate rapid comprehension (or production). Eventually, as speakers of a language eschew difficult constructions and utilize others in their place, the difficult constructions disappear from use because speakers come to consider them ungrammatical. At this point, the grammatical system has been structured according to an extragrammatical constraint.

To the degree that humans share similar processing constraints regardless of the language that they speak, we should expect the same kinds of restrictions to be imposed on the forms of their grammars. Consequently, certain cross-linguistic tendencies arise.

■ 4.3. Economy

Two processes in language tend to be collapsed under the rubric of *economy.* Elements in language that are highly predictable in context tend to be eliminated, and elements that are used commonly tend to be reduced (Haiman 1983). The phenomenon of **pro-drop** is an example of the former. In many languages that have agreement between the subject and the verb, a pronominal subject can be left unexpressed, as in Choctaw (Penutian: United States). The language has a pronoun, *ano,* which is equivalent to the first-person singular pronoun *I* in English; this pronoun, however, is typically not employed in clauses.

(14) Hilha-li-tok
dance-1S-PST
I danced.   (Adapted from Davies 1986, 14)

Because information about the subject is found on the verb in (14), the Choctaw pronoun *ano* ("I") need not be included. In English, there is very little subject-verb agreement. The verb *danced* on its own, for instance, does not reveal whether the subject is *I, you, she,* or something else. Presumably, because information about the subject is unpredictable, subject pronouns cannot be dropped. Thus, there is a split in language types: languages such as Choctaw, which permit pro-drop, and languages such as English, which do not. This split follows from the nature of the verb agreement in language. Languages with robust agreement will be like Choctaw, whereas languages with limited agreement will pattern like English. This universal tendency can be accounted for by appealing to economy. Because robust agreement serves the same function as overt subject pronouns, using both together in the same clause gives rise to **redundancy** in the grammar. Because redundancy is inefficient, it tends to be eliminated from grammar over time.

The other kind of economy in language—that which results from frequency—is readily seen in contractions. In spoken English, the phrases "want to" and "going to" are commonly reduced to "wanna" and "gonna." Over time, they have taken on this form because of the extreme frequency with which they occur. As speakers become accustomed to hearing and using certain words or phrases with great regularity, these expressions can arise in a slightly abbreviated form without any loss of comprehension. The same information is passed but using a reduced (more economical) form. Eventually, the abbreviated form becomes a convention of the language. This process, sometimes referred to as **automization,** is subtle. Speakers are rarely aware of what is happening to their language while the automization is under way.

Because economy can be taken as the driving force behind certain kinds of changes that occur in languages, it can also be used as an explanation for similarities among languages. For example, subject agreement affixes (such as -*li* in (14)) tend to be monosyllabic in the world's languages. This fact can be taken as an instance of economy working in language: Because subject agreement arises with extreme frequency in languages that have it, the forms used to indicate the agreement shrink in size over time.

■ 4.4. Perception-Cognition

Particularly in the realm of **lexical semantics** (i.e., the meanings of words and units smaller than words), researchers have noted the importance of human perceptual and cognitive capacities (Lee 1988). For example, work on basic color terms in language has revealed the following hierarchy (Berlin and Kay 1969):

white-black > red > green-yellow > blue > brown

It should be noted that the hierarchy here does not make claims about color expressions generally but about basic color terms. Basic color terms are, roughly speaking, those words for colors in a speech community that are commonly known and that cannot be divided further into smaller linguistic units. Using English as an example, the latter half of this definition rules out expressions such as "light brown," "hot pink," "blood red," and "navy blue." Although they are all widely used in describing color, they are not basic color terms because they are composed of a modifier + a color term. There are also many color expressions in English that cannot be broken down in this way but are still not basic color terms: salmon, amber, indigo, azure, and so on. They are not considered basic because they are not widely known or used throughout speech communities. On the contrary, they are typically employed only by the well educated and by people who have a personal or professional expertise that requires knowledge of fine distinctions between colors.

The color terms discussed previously are arranged in an **implicational hierarchy.** The symbol, >, indicates that the entity to its left holds priority over the entity on its right. For example, blue > brown on the far right of this hierarchy denotes that the word for the concept "blue" holds priority over the word for "brown."

In the current example, the notion "priority" represents an ontological priority. In simpler terms, this means that a word to the left of a > must exist in a language for the word to the right of the same > to exist. Thus, we can interpret the color hierarchy in the following manner: A language with only three basic color terms will have white, black, and red. If there is a fourth term, it will be green or yellow, and so on.

Kay and McDaniel (1978) have found that this hierarchy is grounded in human anatomy. The way the visual system is structured causes exposure to black and white colors to produce maximally distinctive responses (i.e., measurements reveal that the way in which the visual system reacts when exposed to white and black is as different as it can be). Of all the remaining colors, red produces the most distinctive response from black and white, then green, and so on. The fact that the color vocabularies of the world's languages follow along the hierarchy is simply due to the way the neurons of the visual system work.

■   **4.5. Iconicity**

The form of some linguistic expressions reflects a real-world property of what is being denoted (see Haiman 1980). Some simple cases of iconicity include the following:

(15) a. The movie was so bad that it dragged on and on and on and on.
       b. The ping-pong ball went back and forth, back and forth.

In both these examples, the phrases *on and on* and *back and forth* are repeated to better capture the repetitious nature of the event they are describing. The actual form of the expression, then, is a symbol of the repetition occurring in the actual situations described by the clauses.

This fact of English also holds true as a universal tendency, at least in a general way. When languages indicate plurality or repetition, they tend to do so by adding linguistic forms. For example, languages that make a singular versus plural distinction on nouns frequently add a suffix to the nouns to indicate plurality but simply use the bare noun stems to indicate singularity.

5.0. Summary

Three major theoretical issues were addressed in this chapter: (a) What sorts of universal claims can be made about language?; (b) what constitutes a legitimate database for the formulation of universals?; and (c) how are universals to be explained? Notably, a satisfactory answer was really only provided for the first of these questions. I noted that the notion "universal" was a cover term for essential properties of language (i.e., those that necessarily hold true of all languages) as well as typical properties (i.e., those that may not hold true for every language but still represent the normative case). For typical properties, the universals can be concerned with the presence or absence of an individual linguistic feature or they can be concerned with the connection between two or more features.

In discussing the second and third questions, however, I stopped far short of arguing for definitive answers, opting instead to survey the core problems one would need to address to articulate an answer. My intention in doing this was to represent the current state of affairs within the field. There is a wealth of fascinating discussion surrounding sampling techniques and explanations for universals, but no consensus has emerged that I might present as the perspective of typologists generally.

Having laid out the conceptual basics of typology in the past three chapters, I now move on to specific phenomena of human language to probe for the unity and the diversity that underlie the linguistic system. I begin in the next chapter with universals in the ordering of words and phrases, an area of investigation that has had a high profile within typology since the 1960s.

6.0. Key Terms

Absolute universals   Language sample
Automization   Lexical semantics
Complex implicational universals   Linguistic area
External explanation   Nonabsolute universals
Implicational universals   Pragmatically marked
Independent languages   Pro-drop
Internal explanation   Redundancy
Language genera

Notes

1. Various languages, including Nootka (Almosan-Keresiouan: Canada) and Mohave (Hokan: United States), are said to lack a clear adjective category. In these languages, adjectival meanings are typically expressed by stative verbs. In the final analysis, it may turn out that properties that do in fact identify a unique adjective class have been overlooked. If this is the case, then the nonabsolute universal in (2b) would become absolute. Alternatively, it may be the case that the notion "adjective," which is a relatively clearly defined category in languages such as English, is better analyzed as subclasses of verbs or nouns or both in other languages. In this case, the strong tendency expressed in (2b) would have to be weakened or abandoned. Word classes such as adjective are discussed in the next chapter.

2. Maddieson (1984) included both long and short varieties of [i] in this calculation.

3. This kind of universal is particularly prominent in the work of the typologist John Hawkins (1979, 1983).

4. It should be noted that the order noun-adjective is also found in Tigre, although it is apparently less common (Raz 1983, 32). Moreover, when the preposition *naÿ* ("of") is used in the expression of the genitive, the genitive can come before the noun (80). Raz does not offer comment on this fact.

5. One of the main points of Campbell et al. (1988) is that exceptions to otherwise absolute universals are often the result of borrowing. This appears to be true for Tigre and the universal in (5). Tigre, a Semitic language, has been influenced by Cushitic languages, particularly Bedawye (Hetzron 1972). The Cushitic languages typically have adjective-noun order and may represent the source of this characteristic in Tigre.

6. Rijkhoff, Bakker, Hengeveld, and Kahrel (1993, 171) observe, "in view of recent proposals which suggest still larger genetic groupings, resulting in fewer independent language families, it is clear that it will become increasingly difficult to design representative probability samples in which languages are not genetically related." In other words, it may not be possible to create a sample of 50 genetically independent languages, let alone a sample in which the 50 languages are independent both genetically and culturally. The authors argue, therefore, that the task in creating a sample is not to find languages that are actually independent but to find languages that are maximally diverse genetically.

7. The languages within a genus generally share most major typological characteristics (word order, morphological type, etc.).

8. Greenberg casts the universal as an absolute. Dryer (1989b), however, lists six languages that are exceptions to the claim.

9. The parentheses indicate that the prepositional phrase is optional.

10. Another notable property of the passive construction is that the agent nominal, the doer of the action (Barry in (11b)), is found in a prepositional phrase. Many languages are like English in this respect, or they mark the agent with an oblique case (see Chapters 4 and 7 for a discussion on case). Other languages suppress the agent nominal. That is, they do not allow the agent to be expressed at all in the passive. For the purposes of the discussion here, this property is ignored.

11. Givón (1984/1990) also points out that the verb in a passive commonly takes on a stative form. This is true in English in which the passive verb is a combination of the auxiliary *be* and a participle. He suggests that recasting an active, which typically denotes an agent-oriented process, as a state is another way to background the role of the agent (see Haspelmath 1990, 1994).

4

Basic Categories

Irrespective of theoretical orientation, linguists are involved in creating and applying abstract categories whenever they engage in analyzing language. In this chapter, three rudimentary categories are introduced, all of which play a particularly crucial role in the understanding of human language: (a) parts of speech, (b) semantic roles, and (c) grammatical relations. Because these categories are so fundamental to research on language, it is necessary to be familiar with the terms that are used to describe them. Each of the categories has a strong basis in intuition, but they are notoriously difficult to apply consistently within a language, let alone cross-linguistically. Therefore, another purpose of this chapter is to highlight some of the difficulties involved with treating these basic notions as absolute universals.

The following sentence will function as a starting point for our discussion:

(1) The hosts served sandwiches to their guests.

The word *hosts* can be labeled in several ways: It is a noun, it is the agent of the event described by the verb, and it is a subject of the clause. Each of these labels captures a different perspective about the linguistic identity of *hosts*. To call it a noun is to say something about its membership in a **lexical class** (or as it is more commonly called, its **part of speech**). Lexical classes are sets

54

of words, such as nouns or verbs, that share certain semantic, morphological, and syntactic properties. On the other hand, when *hosts* is referred to as an agent, its semantic role is being described. A **semantic role** is a label that describes the part that an entity plays in developing the meaning of the sentence. Because *hosts* designates that entity that is instigating the action of serving in (1), it is called the **agent.** Compare this with *guests,* which is a **recipient** because it refers to the entity that is receiving the object of the serving. Finally, identifying *hosts* as a subject is to state its **grammatical relation,** or the function that it plays in the grammar of the clause.

Note that these three notions—lexical class, semantic role, and grammatical relation—are independent of one another. Unlike (1), it is possible to have a subject that bears a semantic role other than agent, as in "Sandwiches were served to the guests." In this case, the subject of the clause is *sandwiches.* It does not describe the instigator of serving but rather the thing being served. Hence, it is called a **patient.** Just as subjects do not have to be agents, they also do not have to be nouns. For example, one can say "That the earth is round is believed by everyone," where the subject of the verb *believed* is a whole clause—"that the earth is round"—rather than a nominal expression.

All this perhaps seems straightforward. After all, you probably learned something about things such as nouns and subjects back in grade school. Complications set in, however, when one attempts to provide an explicit definition for the various types of lexical classes, semantic roles, and grammatical relations. Consider the notion "agent." Previously, I identified this role as designating the entity that instigates the action of a clause. What does it mean, however, to say that an entity instigates an action? Does it require the entity to exert some force, to be acting volitionally, to have control over the event, or some combination of these features? In this regard, which of the sentences in (2) might be said to have an agent?

(2) a. Mary angrily rolled the ball down the hill. [+force, +volition, +control]
b. The ball rolled down the hill. [−force, −volition, −control]
c. The wind blew the ball down the hill. [+force, −volition, −control]
d. The bat sent the ball rolling down the hill. [+force, −volition, −control]
e. Mary accidentally rolled the ball down the hill. [+force, −volition, +control]

The sentences in (2) all describe similar events: A spherical object that has the physical properties necessary for movement is propelled down an incline. In (2a), there is a clear example of an agent. The nominal *Mary* refers to an entity that is in control of the event of rolling. If Mary does not act in a particular fashion, then the event of a rolling ball is not possible. To actualize the rolling event, Mary exerts force of some kind, presumably some sort of physical operation. Finally, Mary is making a conscious determination to enact the rolling event. That is, she is volitional. In contrast, it is quite clear that the subject of (2b), *ball*, is not an agent because it lacks any of the semantic components normally associated with agency. What about (2c) through (2e)? The subjects of these sentences possess some of the characteristics present in (2a) but lack others, so how should they be classified? Is there a continuum of agency?

These are difficult questions on which there is no consensus within linguistics. At some level, it may seem that worrying about exactly what is and what is not an agent (or a noun, a subject, and so on) is merely a technical matter of terminology. There is much more at stake, however, than a simple tinkering of the wording used for different terms. If the concept of, for example, a noun is shown to have a significant impact on the grammar of several languages, then it must correspond to some aspect of the basic human capacity for language. Whenever this is true, though, linguists want to know how the concept in question relates to other aspects of linguistic ability, how it develops, how it is stored and processed in the brain, and so on; to explore any of these profound issues, however, one first must know exactly what it is that needs to be investigated. This is partly why notions, such as noun, direct object, and patient, must be made as explicit as possible.

1.0. Lexical Classes

As noted previously, a part of speech is a category of words that share a set of semantic, morphological, and syntactic properties. Some parts of speech relevant to English include the following:

(3) Noun: *dog, Peter, ambition, gravel*
    Verb: *carry, think, hit, appear*

Adjective: *happy, salty, dark, redundant*
Preposition: *between, in, around, to*
Auxiliary verb: *must, do, be, might*
Determiner: *the, those, some, a*
Adverb: *well, quickly, fortunately, too*
Conjunction: *and, or*

Examining the criteria that might be provided to delimit all these categories
would require a lengthy discussion; therefore, to provide a sense for the kinds
of criteria that linguists use, I will briefly note some properties of adjectives
in English. In terms of semantics, adjectives typically denote property concepts. Consequently, they are often used to reveal a specific quality associated
with an object (e.g., *happy* days, *salty* water, *dark* clouds, or *redundant*
answers). One morphosyntactic property generally shared by adjectives is that
they can be placed into a comparative and a superlative form (e.g., *happier* or
happiest).[1] They have a common morphological characteristic of being transformed into adverbs by adding *-ly* (as in *darkly*). Finally, they usually can be
modified by degree adverbs such as *quite* (*quite salty*). On the basis of such
a clustering of properties, linguists feel justified in positing a lexical class
such as "adjective."

It should be observed that there are obvious subdivisions within any of
the lexical classes in (3). For example, nouns could be divided into proper
(*Peter*) versus common nouns (all others), mass (*gravel*) versus count nouns
(others), or abstract (*ambition*) versus concrete nouns (others).

The possibility of forming principled subdivisions often makes it difficult
to give a simple criterion for class membership. For example, one might want
to define nouns as those words that can be placed in the plural. Pluralization,
however, is not possible with mass nouns (therefore, *gravels* is ungrammatical), and it is only possible in extremely limited circumstances with proper
nouns. Subdivisions within categories also leave open the question of whether
the subclasses should be considered parts of the same category (as one might
argue for verbs and auxiliary verbs) or simply two separate categories.

Not all languages employ exactly the same parts of speech. For example,
some languages lack a category of auxiliary verbs (e.g., ancient Greek) or
prepositions (e.g., Japanese), both of which are found in English. Conversely,
English lacks categories found elsewhere. For example, consider **noun classifiers**. In some languages, such as Thai (Daic: Thailand), when a noun is

modified by a numeral, an additional word called a classifier is also required.
Examples include the following:

(4) a. deg   sɔɔŋ   **khon**
       boy   two   CLASS
       two boys
    b. maa   saam   **tua**
       dog   three   CLASS
       three dogs
    c. baan   sii   **laŋ**
       house   four   CLASS
       four houses   (Data from Schachter 1985)

Therefore, it is clear that the particular roster of lexical classes that is
found in any given language is not universal. Within this cross-linguistic
variation, however, some universals do arise. First, all languages make a
distinction between open and closed lexical classes. An **open class** is one
whose membership is in principle unlimited because new items are continu-
ally being added. In English, verbs, nouns, and adjectives (and perhaps
adverbs) are all open classes. Thus, not only do these classes contain a vast
number of members but novel forms are constantly being promulgated by
speakers. Among verbs, for example, one now can use many forms that simply
did not exist in the not-so-distant past: *to journal, to gift, to downsize, to
e-mail, to out,* and *to digitize,* to name but a few.

In contrast, a **closed class** is one in which membership is largely fixed,
such as is the case with determiners, prepositions, and conjunctions. Although
it is true that over time items in these classes can fall into disuse (when is the
last time you heard the preposition *betwixt* in the course of a day?) and that
new forms can be added (usually via grammaticalization from another class),
the transitions to closed classes are slow and imperceptible, and in this way
the process of adding and losing members is quite unlike that of open classes.

There is a strong correlation between the type of lexical class and whether
it is open or closed. In all languages, verbs and nouns are open classes,
whereas all other parts of speech are closed classes with two exceptions—
adjectives and adverbs. The case of adjectives is an intriguing one because
languages vary dramatically in how the category behaves. Many languages
are like English, in which the adjective category is highly permissive in

accepting new members. In other languages, however, the adjective category
has few members and is completely closed. For example, Hausa (West Chadic:
Nigeria) has just approximately 12 adjectives:

(5)	*Adjective*	*Meaning*	*Adjective*	*Meaning*
	babba	big	gajere	short
	sabo	new	fari	white
	qanqane	small	danye	fresh, raw, unripe
	tsofo	old	qarami	small
	dogo	long, tall	mugu	bad
	baqi	black	ja	red

(SOURCE: Dixon 1982 and references therein.)

    Dixon (1982) notes that membership is not arbitrary in the adjective
category in those languages for which it is a closed class. Instead, there is a
pattern to the types of adjectival meanings that are expressed. A closed class
of adjectives, he argues, tends to include expressions of size, color, age, and
estimation of worth (e.g., good and bad). In (5), only the adjective *danye* might
thus be considered to be an unusual member of the class.

    A second universal about lexical classes is that all languages differentiate
between nouns and verbs.[2] The universality of this distinction is grounded in
some elemental functions of linguistic communication. Two of the basic uses
of language are naming objects in the real world (**reference**) and describing
the behavior or properties of these objects (**predication**). The noun-verb
distinction is simply the grammatical manifestation of these communicative
functions. We therefore expect the primary use of nouns to be reference and
the primary use of verbs to be predication.

    The presence of other word classes in the world's languages varies in
frequency. Adjectives, although probably not universal, are still extremely
common. As noted previously, however, the nature of this class (i.e., whether
it is open or closed) and its size differs as one moves from language to
language. In some languages, the concepts that appear as adjectives in English
are mostly lexicalized as verbs (6).

(6) a. əy   mabu   u-de
       I   him-ACC   see-NEG(nonFUT)
       I did not see him.

b. phi   ǝdu   ŋaŋ-de
   cloth that   red-NEG(nonFUT)
   That cloth is not red.   (Data from Bhat 1994)

As these Manipuri (Tibeto-Burman: India) examples reveal, an adjectival concept (6b) is treated in the same way as a verb (6a) in that it takes the same inflectional morphology as a verb.

In other languages, adjectival notions are mostly lexicalized as nouns, such as in Quechua (Quechuan: Peru):

(7) a. rumi-ta   rikaa
         stone-ACC   1S.see
         I see a stone.
     b. hatun-ta   rikaa
         big-ACC   1S.see
         I see a big (one).   (Data from Weber 1983)

The word *hatun* ("big") takes accusative case and functions as the direct object of the clause in (7b). By virtue of these properties, it is indistinguishable from nouns such as *rumi* ("stone") (7a).

Finally, adjectival concepts are distributed between nouns and verbs in other languages. Dixon (1982), in reviewing such languages, found that certain types of adjectival notions such as physical properties are more likely to be expressed by verbs, whereas others such as human qualities (cruel, jealous, happy, etc.) tend to be lexicalized as nouns.

■ 1.1. Defining Lexical Classes

Having looked at some universals of lexical classes, I now turn to the issue of how such classes are to be defined in the first place. There have been four general approaches. As shall be seen, each has some merit, but none of them are sufficient on their own to provide conclusive definitions for parts of speech.

One method is to define word classes in terms of the morphology that their members take. Nouns, then, are those elements that are inflected for case, plurality, class, or all three. Verbs are words that have affixes indicating person, number, tense, mood, voice, or all four. Adjectives can be specified for degree (e.g., *happier* and *happiest*) and so on. Because these types of morphological marking typically arise only on nouns, verbs, and adjectives, this procedure will only be useful for the open classes. It has nothing to reveal about, for example, the difference between demonstratives and prepositions. A method based on morphology also has the shortcoming of not being fully applicable to all languages because some languages do not use affixes to indicate information on plurality, tense, degree, and so on.

The second method is to determine class membership on the basis of syntax. Using this procedure, the distribution of words and their grammatical functions are examined. Nouns, for example, will be those words that can be modified by demonstratives and relative clauses (distribution) and can serve as the subjects and objects of clauses (their function). Adjectives would be those words that can be modified to indicate degree (e.g., *really happy, too big,* and *pickiest*) and in turn function to modify nouns. In languages for which the major classes are highly differentiated, this approach to lexical classes works rather well. It is far less successful when the lines between word classes are blurred.

An analysis of closed class items in terms of distribution generally works rather well, although it often leaves open the question (discussed in the introduction) about whether two elements are members of the same category but belong to different subclasses or whether they are simply members of different categories. As a case in point, compare the distribution of the two English auxiliary verbs *have* and *should.* On the one hand, their distribution is similar: Both may be fronted in forming questions ("Should I go to the bathroom?" or "Have you gone to the bathroom?"); in negative sentences, the negative word follows *should* or *have,* or the negative clitic *n't* is attached to them ("You shouldn't eat unfamiliar mushrooms," or "I haven't eaten a mushroom all day"); and they appear in tag questions ("I shouldn't eat the whole thing, should I?" or "He hasn't eaten the whole thing, has he?"). Because the two words share a number of distributional properties, their inclusion in the same class is justified: Or is it? Note that when the two words co-occur, they have a fixed order ("I should have been there" vs. "*I have should been there"), and the word *have* must co-occur with a past participle ("I haven't eaten"/"*ate"/"*eat"), but *should* never does ("*I should eaten"). (NB: Asterisks are used here and throughout the book to indicate that a sentence is ungrammatical.) On this basis, one could just posit two different subclasses of auxiliary verbs, but one could also simply set up two distinct categories. The syntactic approach to classification does not assist in making this decision.

The third way to go about defining parts of speech is on the basis of semantics. In its simplest form, this method assigns words to lexical classes based broadly on their meaning. Thus, to use some familiar formulae, a noun is "a person, place, thing, or idea," a verb is "an action or a state," an adjective is "a property," etc. By its very nature, this procedure will only be useful for determining the major classes because many minor classes do not have a meaning outside of their use in grammar. The conjunction *and*, for example, cannot be defined without making reference to the role that it plays in linguistic structure (try it!).

A more serious shortcoming with the semantic method is that simple specifications of meaning such as "a person, place, thing, or idea" are vague so that they admit many exceptions. A word such as *polka* is more obviously an action (or an event) than a thing; it is, however, just as easily employed as a noun as it is employed as a verb. Because of rampant exceptions such as this to the traditional semantic method, a number of linguists have suggested that a more complex meaning-based approach is necessary. Givón (1979) has argued that the boundaries between nouns, verbs, and adjectives are fuzzy by nature. Instead of devising definitions for these categories that delineate rigid semantic criteria for membership, he proposes that the definitions set up **prototypes** that particular words will match to varying degrees. A prototype is the ideal example of a category. Concepts such as "chair," "house," and "dog" might be prototypical nouns, and "hit," "go," and "give" might be prototypical verbs. Givón argues further that the basic semantic feature that underlies prototypes in the major lexical classes is **time stability.** He writes,

> Experiences . . . which stay relatively *stable* over time . . . tend to be lexicalized in human language as nouns. . . . At the other extreme of the lexical-phenomenological scale, one finds experiential clusters denoting *rapid changes* in the state of the universe . . . Languages tend to lexicalize them as verbs. (51-2)

Notably, Givón's proposal ties lexical classes directly into human experience.[3] Those sensory experiences that are static and persistent will be named by nouns, whereas those bundles of sensory data that are dynamic and temporary will be named by verbs. Adjectives, says Givón, fall on the middle of this time-stability scale.

The recognition of prototypicality and time-stability are both crucial insights into the nature of lexical classes, but they are not without their own deficiencies. Prototypicality actually does not solve the problem concerning how lexical classes are determined; what it does is to realign the expectations that one has about the predictability of class membership. One still needs to define the prototypes in a satisfactory manner, and this turns out to be problematic.

Regarding Givón's (1979) notion of time-stability, in practice it is very hard to apply. Why should *feast* so easily be used as a noun or verb, whereas *banquet* has a strong predilection for use as a noun. What about verbs that denote highly stable experiences such as *to tower* or nouns that readily denote temporary experiences such as *a fire, a flicker,* or *a glance*? Finally, what about abstractions such as *justice* or *mercy*? In all these cases, the relevance of a time-stability scale is unclear.

Another problem with Givón's (1979) proposal is that adjectives do not appear to fit on the time-stability scale in the way he assumes. As Thompson (1988) points out, the typical properties associated with adjectives involve size, shape, texture, and so on, all of which are relatively stable properties. Conceptually, they do not seem to fall in between nouns and verbs in any transparent way. Moreover, placing adjectives on the middle of the time-stability scale makes inaccurate predictions about their morphosyntactic properties. For example, in a language in which adjectival notions tend to be lexicalized as nouns, one would still expect them to display some morphological or syntactic properties that reflected their relative time-instability. They do not appear to ever act in this way, however.

For this reason, some linguists have suggested that lexical class membership may not be semantic at all but instead be based on discourse properties (Hopper and Thompson 1984; Thompson 1988). As with the morphological and semantic approaches, the discourse perspective on class membership is most directly applicable to the major parts of speech. The central idea is that prototypical nouns tend to introduce participants or props into discourse. Prototypical verbs, alternatively, are those that assert the actual occurrence of events in the discourse. To get a sense for how this system might be applied, examine the following sentences, which are taken from Hopper and Thompson (1984):

(8) a. Early in the chase the hounds started up an old red FOX, and we hunted him all morning.
    b. After the break, McTavish THREW the log.
    c. We went FOX-hunting in the Berkshires.
    d. To THROW a log that size takes a great deal of strength.

In (8a), a new participant, *fox,* is introduced into the discourse. This noun can be singular or plural, it can be modified, marked for case, and so on. Therefore, in this prototypical use, a noun, with all the properties normally associated with a noun, is employed. In (8c), however, the same lexical root has lost its ability to take nominal inflection or be modified (e.g., the form *red-foxes-hunting* is terrible). In (8b), *threw* appears in a prototypically verbal function and thus may appear in a variety of tenses and moods, take agreement, and so on. In (8d), in which the verbal root arises in a nonprototypical function, it has lost these properties.

Certain kinds of concepts are best suited to introduce participants or props, whereas others are better suited to signal events so that over time the respective concept types will form "lexical classes." Because nouns, verbs, and adjectives are primarily epiphenomena of discourse, however, the boundaries between the classes will not be at all sharp. Indeed, certain words may shift their properties quite easily.

In summary, there are a variety of different perspectives from which the determination of parts of speech can be carried out: morphological, syntactic, semantic, and discourse. Each of them has its strengths, yet each of them falls short of applicability across all categories for all languages. Hence, the most fruitful approach has been, and is, to use them in combination.

2.0. Semantic Roles

Whenever we encounter a well-formed sentence, we automatically assign meaning to it. This is part of what it means to know and use language. The comprehension of sentences happens so effortlessly that we might suppose there is not much to this interpretive task. Nothing could be further from the truth. How speakers are able to construct meaning out of sequences of sounds and words remains the single greatest mystery of language.

What linguists do know, however, is that part of what it means to interpret a sentence accurately is to understand the semantic connection that noun phrases have to the rest of the sentence. Consider the sentences, "Spike barked" and "Lenore stretched." Somewhat obviously, yet quite importantly, we understand that in the first case, *Spike* represents an entity carrying out the action of barking, and in the second case *Lenore* represents an entity involved in stretching. Furthermore, despite the fact that barking and stretching are extremely different kinds of action, we also recognize a similarity between the roles that Spike and Lenore play in their respective sentences. In both cases, they are the ones who most directly brought about the occurrence of an event. Therefore, it is desirable to produce a label, such as "agent," that captures the conceptual similarity. Such labels are called *semantic roles*. They indicate the relationship that nominals bear to the clause that contains them.[4]

Sentences often contain multiple noun phrases and, correspondingly, multiple semantic roles can be affiliated with the same sentence. For example, in the sentence, "Last Monday, Mary baked a cake for John's birthday, the noun phrase *Last Monday* has a **temporal** semantic role, *Mary* is an agent of the verb, *a cake* is a **patient**, and *John's birthday* is **purposive.**

These and other common semantic roles[5] are given in (9):

(9) Agent (entity causing action): **The cook** has diced the carrots.

   Benefactive (entity benefiting): The chapter has been written for
    Lindsay.   .

   Comitative (expresses accompaniment): I always go to the store with
    my dog.

   Experiencer (recipient of cognitive stimulus): **Freud** feared his mother.

   Goal (end point of motion): Ms. Marcos arrived at **the store** to buy
    shoes.

   Instrumental (tool used in carrying out a task): Blake is walking with **a
    cane.**

   Locative (point in space): Elvis lived at **Graceland.**

   Patient (entity affected by action): George chopped down **the cherry
    tree.**

   Purposive (reason for action): The pauper washed dishes **for his supper.**

   Recipient (entity receiving object): Ivana will donate her diamonds to
    the Humane Society.

   Source (origin of motion): Whitney entered from **the rear of the stage.**

   Temporal (point in time): Father John left the church **at noon.**

   Theme (object in motion): The Unabomber threatened to send **a
    package** to LAX.

The list in (9) is intended to provide a sense for the types of semantic roles that are commonly employed by linguists. The list is not at all complete nor is it likely to be embraced by all linguists in its current form because there is disagreement over what exactly the roster of roles should be. For example, I have listed the semantic role of *theme* and described it as the label given to an "object in motion." By virtue of this description, the notion of theme is distinct from that of patient. Some linguists, however, have suggested that these two roles should be collapsed into one.

Why should such indeterminacy exist? Part of the problem is that no set method has been agreed upon to define individual semantic roles (see Jackendoff 1987 and Dowty 1991 for discussions). Recall from the introductory section the complications involved in defining the role of agent. If just the semantic properties of volition, force, and control are considered, one might take agent in the most restrictive sense as a nominal that possesses all three of these properties. The nominal *Mary* in "Mary angrily rolled the ball down the hill" would be an agent because it describes a entity who chose to roll the ball (i.e., had the property of volition) and caused the rolling (i.e. has the property of force). On the other hand, in the sentence, "Mary rolled the ball by mistake," the nominal *Mary* could no longer be called an agent because it does not refer to an individual that is acting volitionally. If one followed this tack, then a different semantic role would need to be posited for *Mary.* One might use the label *effector,* for example.

Conversely, one could take a more inclusive approach to defining semantic roles. An agent, using this approach, could be taken as a nominal that possessed any of the three properties of volition, control, and force rather than possessing all of them. In this case, it might also be possible to collapse additional roles, such as *instrument,* into the notion of agent. The trade-off would be that one could not then explain, for example, why some languages treat volitional entities distinctly from nonvolitional entities.

There have been abundant attempts to address this issue, and I will not go through them in any detail here. Suffice it to say that the general approach has been to posit as few roles as possible, identifying a new role only when it seems to be required by the morphology or syntax of a number of languages. For example, although experiencers and agents tend share a great many semantic properties (they are usually animate, conscious beings), the patterns of case marking in some languages suggest that they are best kept distinct. Specifically, quite a few languages can mark experiencers, but not agents, with dative case in transitive clauses, as in Korean (Korean: Korea):

(10) Chelswu-eykey   Swuni-ka   mopsi   kuli-wess-ta
      Chulsoo-DAT   Sooni-NOM   badly   miss-PST-IND
      Chulsoo missed Sooni badly.   (Data from Gerdts 1991)

Similarly, English experiencers, but not agents, are commonly marked by the preposition *to* ("The party was quite pleasing to me"/"exciting to me"/"exasperating to me"/etc.). Because experiencers and agents are often manifested by unique patterns of case marking, there is good reason to posit unique roles.

Although morphosyntactic evidence for distinct roles is a solid methodological requirement, it still leaves open the problem of proliferating semantic roles every time a minute discrepancy between the properties of two nominals is identified. Is a single morphological distinction in a single language enough to determine a unique role? If so, then there are probably tens of thousands of them. If not, then how many different morphological or syntactic distinctions are required and in how many languages? There is certainly no agreement on the answers to these questions at this time. Nevertheless, most analysts tend to argue for somewhere between 8 and 20 unique roles.

3.0. Grammatical Relations

Grammatical relations are functional roles in clauses, such as subject, direct object, and indirect object, identifiable by special morphological and syntactic marking. Grammatical relations are perceptible in language by a cluster of properties associated with a nominal that are not directly relatable to the semantic role of the nominal. In English, for instance, nominals bearing many disparate semantic roles can serve as the subject of a clause: agents (**"John** bought the tickets"), patients (**"The tickets** were bought by John"), recipients (**"John** was sent an anonymous letter"), and so on. In other words, the major purpose of grammatical relations is to neutralize semantic role distinctions for the purposes of morphology and syntax.

The ways in which grammatical relations are marked varies from language to language. *Inter alia,* English subjects are preverbal and trigger verb agreement. If a pronoun is a subject, it will be in nominative case (*he, they, she,* or *we*) rather than objective case (*him, them, her,* or *us*). Moreover, if two sentences are conjoined with *and,* the subject (and not any other relation) of the second can be deleted—for example,"Mary saw John, and then kissed him" is fine, but "Mary saw John, and then she kissed" is unacceptable. Although there are many other such properties that could be listed for determining English subjects, other languages may use very different schemes. For example, in Malagasy (Austronesian: Madagascar), only subjects can be relativized:

(11) ny   mpianatra   [izay   nahita   ny   vehivavy]
     the   student   that   saw   the   woman
     the student who saw the woman   (Data from Keenan and Comrie 1977)

Relative clauses (such as the one bracketed in (11)) are discussed further in Chapter 15; what is important to draw from this example is that the subject of the verb *nahita* ("saw") is the element that is relativized. In English, one could also relativize an object ("the woman whom the student saw"). In contrast, Malagasy restricts relativization to subjects, and therefore the construction serves as one of the ways the subject relation is individuated in the language.

The universality of grammatical relations is a controversial topic. No one doubts that they play a significant role in a wide array of languages. Their status as universals, however, has been questioned on two fronts. First, the specific set of grammatical relations that is found in the world's languages is debated. The problem here is again partly one of definitions, but there are empirical issues as well. (See Keenan 1976 for a well-known attempt to define the notion of "subject.") Second, some have questioned whether grammatical relations exist in all languages or whether there are certain languages for which the concept is irrelevant. Both of these problems are addressed in the following section.

■ 3.1. Grammatical Relations as Universals

Both in traditional grammar and in several contemporary syntactic theories (e.g., Relational Grammar and Lexical-Functional Grammar), it is assumed that there are three primary grammatical relations that can be held by noun phrases in a clause: subject, direct object, and indirect object.[6] The rationale for this presumption is drawn from some recurrent cross-linguistic lexical, morphological, and syntactic facts. The first piece of evidence for a universal set of three grammatical relations comes from the argument structure of verbs. Recall that it is the nature of verbs to express states or actions. In the expression of actions, verbs specify the number and the roles of entities participating in an event. For example, English speakers know that the verb *fly* entails motion by a single participant, and that the verb *devour* requires two participants, the one doing the devouring and the person or thing being eaten. The entities specified by the verb are called **arguments.** An interesting fact about verbs is that they have inherent restrictions on the minimum number of arguments that appear with them. An English sentence headed by *fly* must include at least one argument; thus, the utterance *flew quickly* is immediately recognized by an English speaker to be incomplete. Similarly, the verb *devour* requires two arguments (cf."*John devoured"). Certain verbs such as *give* also require three arguments. One never finds, however, verbs that require four or more arguments, either in English or any other language.[7] Hence, there seems to be an upper limit of three mandatory verbal arguments. Furthermore, the treatment of these required arguments tends to hold a privileged status in the morphology and syntax of languages: They are marked in ways not available to other noun phrases occurring in the sentence, a point I return to presently. The proposal that there are three special functions—or grammatical relations—captures all these facts in a straightforward manner.

At the outset of Section 3.0, I pointed out that grammatical relations are determinable by a cluster of morphological and syntactic properties and subsume nominals with diverse semantic roles. An example of this occurring for English subjects was provided. The same kind of neutralization occurs with direct objects and indirect objects. The following is an example from Spanish (Italic: Spain and Latin America) of the latter:

(12) a. Mi   madre   le   mandó   una   carta a   **Carmita**
      my   mother   3S-DAT   sent   a   letter to   Carmita
      My mother sent a letter to Carmita.

   b. Marta le   recordó   el   asunto   a   **Pablo**
      Marta 3S-DAT   reminded   the   matter   to   Pablo
      Marta reminded Pablo about the matter.

   c. Esa mujer le   robó   un   reloj   a   **mi   padre**
      that woman 3S-DAT   stole   a   watch   to   my   father
      That woman stole a watch from my father.   (Data from Farrell 1994)

The nominals in bold type are all encoded in the clause structure in the same way. They are postverbal and follow the direct object, they are flagged by the preposition *a* ("to"), and they are cross-referenced by the preverbal clitic *le*. This cluster of morphosyntactic properties allows them to be identified as indirect objects. As such, they can bear a number of semantic roles such as recipient (12a), experiencer (12b), and source (12c).

Languages seem to be restricted to three such "slots" for neutralization in their grammars, however, which is evidence again for there being only three grammatical relations in the universal set.[8]

A final reason that subject, direct object, and indirect object have been taken as the universal class of grammatical relations is that verb agreement is often designed to encode these, and not any other, noun phrases. This issue is raised again in detail in Chapter 9. For present purposes, it is sufficient to say that if a language exhibits verb agreement with any nominals in a clause, it will be with those nominals that are typically called subjects, direct objects, indirect objects, or all three, but with no others.

So far, then, several reasons have been furnished for why the class of grammatical relations contains three members. The question has been raised repeatedly, however, as to whether the same three relations appear in every language. This objection can be broken down into two parts. On the one hand, one might ask whether every language uses all three grammatical relations. There is plenty of evidence to show that they do not. In particular, the relation of indirect object does not appear to play a role in every language.[9] Rather, languages tend to fall into two groups—those that use two grammatical relations and those that use three. Following Gerdts (1992), I refer to these types respectively as *direct object-centered* and *indirect object-centered* languages.

Certain morphosyntactic properties characterize each. Direct object-centered languages tend to have very little case marking and have verb agreement only with subjects or only with subjects and direct objects. They also tend to permit recipients to appear as direct objects. In English, for example, recipients may be flagged by the preposition *to* ("I gave the ball to Jim") or they may be treated as direct objects ("I gave Jim the ball").

In contrast, indirect object-centered languages tend to have robust case-marking systems and to allow verb agreement with indirect objects. Moreover, they often permit patients, which are typically treated as direct objects in direct object-centered languages, to be encoded as indirect objects. This, for instance, occurs in Choctaw (Penutian: United States):

(13) a. An-at-o   iskali   chim-a:-li-tok
         I-NOM-CONTR   money   2.DAT-give-1.NOM-PST
         I gave the money to you.
     b. Chim-alikchi-li-tok
         2.DAT-doctor-1.NOM-PST
         I doctored you.   (Data from Davies 1986)

As can be seen in the Choctaw clause in (13b), the patient nominal ("you") is
marked on the verb using the prefix (*chim-*) that is utilized for marking indirect
objects (cf. 13a).

We have seen, then, that languages almost without exception use three or
fewer grammatical relations, and that there is a principled distinction between
languages that use two and languages that use three. Are there languages that
use one or that do not use grammatical relations at all? It is unlikely. Only a
few such languages have been reported in the literature. For example, Van
Valin (1993b) argues that Achenese (Austronesian: Indonesia) grammar
makes no use of grammatical relations. Even in this case, however, Van Valin's
analysis makes reference to two relations (which he calls Actor and Under-
goer) that are not fully semantic. Indeed, his relations are abstract notions that
function to conflate different semantic roles and, in this way, they are very
much like grammatical relations. Hence, his argument is not so much that
grammatical relations are not employed in Achenese, but that the relations
that are used are not fully aligned with what have traditionally been called
subjects and direct objects. This leads us to the second way in which the
universal set of three grammatical relations has been questioned.

One might ask if a language, even if it uses no fewer than two and no
more than three grammatical relations, uses relations equivalent to subjects
and objects as they are normally understood. The answer appears to be that
languages sometimes do employ grammatical relations that differ from the
traditional concepts. For example, consider the following pattern of case
assignment in Kalkatungu (Kalkatungic: Australia):

(14) a. Kaun   muu-yan-ati
         dress.ABS   dirt-PROP-INCH
         The dress is dirty.
     b. Kuntu   wampa-ngku   kaun   muu-yan-puni-mi
         not   girl-ERG   dress.ABS   dirty-PROP-CAUS-FUT
         The girl will not dirty the dress.   (Data adapted from Blake 1994)[10]

The nominals that correspond to subjects are *kaun* ("dress") in (14a) and *wampangku* ("girl") in (14b). Notice, however, that these two "subjects" are case marked differently. Only the latter carries a case suffix (*-ngku*). Consequently, one cannot state a case-marking rule in terms of the notion subject. Rather, Kalkatungu case marking operates on the basis of a different system of grammatical relations. Specifically, for such languages, the relations **ergative** and **absolutive** are invoked. An ergative nominal is equivalent to the subject of a transitive clause in English. An absolutive is equivalent to the subject of an intransitive clause or the direct object of a transitive clause. Do not worry if, at this point, this terminology is confusing. It is described in fuller detail in Chapter 9. What is crucial to grasp here is that the use of "subject" and "object" is not helpful for describing the case marking of core arguments in languages such as Kalkatungu. This is not to say, however, that the notions subject and object are completely vacuous in this language. There are other aspects of the grammar that still revolve around the more familiar grammatical relations, including verbal agreement with pronouns:

(15) a. Nyinti   yapatyarra-thati-nha-mpa-**n**
        you   will-become-PST-PFV-2.SUB
        Are you well again?

     b. Nyinti   waku   ithiti-mpa-**n**
        you   skin   throw-PERF-2.SUB
        You threw away the skin?

     c. Itya-nyin-**kin**   nyini   munthuntu
        biting-2.OBJ   you   bullant
        The bullants are biting you.   (Data from Blake 1990)

The verb suffixes (in bold type) cross-reference the second-person pronoun in each of these clauses. In (15a) and (15b), the suffix (*-n*) is marking subjects versus (15c), in which the suffix (*-ki*) signals that the pronoun is an object. Thus, for this aspect of agreement, the grammatical relations subject and object must be used.

Most languages that evince an ergative-absolutive distinction are like Kalkatungu in also having many aspects of their grammatical system that operate on a subject-object basis. Only a few exceptions to this generalization have been reported, mostly among Philippine languages and Caucasian languages. Even in these cases, however, the analyses that have been furnished are controversial in their details and open to a number of interpretations. At any rate, it is clear that even after one recognizes the existence of ergative and absolutive relations there is still a need to take the notions of subject and object as being somehow more basic to human language.

On the basis of the empirical facts from languages such as Kalkatungu, the universal set of grammatical relations must be extended to include absolutive and ergative. Furthermore, it must be recognized that certain languages will employ up to five relations (subject, direct object, indirect object, ergative, and absolutive) within their grammars. No more than three of these relations, however, will appear in any given clause. Finally, it should be emphasized that the significance of grammatical relations for particular languages is a matter of degree. In a language such as English, the notion of a subject (or object) is crucial in describing a great many aspects of basic clause structure. In other linguistic systems, however, semantic roles may have a greater impact on grammatical constructions, or perhaps discourse notions such as "topic" override the importance of grammatical relations in determining the statement of syntactic rules.

4.0. Summary

Some basic categories of language have been examined. In each case, it was found that the categories are universal in some sense, but that their universal status was subject to substantial caveats and classifications. In particular, it was revealed that the definition that one gives to these categories has implications for whether it can be applied to all languages or applied consistently within languages. The problem of definitions was not so much solved here as introduced so that the reader might be aware of some of the controversies involved in research on lexical classes, semantic roles, and grammatical relations. Nonetheless, the utility of these categories for linguistic analysis should have become clear. Indeed, it will become apparent in the chapters that follow that it is nearly impossible to do typology without making constant reference to the various notions discussed in this chapter.

5.0. Key Terms

Absolutive	Semantic role:
Agent	Agent
Argument	Benefactive
Closed class	Comitative
Ergative	Experiencer
Grammatical relation	Goal
Lexical class	Instrumental
Noun classifier	Locative
Open class	Patient
Part of speech	Purposive
Patient	Recipient
Predication	Source
Prototype	Temporal
Reference	Theme
	Time-stability

Notes

1. For certain adjectives, the comparative and the superlative are formed by the addition of the suffixes *-er* and *-est,* respectively (e.g., *darker* or *darkest*). For others, the comparative and superlative are created by placing the words *more* and *most* before the adjective (e.g., *more redundant* or *most redundant*). The choice between the two options is primarily phonological. The first strategy is employed with one-syllable adjectives and two-syllable adjectives ending in the sound [i] (e.g., *saltier* or *saltiest*). The second strategy is used for others. The picture is actually much more complicated than this, however. There are certain types of adjectives that do not consistently adhere to either of the strategies, such as two-syllable adjectives whose second syllable is a syllabic [n] or [l]. Hence, one hears both *commonest* and *most common* as well as both *subtler* and *more subtle*. There are also individual adjectives that are frequently used in the unexpected form. For instance, American English speakers commonly say *more fun* rather than *funner.* Finally, there is the phenomenon of double comparatives in which both the suffix *-er* and the word *more* are utilized together. It is my impression that the double comparative is rapidly increasingly in use.

2. On occasion, counterexamples to this universal have been proposed, but in general they have been demonstrated to be spurious when additional data are examined. The most celebrated instance of a language that supposedly does not make a distinction between nouns and verbs is Nootka (Almosan-Keresiouan: Canada). The great anthropological linguist Morris Swadesh (1938, 78) claimed that words in this language "do not fall into classes like noun, verb, adjective, preposition, but all sorts of ideas find their expression in the same general type of word, which is predicative or non-predicative according to its paradigmatic ending." Jacobsen (1979) has shown, however, that Swadesh has overstated the case. It is, in fact, possible to locate a distinction between verbs and nouns in the language. The lasting legacy of Swadesh's claim is that the degree of demarcation between categories can differ among languages. The division in languages such as Nootka is slight relative to a language such as English.

3. The tradition in generative grammar has been to treat lexical classes as a basic part of the innate language capacity rather than a direct reflection of sensory experience.

4. One profound question about semantic roles is whether they are purely conceptual notions (and therefore are not really linguistic notions per se) or whether they are truly linguistic notions that relate concepts to linguistic structures. I assume the latter here.

5. A number of terms other than *semantic role* are used in linguistics: *logical role, thematic role, theta role, thematic relation, case role,* and *deep case relation.*

6. It should be noted that in Relational Grammar the set of grammatical relations includes additional members, although the precise number is a matter of debate.

7. Although it is not common, one does find that in some languages verbs require four arguments if they appear with causative affixes or applicative marking. See Chapters 9 and 11 for more details.

8. Kinyarwanda (Niger-Congo: Rwanda) and perhaps other Bantu languages are exceptions to this otherwise absolute statement (see Gerdts and Whaley 1992 and Whaley 1993).

9. See Comrie (1989) who questions the need to posit that English has an indirect object.

10. Blake (1994), following the tradition among Australianists, uses the gloss NOM(inative) rather than Abs(olutive).

PART

Word Order Typology

5

Constituent Order Universals

A prominent area of study within typology deals with the order of elements in clauses and phrases. You have already been exposed to this type of work in the discussion on universals in earlier chapters. Many of Greenberg's (1966) universals, for instance, deal with the ordering of various constituents (1):

(1) Greenberg's Universal 17: With overwhelmingly more than chance frequency, languages with dominant order VSO have the adjective after the noun.

In this chapter, we take a closer look at constituent order universals and some possible explanations for them.

1.0. Order of Clausal Constituents

In typological research, there has been particular interest in the relative ordering of subject (S), verb (V), and object (O). The most prevalent distribution of these three elements in a language is sometimes referred to as the "basic word order" for that language. As many scholars have noted, however, this terminology is improper because subjects (as well as objects) are not always single words (as in 2a), but rather sometimes phrases (2b) or even clauses (2c).

(2)   a. **Phil** seems strange.
      b. **The new neighbor** seems strange.
      c. **That the Red Sox won the pennant** seems strange.

Accordingly, the term "basic constituent order" is used here to describe the dominant linear arrangement of S, V, and O.

For many languages, a basic constituent order can be determined easily and noncontroversially. For example, in English we find clauses with the orders OSV (3a) and VSO (3b), but it is quite clear that these orders are "special" and that SVO is typical (3c).

(3)   a. Beans, I hate.
      b. Believe you me.
      c. Seymour sliced the salami.

In addition to the strong intuition of native speakers, there are many reasons to claim that (3c) is the basic order for English. There is a distinctive intonational pattern in (3a)—a slight pause after *beans*; it also has a specialized use in discourse—for example, to contrast *beans* with something the speaker does not like as in "I like peas, but beans I hate." Indeed, without some discourse context, (3a) sounds odd. Moreover, it is not considered grammatical by all English speakers. Because it is an idiom, (3b) is not representative of basic constituent order. Consequently, there are very few expressions that can occur in the same VSO form (4).

(4)   a. *Believe John Mary.
      b. *Hit Jane Seymour.
      c. *Surrender you your village.

Because orders other than SVO have specific constraints on their use, the order in (3c), which has no such constraints, is identified as the basic order.

Not all languages have as strict a word order as English does, however. These languages often provide a unique challenge to typologists because their basic constituent order is much more difficult to ascertain. In ancient Greek (Hellenic), for example, S, V, and O can potentially arise in any order (5).

(5) a. ho   didaskal-os   paideuei   to   paidi-on   [SVO]
        ART   teacher-NOM   teaches   ART   boy-ACC
        The teacher instructs the boy.
     b. ho didaskalos to paidion paideuei   [SOV]
     c. paideuei ho didaskalos to paidion   [VSO]
     d. paideuei to paidion ho didaskalos   [VOS]
     e. to paidion ho didaskalos paideuei   [OSV]
     f. to paidion paideuei ho didaskalos   [OVS]

Despite the variation in word order, there is no confusion over the intended meaning of the sentences in (5) because nominals in Greek are marked for **case** (case is a system of marking noun phrases for their grammatical function in a phrase or clause—see Chapter 9 for a complete description). In (5) there is a nominative case suffix (*-os*) attached to the noun *didaskal-* ("teacher") that indicates that this nominal serves as the subject of the clause. Similarly, *-on,* which is an accusative case suffix, is attached to the noun *paidi-* ("boy") to signal that it is the direct object of the clause.

Although some of the word orders clearly serve special discourse functions in Greek (e.g., (5e) and (5f)), not all of them do in a straightforward way. Consequently, there is disagreement over which of the orders, if any, is basic. For now, I simply raise this as an issue to be kept in mind. In the next chapter, how one might make a decision on the dominant order of V, S, and O in a "free" constituent order language is examined.

There are six logically possible orders of S, V, and O, and all of them have been claimed to serve as the basic constituent order for at least one language in the world. An example of each is provided in (6).

(6) SOV: Taro   ga   inu   o   mita (Japanese [Japanese-Ryukyuan: Japan])
           Taro   SUB   dog   OBJ saw
           Taro saw the dog.
     SVO: Umugore   arasoma   igitabo (Kinyarwanda [Niger-Congo: Rwanda])
           woman   3S-read   book
           The woman is reading a book.

VSO: Bara   Elohim   et   ha-shamayim
     created   God   OBJ   ART-heavens
     God created the heavens.

                                   (Biblical Hebrew [Semitic])

VOS: Manasa   lamba   amin'ny   savony   ny   lehilahy
     washes   clothes with.the soap   the   man
     The man washes clothes with the soap.

              (Malagasy [Austronesian: Madagascar])

      (Adapted from White, Travis, and MacLachlan 1992)

OVS: Toto   yahosiye   kamara
     man   it-grabbed-him   jaguar
     The jaguar grabbed the man.

                           (Hixkaryana [Carib: Brazil])

                             (Data from Derbyshire 1985)

OSV: pako   xuã   u'u
     banana   John   he.ate
     John ate bananas.

           (Urubú [Equatorial-Tucanoan: Brazil])

     (Data from Kakumasu as cited in Derbyshire and Pullum 1981)

Although each of the six possible orders of these major clausal constituents have been attested, they are not evenly distributed among the languages of the world. This provides a clue to a significant organizational principle of human language—if the ordering of S, V, and O were random, we would expect each of the constituent order types to appear with about the same frequency. In fact, some orders turn out to be relatively common, whereas others are remarkably rare. Table 5.1 captures the relative frequency of each word order type.

The frequency with which SOV and SVO occur is startling. If basic constituent order were not governed by some principle or principles of language, then each of the six potential orders would occur with roughly the same statistical frequency (16%). SOV and SVO are found in over 40% of the languages in the sample, however, and together they comprise almost 90% of the total. Clearly, then, the distribution cannot be taken as random, and some explanation must be determined for their statistical dominance.[1]

A slightly different arrangement of the data in Table 5.1 comparing the relative ordering of just two of the basic constituents, S and O, reveals another striking pattern (Table 5.2).

TABLE 5.1 Frequencies of Basic Constituent Orders

	Languages	
Word Order	*Number*	*%*
SOV	180	45
SVO	168	42
VSO	37	9
VOS	12	3
OVS	5	1
OSV	0	—
Total	402	

SOURCE: Adapted from Tomlin (1986, 22).

TABLE 5.2 Relative Frequencies of the Order of S + O

	Languages	
Word Order	*Number*	*%*
SO	385	96
OS	17	4
Total	402	

Languages that place the subject before the object (96%) are quite conspicuously more common than those that place the subject after the object (4%). This distribution was also noted by Greenberg (1966) and captured by his Universal 1:

(7)   Greenberg's Universal 1: In declarative sentences with nominal subject
      and object, the dominant order is almost always one in which the
      subject precedes the object.

Although this universal stipulates the linear precedence of subjects over objects, it does not explain why it should hold true in language. Comrie (1989, 93) suggests that this glaring priority of subject over object has a functional explanation. Presumably, a deeper cognitive organization of information underlies the pattern. In a transitive clause (that is, a clause with both a subject and an object), the subject generally is the initiator of the action expressed by the verb and the entity in control of that action, whereas the object is the entity being acted on. These properties of the subject make it more salient than the object in human cognition, and the saliency is reflected in languages when they develop a constituent order that puts subjects before objects.[2]

Table 5.1 reveals another remarkable pattern. The data reveal that languages in which O and V are contiguous are highly preferred. That is, basic constituent orders in which V and O are not separated by S occur far more commonly. Specifically, they are found in 365 (91%) of the languages. The tight bond between V and O as opposed to V and S or O and S has been recognized in linguistics for some time. In Government and Binding Theory, the close association is formalized in universal rules of phrase structure. Although the particular form that these rules take in Government and Binding would require a great deal of explanation, they can be presented as in (8).

(8) S → NP(sub); VP
     VP → V; NP(obj)

These rules dictate the organization of constituents in clauses. The first rule can be read as "a clause consists of a noun phrase (which is the subject) and a verb phrase." The second rule states that "a verb phrase consists of a verb and a noun phrase (object)." The semicolons that occur in the right-hand portion of the rules indicate that the two constituents may arise in either order. Together, the rules generate the following structures:

(9) NP(sub) V NP(obj)   [=SVO]
     NP(sub) NP(obj) V   [=SOV]
     V NP(obj) NP(sub)   [=VOS]
     NP(obj) V NP(sub)   [=OVS]

The phrase structure rules, which are presumed to be innate aspects of the human language capacity, do not generate OSV or VSO structures. Therefore, some exceptional linguistic property would be required to motivate these two orders and, as a consequence, they are less common.

You may have noticed that the rules in (8) do produce VOS and OVS sequences, and these are very uncommon orders. How can this fact be accounted for? If one assumes that the order of S, V, and O is sensitive not just to the phrase structure rules but also to other principles such as Comrie's notion of subject saliency, the rarity of these orders is understandable. As a demonstration (similar to a proposal made by Tomlin 1986), assume that just the two principles that have been discussed interact in establishing preferred

TABLE 5.3 Ordering Principles for S, V, and O

Word Order	Subject Saliency	Phrase Structure Rules
SVO	+	+
SOV	+	+
VSO	+	−
VOS	−	+
OVS	−	+
OSV	−	−

constituent order patterns. Table 5.3 reflects whether a given constituent order adheres to the principle (+) or fails to adhere (−).[3]

Those constituent orders that adhere to both principles are most common, those adhering to one of the principles less common, and OSV, which violates both principles, is extremely rare or nonexistent. Following Song (1991b), this approach can be further refined and made more accurate by giving more weight to the subject saliency principle. With this emendation, SVO and SOV would be most preferred, followed first by VSO, which adheres to the weightier principle, and then by VOS and OVS, which are in line with the unweighted principle. OSV would remain the least preferred type. Notice that these predictions correlate perfectly with Tomlin's (1986) data in Table 5.1.

The accuracy of this approach to word order suggests that it has merit. A few outstanding problems remain, however. First, the data in Table 5.1 are based on a sampling method that selects languages according to the size of the language family from which they come. For example, if Austronesian languages comprise 10% of the total number of languages in the world, then 10% of the languages in Table 5.1 would be Austronesian. Recall from Chapter 3, however, that this method does not necessarily indicate pure linguistic preference for a trait such as word order because language family size is partly due to nonlinguistic factors such as historical interactions between people groups. It should be noted, however, that other studies on the relative frequency of basic constituent orders that are grounded in different sampling techniques provide results that are consistent with the data in Table 5.1 in the relevant ways. That is, they indicate a dominance of SOV and SVO languages, a spattering of VSO, very few VOS and OVS, and almost no OSV.

A second problem is that there is no explanation as to why dispreferred languages ever arise in the first place. After all, if subject saliency and the phrase structure rules are essential aspects of the way that language is

TABLE 5.4 Lehmann's Constituent Order Correlations

Word Order	Correlation
VO	OV
Preposition + noun	Noun + preposition
Noun + genitive	Genitive + noun
Noun + adjective	Adjective + noun
Noun + relative clause	Relative clause + noun
Sentence-initial question word	Noninitial question word
Prefixes	Suffixes
Auxiliary verb + main verb	Main verb + auxiliary verb
Comparative adjective + standard	Standard + comparative adjective
Verb + adverb	Adverb + verb
Negative + verb	Verb + negative
Subordinator + clause	Clause + subordinator

organized, what would cause a language to develop in conflict with one or even both of them? Ultimately, the answer to this question would depend on looking at each of the languages in question. Work on VOS languages (Dik 1978, 176-77) and object initial languages (Derbyshire 1985, 101-04), however, has accounted for the "unexpected" word orders in terms of an atypical set of historical factors.

2.0. Constituent Order Correlations

With Greenberg's universals, it is striking how often the order of V, S, and O is used as a precondition in statements about the order of other constituents (Universals 3-5, 7, 10, 12, 13, 15-17, and 21). This fact led Lehmann (1973, 1978a) to conclude that the order of verb and object in language is somehow basic to the ordering of constituents in general for any given language.[4] Therefore, if one knows the relative ordering of V and O, one can predict the ordering of other pairs such as nouns and genitives, adpositions and nouns, nouns and adjectives, question words and clauses, affixes and roots, and so on. Lehmann's correlation pairs are given in Table 5.4.

A language such as Oroqen (Manchu-Tungus: China) nicely exemplifies the correlations given previously. It is SOV (10a), has postpositions (10b), possessors (genitives) before nouns (10c), adjectives before nouns (10d), relative clauses before the nouns they modify (10e), and so on.[5]

(10)

	S	O		V		N	Postposition
a.	∫i:	əri	t∫ɔmɔ araki-wa	umt∫aj	b.	kɔ:kanmi	dʒa:lin
	you	this	cup liquor-OBJ	drink		children	for
	You drank this cup of liquor.					for the children	

	Gen	N		Adj N	
c.	minɲi	araki-w	d.	ɔrɔbkun	tə:tiwə
	my	wine-1S		wet	clothes

	Relative clause		N		Qword	Qparticle
e.	bu:	ugt∫i-rə-t∫ə-wun	murin	f.	∫i: irə ŋənəni	jɛ
	we	ride-REL-PRES-1P	horse		you where go	QUES
	the horse we often ride				Where are you going?	

	Std	Comp. Adj		Adv	V
g.	∫in-du	gugda	h.	nɔ:nin əlkədʒi	gətet∫ən
	you-DAT	tall		he slowly	wake.up
	taller than you			He slowly woke up.	

		Neg V
i.	bi:	ə∫i-m umna
	I	not-1S drink
	I don't drink.	

Lehmann's proposal, in the simplified manner it has been presented so far, seems to capture an astonishing fact about the way that language behaves: Certain categories in language pattern like verbs and others like objects with respect to their relative ordering. Hence, the relationship between verbs and objects may represent a key organizing principle of language.

Unfortunately, the empirical evidence for Lehmann's correlations is not so straightforward. First, it is common for languages not to be fully consistent in following the expected patterns. English is one such example. In some ways, English manifests the patterns predicted for VO languages: It has prepositions, can use noun-genitive order ("house of John"), places relative clauses after nouns, puts auxiliaries, manner adverbs, and negatives before the verb, uses clause initial subordinators, and sets up comparative adjectives before the standard of comparison. It violates Lehmann's predictions, however, by employing the adjective-noun order, having a genitive-noun pattern ("John's house"), and being predominantly suffixing.

To account for these typological "inconsistencies," Lehmann (1973) invokes a historical explanation: "When languages show patterns other than those expected, we may assume that they are undergoing change" (55). Therefore, consistent OV-patterning and consistent VO-patterning languages are the ideals, but languages in the process of changing from one type to another exhibit properties of both.

Even after making such a provision for typologically inconsistent languages, there are still problems with Lehmann's proposal concerning word order correlations. Perhaps most significant, some of the patterns that he assumes to hold in language are not actually statistical correlations at all! For example, Dryer (1988a) shows that evidence is lacking for a correlation between verb-object order and noun-adjective order. As noted in Chapter 3, in most regions of the world OV languages are more likely to place adjectives after the noun rather than before it as the correlation pair in Table 5.3 suggests. Additionally, Lehmann's claims about affix ordering, the order of negatives and verbs, and the order of relative clause and noun have been called into serious doubt.

A second problem with Lehmann's list of correlation pairs is that he offers no explicit explanation for why they should occur. What is it about nouns and relative clauses, verbs and auxiliaries, and so on that cause them to pattern in accordance with the order of V and O? Perhaps the explanation that has been circulated most extensively is that of Venneman (1973, 1974b, 1976). He claims that underlying these correlation pairs is a deeper functional relationship: Languages have a propensity to consistently order **heads** and **dependents** regardless of the word class into which they fall.[6] Broadly speaking, a head is the central element of a construction. Dependents, on the other hand, generally modify the head or serve as one of its arguments.

Using the notions of head and dependent, Vennemann captures Lehmann's roster of correlations with a single generalization.[7] Like Lehmann, Vennemann allows for typologically inconsistent languages by setting up dependent-head and head-dependent as ideal language types that actual languages gravitate toward.

Vennemann's explanation leads him to depart from Lehmann's claims in one crucial respect. By framing word order universals in terms of heads and dependents, Vennemann has made all the correlations bilateral. This means that if one knows the order of adpositions and nouns in a language, one can predict the order of verb and object. In an important sense, the verb-object order is no longer basic to the correlations but is on a par with all other head-dependent pairs. Because the ordering of elements is now grounded in the abstract notions of dependent and head, there is no longer any need to explain why verbs and objects should serve as the basis of constituent order correlations.

The appeal to this deeper functional principle of organization has potential problems of its own, however. What about violations to the head-dependent predictions such as noun and adjective ordering? If languages that are consistently head-dependent or consistently dependent-head ideals, why are there so few languages that are actually ideal?

One linguist who has offered some important insights to these questions is John Hawkins (see, in particular, Hawkins 1983).[8] One of his most significant proposals is that the distinction between VO and OV languages used by Lehmann and Vennemann is not quite right (a point also made by Mallinson and Blake 1981 and Comrie 1989). Instead, he suggests that there is a three-way distinction between verb-initial languages, verb-final languages, and verb-medial languages (i.e., SVO and OVS). Although it is debatable whether this three-way distinction is actually empirically justified (see Dryer 1991), the significance of Hawkins's proposal has been that word order typologists have been led to reassess some long-held assumptions about constituent order correlations.

Second, Hawkins argues that the organizing principle for syntactic elements is not best described simply as dependent-head but by a principle of **cross-category harmony,** which states roughly that we should expect the most frequent types of languages to be those in which the proportion of dependents preceding one category of head is the same as the proportion of dependents preceding other categories of heads.[9] According to this principle, if a language places all its noun dependents (genitives, adjectives, and relative clauses) before the noun, then it will place all verb dependents (objects, adverbs, negatives, etc.) before the verb. Similarly, if most of the noun dependents appear before the noun, then most verb dependents will appear before the verb. If no dependents appear before the noun, then no dependents will appear before the verb. This principle is similar in spirit to that of Vennemann's, but it broadens the notion of what is considered a consistent language with respect to ordering. Thus, there arise fewer exceptions.

One final contribution of Hawkins must be noted. He also recognizes that there is no single principle responsible for the linear order of head-dependent pairs. Perhaps the best known example of competing principles is found in the interaction of nouns and relative clauses. As noun modifiers, one expects relative clauses to pattern according to the head-dependent principle (or the updated cross-category harmony principle). While there is a strong preference for VO languages to place relative clauses after nouns, the mirror image pattern (OV and relative clause + noun) does not hold. In fact, in many areas of the world there is a marked prominence of OV languages that place the relative clause after the noun, and when one considers all OV languages together, there is a slight preference for OV languages to have postnominal relative clauses (Dryer 1992). This constitutes an exception to the expected pattern. Hawkins proposes that, in the case of relative clauses, there is a second functional principle that must be considered: the **heavy constituent principle.**

Heavy constituents are those that contain a large number of grammatical elements. Relative clauses, as a class, certainly qualify because they usually consist of a number of phrases. The heavy constituent principle states that heavy constituents tend to be placed after the head that they modify. Therefore, although the head-dependent principle would lead to a relative clause + noun order, the heavy constituent principle would lead to noun + relative clause. Because of this conflict, OV languages are inconsistent in the way that they order these two elements.

Two of the problems with Vennemann's initial proposal, then, have been given at least partial solutions by Hawkins. First, some of the violations to the supposed correlations may be explicable in terms of competing organizing principles. Second, the relative frequency of inconsistent languages might be accounted for by allowing for a less rigid organizing constraint than the head-dependent principle.

Nevertheless, there remain some nagging issues. Are the categories defined as head and dependent the right ones? What about head-dependent pairs, such as nouns and adjectives, that simply do not seem to reflect any consistent patterns? For the remainder of this chapter, I outline a recent approach to constituent order correlations that appears to provide promising answers to these questions.

3.0. Branching Direction Theory

Matthew Dryer has re-examined two of the basic assumptions behind the head-dependent-based approaches discussed previously (in particular, see Dryer 1992). In addition to pointing out the lack of expected patterning by certain head-dependent pairs (including adjective-noun and demonstrative-noun), he draws attention to the fact that the predictive power of these explanations depends entirely on one's assumptions about which element in a given pair is the head. This is not controversial in some instances (e.g., verbs and adverbs) but is a matter of some debate in others (adpositions and nouns, subordinators and clauses, verbs and auxiliaries, etc.).

As a counterproposal, Dryer has outlined the branching direction theory (11).

(11) The Branching Direction Theory (BDT): Verb patterners are nonphrasal (nonbranching) categories and object patterners are phrasal (branching) categories. That is, a pair of elements X and Y will employ the order XY significantly more often among VO languages than among OV languages if and only if X is a nonphrasal category and Y is a phrasal category.

The version of the BDT provided here is syntactically based in that it makes reference to phrase structure. The crucial distinction is between branching and nonbranching categories. A branching category is one that has internal structure. For example, a noun phrase such as "books about the war" is not an atomic unit; it can be broken down further into parts: *books* is the head of the phrase and *about the war* is a prepositional phrase that modifies the head. Their relationship can be captured using a tree diagram as in Diagram 5.1.

As the diagram reveals, the noun phrase (NP) branches into its two constituents. The noun *books* is nonbranching because it has no internal syntactic structure. The prepositional phrase, in contrast, is branching because it can be further analyzed as having a prepositional head and an NP complement. As a further stipulation, a category is only considered branching for the purposes of the BDT if it consists of a nonbranching head and a phrasal complement. For example, the adjective phrase "very quiet" will not be considered a branching category because the degree word *very* is not a full phrase. That is, *very* cannot be modified or expanded in any way.

```
                    NP
                   /  \
                  N    PP
                  |    / \
              books   P   NP
                      |   / \
                  about  the war
```

Diagram 5.1

```
       VP                        NP
      /  \                      /  \
     V    NP                   N    RelCl
     |    / \                  |    /  \
   hit the  boy              man  Rel   Clause
                                  whom   / \
                                        I   hit
```

Diagram 5.2

With this terminology in place, consider the claims of the BDT. It pre-dicts that a language will tend to consistently place branching categories after nonbranching categories or vice versa. Another way to phrase this is that languages tend to be consistently **right branching** or consistently **left branching.** English is a good example of a right-branching language (Dia-gram 5.2).

In the first construction in Diagram 5.2, the verb *hit* is found before the noun phrase *the boy*. This noun phrase has internal structure; therefore, it is a branching category. Thus, for the combination of elements, *hit* and *the boy,* the branching category is to the right of the nonbranching category. For the structure on the right, the relative clause has internal structure; therefore, it is considered a branching category. Once again, then, the branching element occurs to the right of the nonbranching structure. Within the relative clause,

```
              VP                              NP
            /    \                          /    \
         NP       V                    RelCl       N
        /  \      |                   /    \       |
  tʃɔmɔ araki-wa  umtʃaj       bu: ugtʃirətʃəwun   murin
  cup  of liquor  drink          we ride          horse
                                (the horse we often ride)
```

Diagram 5.3

the relative pronoun, which has no internal structure, is placed before the clause *I hit*.

Contrast this to Oroqen, which is left branching (Diagram 5.3). In both the constructions in Diagram 5.3, the structurally more complex element is to the left. Therefore, they are left branching.

The BDT has two advantages over the proposals of Vennemann and Hawkins. First, rather than employing the notions head and dependent, which can be difficult to justify independently of the word order facts, the BDT makes reference to syntactic notions. In this way, the BDT constitutes an internal explanation (see Chapter 3) of the word order facts.

Second, the BDT provides a potential explanation for why pairs of elements such as adjective-noun do not pattern in the expected way. When adjective phrases are used in the modification of a noun, they are extremely limited in what form they can take. In English, for example, they can consist of the adjective alone (12a), an adjective modified by a degree word (12b), or an adjective with an infinitival complement (12c).

(12) a. the **happy** scholar

b. the **very happy** scholar

c. the scholar **happy to help others**

Recall that in Vennemann's constituent order scheme, the examples in (12a) and (12b) are exceptional because English is a language that places dependents after heads. In the view of the BDT, however, no ordering predictions hold for the adjectival expressions used in the first two examples. Dryer (1992) argues that prenominal adjectives are not full branching categories because they cannot take phrasal complements (e.g.,"the happy to help others scholar" is not well formed). In (12c), however, where the adjective phrase is a full branching category, it is placed after the nonbranching head, which is precisely what is expected.

Although the branching direction theory is framed as an internal explanation of constituent ordering, Dryer (1992, 128-32) speculates about more conventional functional explanations that might underlie the BDT. He suggests that uniformity in branching may increase the efficiency of processing language (see Kuno 1974 and Hawkins 1990). That is, if a language is consistently left branching or consistently right branching, then structures that are difficult to interpret are less likely to result.

4.0. Summary

Basic constituent order and parallels in ordering between syntactic categories have been a central concern of typology since Greenberg's (1966) seminal study. Although not all the complications confronting research on basic constituent order have been fully resolved, there is consensus on the fact that subject initial languages and languages in which V and O are contiguous are linguistically preferred. These preferences can be accounted for by the interaction of several functional principles.

Correlations in the ordering of certain elements in language are striking. Explaining these correlations, however, has proved to be a complex process. A relatively recent proposal, the branching direction theory, offers a promising avenue for further research. Although the BDT is not without its own problems,[10] it suggests that many word order patterns might be related to the configurational structure of clauses, and that ultimately configurational structure might be rooted in principles of language processing.

5.0. Key Terms

Case	Heavy constituent principle
Cross-category harmony	Left branching
Dependent	Right branching
Head	

Notes

1. Most of the discussion in this section will rely on an intuitive notion of "significant" patterns. I do this to avoid introducing standard statistical tests that might be used to demonstrate the quantitative significance of the numbers. In a thorough treatment of word order, however, one would want to apply such tests to the relative frequencies to demonstrate that they are indeed statistically significant patterns that require explanation and not simply random fluctuations from the expected frequencies.

2. An anonymous reviewer of this chapter rightly notes an alternative explanation to the predilection to place subjects before objects. In (overly) simple terms, subjects of clauses tend to be topics of discourses because there is a general tendency in language to place topics clause initially. Given the high incidence of subjects as topics, they will consequently arise clause initially more than objects (or any other core constituents). In many languages, this clause-initial position becomes the standard slot for subjects over time. Kayne (1994) reaches the same conclusion but from a very different perspective. On the basis of considerations internal to the theory of Government and Binding, he argues that the order SVO is part of Universal Grammar.

3. Tomlin (1986) uses precisely this sort of interaction between principles. His scheme is slightly more complicated, however, in that he uses three principles rather than two.

4. Greenberg rarely made claims on the basis of V and O alone; he almost always included S. Lehmann, on the other hand, does not attempt to fit S into his proposal about correlations.

5. I have not provided data on auxiliary verbs or subordinators because the two grammars of Oroqen that exist, Hu (1986) and Zhang, Li, and Zhang (1989), do not provide enough information on how they are used in the language. It should also be noted that the Oroqen relative clause (10e) has traditionally been described as an adjectivalized verb. Finally, I have not given a separate example to demonstrate the suffixing preference of Oroqen because this information can be found in most of the data in (10).

6. Vennemann refers to heads as "operands" and adjuncts-modifiers as "operators." This terminology is avoided here in favor of the more common terms "head" and "dependent."

7. In point of fact, Vennemann never attempted to fit all of Lehmann's correlation pairs into his schema—for example, the prefixes versus suffixes distinction.

8. Hawkins differs from Vennemann in the following important respects: (a) he rejects the use of bilateral implications, (b) he seeks absolute universals rather than simply statistical distributions of languages, and (c) he reintroduces the importance of S in word order correlations.

9. Hawkins (1990, 1994) has attempted to account for word order correlations by reference to sentence processing.

10. Dryer (1992, 115-28) outlines some complications and potential objections to the branching direction theory.

6

Determining Basic Constituent Order

Although constituent order typology has proved to be a powerful line of research in answering the question, "What is language?," there are some rather basic issues in constituent order research that remain controversial. Many of these issues have been raised, however briefly, in previous chapters: the composition and size of the database, the accurate determination of correlation pairs, and the explanation for constituent order patterns. In this chapter, I address an additional concern—the very practical problem of how one goes about determining the basic constituent order in a given language, particularly if that language has a fairly flexible constituent order.

1.0. Constituent Order Variation

Most (probably all) languages have more than one way to order subject (S), verb (V), and object (O). In languages with a fairly rigid constituent order, certain variations are clearly employed for special functions in constructing

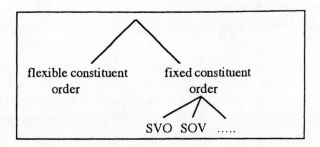

Figure 6.1. Typology of Basic Constituent Order

a discourse. For example, in English when OSV ("beans, I like") arises, it is clear that this order should not be taken as basic to the language because it is used in a very restricted context. For many languages, however, two (or more) word orders may occur frequently and not seem to have any unique discourse function. In these instances, how do we decide what the basic word order is? Some linguists have proposed that in classifying languages according to basic constituent order, a category should exist for languages that do not have a basic constituent order at all (Thompson 1978) (Figure 6.1).

The primary split in language types in this view is rooted in whether constituent order is primarily sensitive to pragmatic considerations (flexible order) or syntactic considerations (fixed order).[1] The proposal is an attractive one in that the linguist does not need to impose a rigid constituent order classification on a language that does not manifest any obvious rules for the linear arrangement of clausal units. Nonetheless, the extended typology faces certain problems of its own.

The first problem is that languages reveal degrees of flexibility in the ordering of constituents. On the one extreme are languages such as English that are quite rigid. The SVO pattern is imposed stringently on clauses with a small set of principled exceptions (such as the one noted previously). At the other extreme, one finds languages such as Warlpiri (Pama-Nyungan: Australia). In the following sentence, the only restriction on the order of the clause units is that the auxiliary must occupy the second position in the sentence:

(1) a. Ngarrka-ngku   ka   wawirri   panti-rni
         man-ERG   AUX   kangaroo   spear-nonPST
         The man is spearing the kangaroo.

b. Wawirri ka panti-rni ngarrka-ngku.

c. Panti-rni ka wawirri ngarrka-ngku.   (Data from Hale 1983)

In addition to displaying freedom in the positioning of the major constituents of a clause, Warlpiri manifests two other properties typical of languages with extremely flexible constituent order. First, it permits **discontinuous constituents**; for example, in (2) the determiner *yalumpu* ("that") is not adjacent to the noun that it modifies, *wawirri* ("kangaroo"). Thus, the noun phrase is considered discontinuous.

(2)	**Wawirri**	kapirna	panti-rni	**yalumpa**
	kangaroo	AUX	spear-nonPST	that

I will spear that kangaroo.

The other property of Warlpiri that is characteristic of flexible constituent order languages is the extensive use of pro-drop (see Chapter 3, Section 2.0). As shown in (3), verbs can be employed without the presence of overt noun phrase arguments. In the following example, the arguments are understood as third-person singular pronouns because of the form of the auxiliary verb:

(3)	Panti-rni	ka
	spear-nonPST	AUX

He or she is spearing him or her or it.

For many reasons, then, it becomes clear why Warlpiri might be best classified as a flexible constituent order language, just as it is clear that English has fixed order. It is much more problematic to determine a classification for languages that fall somewhere between the two extremes. At what point between the extremes does one consider a language to carry a flexible constituent order?

The answer to this question becomes further obscured by the existence of languages that ostensibly have flexible constituent order, but have certain properties that indicate that they are more highly structured. 'O'odham (Uto-Aztecan: United States/Mexico) is one such language.[2] Like Warlpiri, all possible orders of S, V, and O are found in 'O'odham, although certain orders are much more frequent than others.[3] The arrangement of the constituents is guided by pragmatic considerations (see Payne 1987, 1992a). Certain properties of 'O'odham grammar, however, suggest that it maintains an SOV order

(Hale 1992) at an abstract level of grammar. Hence, the following picture of 'O'odham constituent order arises:

(4) Abstract level   SOV

     Surface level   Flexible order

If this picture accurately describes the language, at which level of grammar does the notion "basic constituent order" hold?

At this stage in typological research, there is little place for dogmatism in answering these difficult questions. Several observations can be made, however, that offer some tentative solutions. Recall that in the previous chapter it was noted that recent attempts at accounting for constituent order correlations have not granted primacy to O and V in predicting the patterns. Dryer's (1992) branching direction theory, for example, is based on the configurational relationship between constituents. As such, it predicts correlations between the order of branching and nonbranching elements. V, as a nonbranching category, and O, as a branching category, are just one instance of a pair of elements for which the theory makes predictions, but they are not basic to it. For this reason, then, the concept of a flexible constituent order language should not be defined solely in terms of S, V, and O. Instead, languages should be identified as employing flexible order when most of the relevant pairs of constituents exhibit freedom in their placement.

Furthermore, although abstract levels of syntax are clearly significant for understanding the nature of language, the patterns that hold at this level must be clearly distinguished from surface syntax. What this means is that there exist two notions of "basic constituent order," one that is defined on the basis of abstract syntax and one that is defined on the basis of surface syntax.[4] It is important to note that in typology the notion basic constituent order has traditionally been concerned with the organization of words and phrases at the most superficial level of language. For the purposes of this book, I will continue to examine constituent syntax only at this level unless otherwise indicated.

A final observation: Even in languages in which multiple orders for constituents arise, it is often possible to determine a basic order using several diagnostics (which will be described later in this chapter). Therefore, the label "flexible order" must be reserved for cases in which two or more patterns arise where it is not possible to make a principled determination of what is basic.

Thus, the typology presented in Figure 6.1 provides an important contribution to constituent order studies by allowing for languages in which the linear order of clause elements is flexible. In a very obvious way, these languages are different from those such as English, in which restrictions on linear order play such a crucial role.

2.0. Determining the Basic Order

In languages that have relatively flexible constituent order, the practical problem arises as to how one can make a determination on whether any particular order is basic. Often, native speaker intuitions are very helpful in providing an answer to this question. Certain orders may seem "less acceptable" or "more awkward." In working on Kinyarwanda constituent order, I found my language consultants to express such sentiments commonly and strongly when looking at sentences in their language that had been extracted from their original contexts. The reliability of such intuitions, however, varies dramatically depending on the language, on how sensitive the speaker is to constituent order distinctions, on how well you are able to communicate what it is you want to know about constituent order, and so on.

Fortunately, there are several further "tests" that one can use to aid in the determination. The effectiveness of each of these tests will of course depend on the language to which they are being applied. Although a single test may be sufficient to determine the basic constituent order in some languages, several must be utilized in others.

■ 2.1. Frequency

A good place to begin an analysis of basic constituent order is by choosing a text or texts and simply counting the number of occurrences of each constituent order type (Hawkins 1983).[5] This procedure may reveal that one of the types is clearly dominant. If VSO occurs, for example, 70% of the time, and no other type occurs more than 15% of the time, VSO is almost certainly the basic word order. Unfortunately, the statistical difference between types is rarely this great in languages in which the basic constituent order is in question.

There are several considerations to keep in mind when making text counts. First, not all parts of a text are equal in terms of their typical discourse function. The beginning of a text, or the beginning of each major episode in a text, frequently describes a setting and introduces characters. Such introductions can be marked by special constituent order. This is true to a limited extent in English. Setting changes can be accompanied by an XVS order, where X is some kind of adverbial expression (5).

(5) Over the hill came the troops.

Therefore, when making text counts it is vital to be aware of the discourse mechanisms that are employed to create a coherent text in the first place.

In a similar vein, the statistically most frequent order may be different in different genres of text. In Agutaynen (Austronesian: Philippines), verb-initial clauses dominate narrative texts, whereas SV order is most common in expository discourse (Quakenbush 1992). This alternation is due to certain properties of the two types of discourse. Among others, two facts are relevant in this case: The fact that narrative texts involve a number of temporally sequenced events and the fact that **highly informative** textual entities tend to be placed clause initially in many languages. With respect to the first, Myhill (1992a, 1992b) has shown that verb-initial languages tend to use VS ordering in clauses that express temporal sequencing and SV in clauses that are not temporally sequenced. With respect to the second, it has been noted by many linguists that certain elements of a text tend to occur preverbally—those that add new information to the discourse, information that likely contradicts the expectations of the listeners, and information that contrasts with previous elements in the text. In Agutaynen expository discourse, subjects frequently represent highly informative information of this sort. These two facts together, then, offer some account for the correlation of VS and SV with particular genres (see Dryer 1995 for a discussion on how the interaction between frequency of genre might affect the notion of basic constituent order).

In some languages, the usefulness of text counts is lessened because S and O seldom both occur in a single clause as full noun phrases. In these languages, full noun phrases may be used mainly to introduce new participants into a text. After their introduction, these participants are then referred to using agreement markers or clitics as in Cayuga (Almosan-Keresiouan: Canada):

(6) Shakó-ñǫhwe'-s
     he/her-like-HAB
     He likes her.   (Data from Mithun 1992)

If sentences such as (6) are common in a language, a great many texts may be
required to establish patterns of S, V, and O, or the analyst may need to use
alternative methods to determine the basic constituent order.

■ 2.2. Markedness

The basic constituent order of a language typically occurs in utterances
that have the least formal marking. This is true on all levels of grammar—
phonology, morphology, and syntax. An example of English sentences that
differ with regard to phonological markedness was provided in Chapter 5.
This example is repeated in (7):

(7) a. I like beans.
     b. Beans, I like.

These two sentences differ with respect to their intonation contour. Neutral
intonation—a slowly falling pitch that drops more sharply at the very end of
the utterance— is used in (7a). Alternatively, (7b) begins with a short intense
pitch (due to the heavy stress on *beans*) that is followed by a brief pause and
then the same neutral intonation that is found in (7a). Because (7b) has extra
phonological material "added," it is said to be **marked.** On the other hand,
(6a) is said to be **unmarked.**[6] Consequently, we hypothesize that the word
order of (7a) is basic.[7]

Kutenai (Almosan-Keresiouan: Canada/United States) provides a good
example of morphological markedness:

(8) a. wuꞏkat-i   palkiy-s   tiqat'
         see-IND   woman-OBV   man
         The man saw the woman.
     b. wuꞏkat-aps-i   tiqat'-s   palkiy
         see-INV-IND   man-OBV   woman
         The man saw the woman (or the woman was seen by the man)
                                                                (Data from Dryer 1994)

The sentences in (8) present two constituent orders, VOS in (8a) and VSO in (8b). In (8b), however, there is a suffix on the verb that is absent in (8a), the inverse marker *-aps*. The additional formal marking helps to identify (8b) as the marked structure. For this reason, (8a) can be taken to manifest the basic constituent order.

Finally, there are cases in which syntactic markedness may reveal basic constituent order. German (Germanic: German) has the order SVO in main clauses but SOV in subordinate clauses:

(9) a. Der   Mann   sah   den   Jungen
       the   man.NOM   saw   the   boy.ACC
       The man saw the boy.

   b. Ich   weiss,   dass   der   Mann   den   Jungen   sah
       I   know   that   the   man   the   boy   saw
       I know that the man saw the boy.   (Data from Comrie 1989)

There are two reasons to consider SVO basic in German. First, although a subordinator is employed to introduce a subordinate clause (*dass* in (9b)), no special morphology appears on main clauses. Therefore, subordinate clauses are marked. Second, cross-linguistic evidence about historical change reveals that subordinate clauses tend to be more conservative of older ordering patterns. Thus, we predict that German used to be SOV in all clauses, but the basic order has changed to SVO. This newer order appears in the main clause, although the subordinate clauses have resisted the change and remain SOV.

Markedness serves well as an indicator of the basic patterns in language. Keep in mind, however, that different constituent order patterns are not always accompanied by differences in formal marking. Hence, the markedness test is often irrelevant. Moreover, the rule of thumb that less marking equals the basic constituent pattern does have many exceptions. Finally, markedness considerations can be in conflict with textual frequency. Consider the following case of Yagua (Equatorial-Tucanoan: Peru):[8]

(10) a. Rospita   suuta   Anita
        Rospita   washes   Anita
    b. Sa=suuta   Rospita=níí   Anita
        he-washes   Rospita-her   Anita
        Rospita washes Anita.   (Adapted from Everett 1989)

In terms of markedness, the SVO order in (10a) is basic because it is not accompanied by the extra clitics that appear with the VSO order in (10b). In terms of frequency and pragmatics (see Section 2.3), however, it is the VSO order that is basic (Payne 1985).[9]

Cases in which there is a conflict between the various diagnostics for basic constituent order must be examined individually. As a general rule, however, markedness is the least reliable of the tests.

■ 2.3. Pragmatically Neutral Contexts

A further consideration in making hypotheses about the basic constituent order of a language is the pragmatic function(s) of the clauses being investigated. In general, sentences in which a speaker (or writer) is highlighting a particular constituent are not good exemplars of the basic constituent patterns of the language. More useful are clauses that are more neutral in this regard.

For this reason, it is often useful to elicit sentences out of any particular discourse context, although this practice carries inherent shortcomings. In certain languages, what is arguably the basic constituent order and the order that seems to have no special discourse motivation can be difficult to elicit in isolation. In such cases, the next best option is to use data that are provided in a context but that do not occur at points in the text that typically are characterized by specialized clause patterns such as the beginnings of major discourse units.

3.0. Further Issues

The previous discussion provides some beginning points in the analysis of basic constituent order. As can be realized by now, determining the basic order is rarely as simple as eliciting a few sentences from a language consultant. To conclude the discussion of constituent order typology, a few further issues must be raised.

Among others, Comrie (1989) has pointed out that determining the basic order is complicated by the fact that it is not easy to define the notions "subject" and "object." In some languages, the typical criteria used to decide on a subject (case affixes, agreement, control of reflexive pronouns, etc.) may be split across two noun phrases, A and B. Whether one claims that A is the subject, B is the subject, or that neither can be labeled subject in these languages often depends on one's theoretical orientation. This has been a particularly thorny problem in certain languages of the Philippines and Australia as well as in so-called ergative languages. I return to this problem in Chapter 9.

In this chapter, I have focused almost exclusively on the order of S, V, and O. Flexible constituent order, however, also exists in smaller linguistic units. On occasion, one even comes across affixes whose order is not fixed in a word. In Kirundi (Niger-Congo: Burundi), the locative affix *ha-* does not have a set position with respect to certain object affixes (11).

(11) a. Y-a-rá-**ha**-zí-shize
         He-PST-LOC-there-it-put
         He put it there.

     b. Y-a-rá-zi-**há**-shize
         he-PST-LOC-it-there-put
         He put it there.   (Data adapted from Sabimana 1986)

More commonly, there is flexibility at the phrasal level. In ancient Greek (Hellenic), for example, the order of adjective and noun is variable (12).

(12)   kalon   karpon   karpon   kalon
        good   fruit   fruit   good

In such a case, the basic order would be determined as it would for S, V, and O.

4.0. Summary

The notion of a basic constituent order, which has been reviewed in the past two chapters, is clear enough. However, it is not always easy to establish in languages that readily permit several possible variations of S, V, and O. I have examined the following methods that can be employed together to discover the basic constituent order of a language:

- — An order that is strongly felt to be the basic order by native speakers tends to be the basic order.
- — The most frequent order tends to be the basic order.
- — The order that is least marked tends to be the basic order.
- — The order that arises out of context or in the pragmatically most neutral portions of texts tends to be the basic order.

Of course, even with these diagnostics one encounters languages for which no basic order can be determined, and in such instances it is perhaps best to acknowledge that the language has free constituent order, thereby extending the typology presented in Chapter 5.

My concern in this chapter has been to lay out some analytical tools for recognizing the basic constituent order at the surface level of grammar. As noted previously, however, it appears possible, and for many linguists likely, that the notion of a basic constituent order also holds at an abstract level of grammar. Indeed, Kayne (1994) has presented a case for a universal SVO order that underlies all languages (see Note 4 for more details).

Regardless of whether linguists are after a basic order that holds at a surface level or an abstract level, there is consensus that the linear sequence of constituents is not an autonomous aspect of linguistic structure; it is associated with other formal properties of language. One such property is the morphological structure of languages, and it is this topic that is discussed in Chapter 7.

5.0 Key Terms

Discontinuous constituents	Marked
Highly informative	Unmarked

Notes

1. The papers in Payne (1992b) and Downing and Noonan (1995) provide a wealth of data and analysis on flexible constituent order.

2. 'O'odham is commonly referred to as Papago in linguistic literature.

3. Dryer (1989a) identifies VS and VO as the most common orders in texts. Saxton (1982) states that the language is verb initial.

4. This fact is made explicit in Government and Binding Theory. In most versions of phrase structure in the theory, basic constituent order is highly constrained such that only the orders SVO, SOV, OVS, and VOS are possible at an underlying level. Variations on these orders in surface grammar are permitted through movement rules. An even stronger statement about abstract constituent order has been made by Kayne (1994). He argues that all languages are underlyingly SVO and that variations on this order occur due to movement operations. Although he does not discuss the nature of this movement in detail, it appears that he takes the relative paucity of OVS, OSV, and VOS languages to partly follow from the excessive movement required to derive them from the underlying SVO order. To oversimplify, a surface order of SVO would entail no movement. SOV and VSO would necessitate the movement of a single constituent across one other constituent. OSV, however, would require the O to move across both the S and the V. OVS and VOS would require both the V and the O to move.

5. Although this test is in principle applicable to any language, it is not possible in practice to apply it to many languages because few or no texts have yet been gathered.

6. The terms *marked* and *unmarked* are perhaps among the most inconsistently used terms in all linguistics. Originally, the terms were employed in phonology (Trubetzkoy 1931, 1939) in which they had a relatively clear meaning (see Croft 1990 for a good overview of markedness). Since then, they have been adopted into generative grammar, generative phonology, typology, and discourse studies all with slightly different uses. In this chapter, I use *marked* to refer only to the presence of extra formal marking (additional morphemes, words, intonation patterns, etc.).

7. Crucially, (7b) is not a passive clause, and it behaves as a transitive clause.

8. An equals sign in (10b) indicates that the morpheme that follows is a clitic rather than an affix. Clitics are morphemes that are phonologically dependent on an adjacent word although they may not be syntactically dependent. For instance, in (10b) *níí*, which I have glossed as "her," has no direct syntactic affiliation with the subject noun phrase (NP), but it forms a single word with the NP in terms of Yagua phonology.

It should be noted that the clitics in the original data are not specified for gender. Rather, they are glossed simply as third-person singular clitics by Everett (1989). I have altered the gloss to make the data more transparent.

9. It is likely that Yagua represents a language in which there is a discrepancy between the order of clausal elements at the surface level of grammar (where VSO appears justified) and at the abstract level of grammar (where SVO appears justified).

PART

Morphological Typology

7

Morphemes

The minimal unit that bears meaning in language is called the **morpheme.** In a word such as *uncovers,* there are three morphemes: *cover,* which is the verbal root of the word, the prefix *un-,* and the suffix *-s.* Each of these parts of the word contributes meaning to the whole. As the **root,** *cover* establishes the central notion that is being expressed—namely, that some entity (it could be a blanket, dust, or a hand) is resituated so as to occlude the surface of a second entity (a bed, a table, a drawing, etc.). The morpheme *un-* indicates that the process of covering has previously occurred and is now being reversed to remove the occlusion. The contribution of the morpheme *-s* is to identify certain features about the subject involved in the action of uncovering. Specifically, it requires that this subject be third-person singular (i.e., it must be equivalent to a "he," "she," or "it" and not a "you," "I," "we," or "they").

As this example reveals, morphemes are of very different types. Some form the basis of words (such as *cover*), whereas others modify the meaning of this base in some way (such as *un-* and *-s*). Moreover, the semantic contribution of modifying morphemes can be of different sorts. The prefix *un-,* for instance, revealed something about the nature of the activity itself, whereas *-s* provided information about the agent effecting the activity. Thus, even within a single language there is variety within the morphology that needs to be described.

When morphemes are examined cross-linguistically, the variation becomes more dramatic. Indeed, the languages of the world showcase an impressive array of morphology, ranging from common plural morphemes (such as the *-s* in *cats* in English) to seemingly exotic morphemes such as the Atsugewi (Hokan: California) directional suffix *-ict,* which means "into liquid" (1).

(1)   cwa-staq-ícta
      it.by.wind-guts-into.liquid
      The guts blew into the creek.   (Data adapted from Talmy 1985)

It would be impossible to examine each of the millions of morphemes that occur in languages around the world. Out of all these morphemes, however, we find certain cross-linguistic regularities in the kinds of morphemes one encounters and patterns in the ways these morphemes are combined. This suggests that there are principles that restrict the conceivable options open to the morphological systems of human language.

In this chapter, the basic distinctions between morpheme types are introduced. Note that the goal is not to classify languages in terms of morphology (which is the topic of Chapter 8) but rather to classify the sorts of morphemes that appear in language. This being the case, one should keep in mind that the distinctions discussed here are not relevant in each language, but it is not expected that any language for which the distinctions are inaccurate will be encountered.

1.0. Bound Versus Free Morphemes

The first parameter that has traditionally been employed in describing morphemes is whether they are bound or free. In general terms, a morpheme is **bound** if it cannot appear in isolation but rather must co-occur with another morpheme to constitute a word. A morpheme is **free** if it can appear on its own without the presence of another morpheme. In English, *dog, the, and, walk,* *very, happy,* and *must* are all examples of free morphemes, whereas *-s* (as in *dog-s*) and *un-* and *-ed* (as in *un-cover-ed*) are bound.

Although boundedness can have consequences for the syntax of language, the property of being bound is phonological. Thus, grammatical dependence alone is not sufficient to determine whether a morpheme is bound or not. For example, although *the* must occur with a head noun in the syntax of English, it is not considered a bound morpheme because (a) other words can intervene in between *the* and the head noun (e.g., "the black dog"), (b) *the* can get its own stress in certain contexts ("Caren is *the* woman for me"), and (c) it can be separated by a pause in hyperarticulated speech. For example, imagine a scene in which two children are conversing. Little Jenny has become irritated with her brother because he has failed to understand a sentence that she has now repeated for him three times. On the fourth repetition, she rolls her eyes and slowly phonates each word, placing a pause between them: "Mom_said_to_take_out_the_garbage." In such a context, the pause between *the* and *garbage* sounds natural.

Compare these properties of *the* with the plural marker *-s*. No words can separate *-s* from the noun it modifies, it cannot be stressed, and no pause can separate it from the nouns to which it is affixed.[1] For these reasons, it is clear that *-s* is a bound morpheme.

The determination of whether a morpheme is bound or free is also not fully derivable from its semantics.[2] Hence, in some languages, such as Danish (Germanic: Denmark), definiteness is marked by a bound morpheme rather than a free morpheme, such as *the,* in English (2).[3]

(2) dag   "day"   park   "park"   vise   "song"
     dag**en** "the day" park**en** "the park" vis**en** "the song"

                                             (Data from Haugen 1987)

Conversely, the marking of plurality is not always accomplished by affixation as it is in English. Instead, a separate plural word can be utilized as in the following (3):

(3) Gurung (Tibeto-Burman: Nepal)

     cá   pxra-báe   mxi   **jaga**
     that   walk-ADJ   person   PLURAL
     those walking people   (Data from Glover as cited in Dryer 1992)

The notion of a free morpheme is often confused with the notion of a root, but the two terms are not equivalent because not all roots are free. In ancient Greek, for example, most noun roots must be considered bound because it is obligatory for them to occur with a case suffix (4).

(4) log-os   'word (NOM)'   log-oi   'words (NOM)'
     log-ou   'word (GEN)'   log-ōn   'words (GEN)'
     log-ō   'word (DAT)'   log-ois   'words (DAT)'
     log-on   'word (ACC)'   log-ous   'words (ACC)'

In (4), the noun root *log-* is clearly identifiable, but it never appears in a bare form. Therefore, it is a bound morpheme.

A predominance or paucity of bound roots in a language is one of its morphological signatures. In some languages (e.g., Mandarin Chinese), there are very few or no bound roots. Others, such as English, have a handful of bound roots (consider *-logy,* which appears in *geology, zoology, biology,* and *morphology* but never in a bare form). Still other languages (such as Greek) possess primarily bound roots, particularly among the open word classes.

2.0. Prefixes and Suffixes

One way in which bound morphemes are classified is in terms of their formal relationship to roots. The simplest relationship is affixation. A bound form that is not itself a root and that is affixed to the front of a root is called a **prefix** (5). A bound form that is affixed to the end of a root is called a **suffix** (6).

(5) **in**-adequate, **re**-use, **pro**-life

(6) pleas-**ing**, institut-**ion-al-ize-s**

As can be seen in (6), more than one affix can occur on some roots. Usually, the order of these affixes is fixed, although there are exceptions [see (10) in Chapter 6]. A complete morphological description must, therefore, include statements about affix ordering.

Suffixation and prefixation are both widely attested in language, but there is a notable cross-linguistic preference for suffixes. Bybee, Pagliuca, and Perkins (1990) found that suffixes were more common than prefixes at a ratio of almost three to one.[4] Significantly, the preponderance of suffixation was also found to vary according to basic constituent order such that the ratio of suffixes to prefixes in verb final languages was approximately five to one, approximately two to one for verb medial languages (subject, verb, object [SVO] and object, verb, subject [OVS]), and approximately even for verb-initial languages. Two questions arise, then: Why is there an overall preference for suffixing in language and why is there variation between constituent order types?

The answers to these questions appear to rest partially in language change and partially in the manner by which language is processed by the human mind. The historical dimension is examined first. One process that has been discovered to occur as languages change is **grammaticalization.** In grammaticalization, a free lexical morpheme becomes semantically generalized and phonologically reduced. Over time, it can become a bound affix.

The future tense marker *ta-* in Swahili (Niger Congo: Central Africa) provides an example of these developments (7).

(7) a. n-a-taka   ku-la
      I-PST-want   INF-eat
      I wanted to eat.
   b. ni-ta-ku-la
      I-FUT-INF-eat
      I will eat. (Data from Givón 1973)

The future affix is historically derived from the verb *-taka* ("want"), which is still employed in the language, as can be seen in (7a). Notice that when the full verb is used, it can be marked for tense (in this case by the prefix *a-*), and it introduces an infinitive (*kula;* "to eat"). Over time, the meaning of the verb in certain contexts became generalized from the more robust "have a desire that X take place in the future" to "X takes place in the future," as can be seen in (7b). Parallel to the semantic reduction was a phonological reduction—that is, the disyllabic *-taka* dropped its second syllable. Because such alterations in the form and meaning of the morpheme occurred, it took on the properties of a tense affix and became a productive member of the tense-marking system. The fact, then, that the future tense morpheme in Swahili is a prefix rather than a suffix follows from the fact that its historical source, -taka, occurs before the infinitive it introduces rather than after.

Examples such as that in (7) are common enough that some linguists have subscribed to the position that morpheme ordering follows largely from the word order of previous stages in a language's history. As Givón (1971) puts it,

> If it is true that bound morphemes . . . arise from erstwhile free 'lexical' morphemes, and it is further true that the syntax of the language, at some point of the derivation, determines the free 'lexical' morphemes, then the syntax of the language ultimately also determines the [arrangement of morphemes] which ultimately evolves. (409)

The overall suffixing preference that is found in language may simply result from the fact that the free morphemes that tend to develop into bound morphemes occur more often when they follow the material they eventually affix to than before. This is, in fact, precisely what Bybee et al. (1990) discovered. Given this observation, the predilection for morphemes to be suffixing is primarily an historical accident. If this perception about the origin of bound morphology is correct, or at least partly correct, it also provides an explanation for why the suffixing preference varies among languages with differing basic constituent orders. It is strongest in verb-final languages, which also happens to be the constituent order type with the greatest percentage of postponed grammatical material. This is to say that those morphemes that are most likely to become bound affixes in the process of grammaticalization occur after the words they modify. Therefore, if they do become affixed, they will be suffixes.

It is likely, however, that the historical explanation is only part of the reason that languages exhibit a strong tendency toward suffixation. In addition, one must consider certain aspects of the way that the human mind processes linguistic input (Hall 1988). Because language is encoded by use of sounds occurring in sequence, it is necessarily true that the first part of the word (or phrase or sentence) reaches a listener before latter parts. Rather than waiting until entire words have been uttered, the brain begins to interpret the acoustic data it receives almost immediately (e.g., Marslen-Wilson and Tyler 1980). In other words, the brain attempts to "guess" what a word will be before all of the sounds that the word contains are actually heard. There is great benefit in processing language in this way because it permits faster comprehension than if one had to wait for an entire word to be uttered before attempting to process it.

Cutler, Hawkins, and Gilligan (1985) propose that this method of language comprehension becomes optimally efficient only when the most significant information about a word occurs at the beginning of the word. Furthermore, backed by a good deal of experimental evidence, they argue that the information contained in the stem of a word is more critical to comprehending it than the information contained by any affixes on the word. Therefore, the processing of words will be most efficient when stems occur first in a word. On this basis, then, languages will tend to resist historical processes that might give rise to prefixing in a way that they do not for suffixing.

■ 2.1. Other Types of Affixation

In addition to prefixation and affixation, several other kinds of nonroot morphemes occur in the languages of the world. One fairly infrequent type of affixation is called **infixing**. Infixes are placed within the root, as the following Akkadian (Semitic) data exhibit:

(8) išriq   "he stole"   imḫas   "he struck"
     ištariq "he stole for himself" imtaḫaš "he fought" (lit. "he struck
                                               others")

(Data from Marcus 1978)

In (8), the infix *-ta-* is placed after the first syllable of the root to indicate a reflexive or reciprocal meaning. It is crucial to keep in mind that the definition of an infix is an affix that arises inside the root. Hence, in an English word such as *institut-ion-s,* the morpheme *-ion* is not an infix, even though it does not occur on the periphery of the word, because it is placed after the root.

Two other affix types that are not common but do occur in diverse languages are **circumfixes** and **reduplicated** affixes. Circumfixes consist of two (or more) parts that can be separated by intervening material (either affixes or roots). The following is an example from Kaiowa-Guarani (Equatorial-Tucanoan: Brazil):

(9) a. o-g^w api-ta
        3-sit-FUT
        He will sit.

b. ⁿd-o-gʷapi-ta-i
NEG-3-sit-FUT-NEG
He will not sit.

In this example, negation is signaled by a discontinuous morpheme. We determine that this is an example of a circumfix rather than the co-occurrence of two morphemes because the ⁿd- and the -i must occur together and because there is no way to distinguish between them in terms of meaning.

Reduplication is a type of morphological marking in which the form of the affix is determined by repetition of part (or all) of the root. This process occurs, for example, in the formation of perfect verbs in ancient Greek (10):

(10)	Root	Perfect	Meaning
	paideu-	**pe**-paideuka	"I have taught"
	de-	**de**-deka	"I have bound"
	keleu-	**ke**-keleuka	"I have commanded"
	lu-	**le**-luka	"I have set free"

Note that the prefixes in these data have a consistent meaning (they indicate the verb is perfect), but they have a different phonological makeup for each root. The form of the prefix is determined by the root to which it attaches. If the root begins with a [p], then so will the prefix. If the root begins with a [d], then so will the prefix, and so on. In each case, however, the vowel of the prefix remains the same. Thus, if certain complexities of the process that are irrelevant here are ignored, the prefix can be described as taking the form "Ce, where C = the initial consonant of the verb root."

At this point, it should be noted that not all bound morphology is as easily segmented off from the root as the types of affixation discussed so far. Sometimes, suprasegmental elements, such as tone or stress, are used to manipulate the meaning of a root. For instance, a certain class of English verbs can be nominalized (i.e., turned into nouns) by switching the stress from the second syllable to the first:

(11)	Verb	Noun
	convíct	cónvict
	convért	cónvert
	rejéct	réject
	pervért	pérvert

The stress shift affects the root very much like an affixal morpheme (cf. *-tion*, which also turns verbs to nouns—*pollute/pollution*). Therefore, this type of morphological process is sometimes called **suprafixing** (from Latin *supra* ["over"] + *fixus* ["fastened"]).

The discussion on morpheme types in the past two sections has only touched on the variations that exist in the structure of words cross-linguistically. However, the information is sufficient to identify the major affix types and to point out that these types are not distributed evenly across languages. With respect to this latter point, the question should be raised as to why infixing, circumfixing, and reduplication are less common than prefixing or suffixing.

The relative infrequency of infixes is perhaps due to the way in which language is processed. Languages, it seems, tend not to disrupt units. In the case of infixes, a morpheme is breaking up the sequence of sounds that comprise a root. Furthermore, as Hawkins and Cutler (1988, 309) point out, the middle of a word, which is the position in which infixes arise, is the least salient part—that is, the part that receives the least amount of attention in processing words. For this reason, infixes may be rare because affixes are generally "too informative to be inserted into the least salient position in a word" (309). In addition, or perhaps alternatively, infixing may be uncommon simply because the historical processes that develop it in a language are uncommon. Indeed, it is a fascinating question how infixes get incorporated into stems in the first place.[5]

Circumfixes may be uncommon for a similar reason. Recall from previous discussion that circumfixes involve two affixes that are being used to signal a single piece of information. In a sense, these two affixes comprise a coherent unit of information and so should not be separated. In addition, circumfixes violate the tendency in language that structure be economical (see Chapter 3, Section 4.3). Because the meaning indicated by circumfixes can be gathered from one portion of the circumfix alone, it is uneconomical to use both portions.

The reason for the relative rarity of reduplication is less obvious. The initial observation might be made that reduplication cannot be an instance of former lexical material that has developed into bound morphology. If the majority of bound morphology does indeed arise from erstwhile free morphemes, then the infrequency of reduplication may simply be a function of the fact that it originates from a less common historical process. Furthermore, the kind of range of semantic notions that reduplicative affixes typically possess is fairly limited. For example, reduplication, when it appears in languages, often indicates plurality, iterativity (i.e., the repeated nature of an event), or progressive aspect (i.e., the continuity of an event over time). Notably, these categories are alike in that they all indicate "repetition" of a sort. It is tempting, therefore, to identify an iconic relationship between these categories and reduplication, which consists of repeating part or all of a stem. If such an iconic relationship to meaning is typical of reduplication, then the occasions in which it may arise in language are quite restricted. For these reasons, reduplication is typologically less common than suffixation and prefixation.

3.0. Derivational Versus Inflectional Morphology

In Section 2.0, some of the structural relations that hold between roots and affixes were examined. In addition, affixes can be categorized as to whether they are **derivational** or **inflectional.** In the most general of terms, derivational morphemes purvey robust semantic information (e.g., English *un-, re-, -tion,* and *-ly*) and inflectional morphemes primarily provide grammatical information (e.g., English *-s, -ed,* and *-ing*). In this section, the distinction will be made more explicit.

The word *establishments* has three morphemes: the root *establish* and the two suffixes *-ment* and *-s.* In the formation of the word *establishments,* the contribution of the two suffixes is quite different. The suffix *-ment* transforms a verbal notion (*establish*) into a noun. In this way, it derives an entirely new concept. Instead of an action, *establishment* depicts an object. Accordingly, *-ment* is classified as a derivational morpheme. In contrast, the suffix *-s* does not derive a new concept from *establish.* Rather, it indicates multiple instances of the same concept, and it is classified as an inflectional affix. Thus, although both suffixes contribute semantic information to the word, the nature of this information is qualitatively different.

As one further explores the division between derivational and inflectional morphology, one finds a set of properties that correlates with each of the categories. These properties are listed in Table 7.1.

Whether the semantic effect of the addition of an affix is substantial or minor is, of course, somewhat subjective. When used in conjunction with the other criteria, however, the difference is generally apparent. It should be

TABLE 7.1 Diagnostics for Derivation and Inflection

Property	Derivational	Inflectional
Semantic effect	Substantial	Minor
Effect on word class	Can alter	Never alters
Productivity	Restricted	Unrestricted
Paradigm of opposites	No	Yes
Semantic predictability	Idiosyncratic	Predictable
Location	Inner	Periphery

pointed out that the most dramatic shift in meaning is when a root changes its word class, which is the second diagnostic listed in Table 7.1. The example with *establishment* is a case in point. When *-ment* is affixed to the verb root, the resultant stem is a noun. Such shifts in word class are typically sufficient to determine that a morpheme is derivational, but they are not necessary. Consider the prefix *re-*. Although it is uncontroversially a derivational morpheme, it does not alter the word class of the verb roots to which it is attached. In other words, it derives new verbs from verbs, as shown in the following list:

(12)   turn   return
        distribute   redistribute
        mold   remold
        seed   reseed
        type   retype

Derivational morphemes tend to be only partially productive. That is, they can be affixed only to a subset of the roots on which one might expect them. Consider the nominalizing suffix *-ness*. The function of *-ness* is to create nouns from adjective roots. Although *-ness* is far more productive than most derivational morphemes, there is still quite a number of adjectives it does not attach to, including *?beautifulness, ?bigness, *floralness, *volcanicness,* and so on. Significantly, the adjectives that *-ness* fails to attach to do not seem to form any coherent class based on their meaning; therefore, it is unclear why the morpheme cannot co-occur with these roots. Compare this to the plural marker *-s*—a quintessential inflectional morpheme—which can attach to all nouns except for well-defined classes of exceptions (e.g., proper nouns and mass nouns) and a few odd words that have retained irregular plurals (*child, ox, datum, mouse*, etc.).

Often, inflectional morphemes occur in a paradigm of opposites. A paradigm of opposites simply means a set of mutually exclusive morphemes that have conflicting meaning. Tense markers, for example, often form a paradigm of opposites. Because a verb cannot be simultaneously past and future, or past and present, the morphemes marking these categories cannot co-occur. One does not find derivational morphemes that fall into a paradigm of this sort.

Another difference between inflectional and derivational morphemes is how predictable the meaning is that they bring about. With an inflectional morpheme, such as the comparative *-er* (e.g., *tall-er, happi-er,* and *dumb-er*), the meaning that results when affixation occurs is 100% predictable. This is much different than derivational morphemes such as *-age*. When the morpheme is attached to *leaf*, the consequent meaning is "the congregate of foliage on or from a deciduous tree or leaf-bearing plant." When the suffix appears on the root *orphan*, however, it takes on a related but distinct meaning: "the building which houses a congregation of orphans." When *-age* appears with *suffer, bond,* or *pilgrim*, still further meanings of *-age* arise.

A final criterion for classifying morphemes as inflectional or derivational is their relative distance to the root on which they occur. The general rule of thumb is that derivational morphology is placed closer to the root than inflectional morphology. Therefore, in the word *institut-ion-al-ize-s,* the only inflectional morpheme (the plural marker *-s*) is found outside the string of derivational suffixes.

The diagnostics of Table 7.1, when applied together, provide a generally reliable method for categorizing an affix as an inflectional or derivational morpheme. Nevertheless, there are notorious examples of morphemes whose status is less than obvious when the tests are used. For example, the English nominalizing suffix *-ing* (as in "their constant fight-*ing* kept us awake all night"). This suffix is completely productive; it can be applied to any verb root in English. Its meaning is also almost fully predictable. By these tests, the suffix appears to be an excellent candidate for an inflectional morpheme, but it does not occur in a paradigm of opposites; it occurs inside inflectional morphology such as the plural *-s* (cf. "these happen-*ing*-*s* are hard to explain") and, most significantly, it alters the word class of the verbs to which it is affixed. Previously, I suggested that the "switch of word class" diagnostic was sufficient to establish that a morpheme is, in fact, derivational. On this basis alone, then, *-ing* would be derivational. One might question, however, whether this test really is sufficient to determine derivational morphology. If it is not, then the classification of affixes such as *-ing* become even more ambiguous.

Because of the existence of suffixes such as *-ing,* some linguists have argued that there is no categorical distinction between inflection and derivation, but instead a continuum with some morphemes being more derivational and some more inflectional, and still others sharing derivational and inflectional properties equally (Bybee 1985).

There are, however, several reasons to believe that despite the problems in classification raised by affixes such as *-ing,* the division between inflection and derivation is categorical. First, Greenberg (1963) found that the presence of inflectional morphology in a language implied the presence of derivational morphology, leading him to propose the following absolute universal:

(13) Greenberg's Universal 29: If a language has inflection, it always has

derivation.

Admittedly, Greenberg established this universal on the basis of clear instances of derivation and inflection. The fact that there is an implicational relation of this sort between inflectional and derivational morphology, however, is at least weak evidence that they have categorical status.

Second, as Anderson (1992) points out, the behavior of **portmanteau** morphemes suggests a separation between inflection and derivation. A portmanteau morpheme is a single unit that signals two semantic categories. For example, the French *du* ("of the") cannot be analyzed into discrete parts and therefore is a single unit, even though it represents the combination of the preposition *de* ("of") with the masculine article *le* ("the"). Anderson notes that portmanteau morphemes never seem to combine inflectional and derivational categories. This segregation has at least some account if a strict division is maintained between inflection and derivation.

Finally, work with aphasic patients (patients who have lost some aspect of the ability to produce language due to a brain lesion) has revealed cases in which an individual loses the capacity for use of inflectional morphology while the capacity for derivation remains intact (e.g., Micelli and Caramazza 1988). This pattern of linguistic behavior suggests that inflectional and derivational morphology are stored in separate areas in the brain.

4.0. Affix Ordering

A final characteristic of affixes that holds cross-linguistically is that there
tends to be predictable ordering among them. This was noted previously in a
general way in Table 7.1, in which it is noted that inflectional morphemes tend
to occur farther away from the root to which they are affixed than derivational
morphemes. Even within the set of inflectional morphemes in languages,
however, certain sequences of affixes are most commonly found. For example, consider the following observation by Greenberg (1963):

(14) Greenberg's Universal 39: Where morphemes of both number and case
     are present and both follow or both precede the noun base, the
     expression of number almost always comes between the noun base and
     the expression of case.

Armenian (Armenian: Middle East) exemplifies this universal tendency:

(15) ənker-ner-ic
     comrade-P-ABL
     by the comrades   (Data from Kozintseva 1995)

In (15), the noun root is followed directly by the expression of number—the
plural suffix -ner—which is in turn followed by the ablative case marker -ic.

Verbal inflection also tends to follow a set order. For example, Bybee
(1985) found a strong tendency for languages to follow the following order
(or the mirror image):[6]

(16) Verb root + voice + aspect + tense + mood + person/number.

Rarely does one find a language in which each of these categories is marked
by a unique overt affix. Furthermore, even in languages in which several of
the categories are marked by overt affixes, these affixes may not all arise on
the same side of the verb root. Therefore, Bybee's prediction is that for
whichever subset of the categories do appear in a given language on the same
side of the verb root, they will tend to follow the order in (16) as shown in the
following:

(17) muŋda-w-dʒa-ra-n
    beaten-PASS-PROG-PRES-3S
    He is being beaten.

The Oroqen (Manchu-Tungus: China) verb in (17) follows along the ordering laid out by Bybee. Following the verb is the passive suffix *-w*, which is a type of voice marker (voice markers indicate whether a verb is active, passive, or middle). Then in turn come the suffixes indicating progressive aspect, present tense, and the number and person of the subject.

5.0. Summary

Unlike most of the other chapters in this book, I have explicated some fairly rudimentary notions in this chapter. I have done so intentionally with an eye toward demonstrating that even commonplace notions, such as "prefix," "bound morpheme," and "inflection," generate a number of intriguing typological issues. Hence, in the preceding sections, typological questions at the most fundamental level were entertained. The goal was not so much to classify languages or even constructions as to determine the distribution of basic language categories (this was also done in Chapter 4). In Chapter 8, I continue examining morphology but from a very different perspective. Chapter 8 returns to one of the more enduring questions of typology—Can languages be classified into types in terms of the types of morphology they use?

6.0. Key Terms

Bound morpheme	Morpheme
Circumfix	Portmanteau
Derivational	Prefix
Free morpheme	Reduplication
Grammaticalization	Root
Infix	Suffix
Inflectional	Suprafix

Notes

1. The tests outlined here are indicative of whether a morpheme is bound or free, but they are not sufficient to establish it. Take the prefix *un-*: It is uncontroversially a bound morpheme, but it actually behaves somewhat like the word *the* with respect to the three diagnostics mentioned here. In nonstandard speech, it can be separated from the root it modifies, as in the expression *un-freaking-believable*. It can be stressed in some contexts (e.g., "I didn't say I was happy, I said I was *un*happy"). Finally, in those instances in which it is stressed, it may also be separated from the root by a very brief pause.

2. One cannot, therefore, determine a priori whether a morpheme will be bound or free. This is an empirical question that must be established on a case by case basis. Nonetheless, certain correlations between boundedness and meaning have been observed. For example, Dahl (1985) notes that perfective aspect (see Chapter 12) tends to be expressed through bound morphemes.

3. The indication of definiteness in Danish is more complicated than these data reveal. There is also a definite article in Danish that is a free morpheme. The free definite marker is employed when the noun is modified by an adjective—for example, *det store hus* ("the big house").

4. The database used in this study consisted of 71 languages that were randomly selected within prespecified genetic groupings. This approach is meant to control for any genetic biases in the database. It is less effective in controlling for broad areal biases (see Chapter 3 for a more complete discussion).

5. One reviewer of this chapter identified two historical processes that might give rise to infixes. First, the phonological process of metathesis could potentially produce an infix. In metathesis, two sounds (or syllables) switch places within a word. Given a sequence of sounds (or series of sounds) ABC, metathesis between B and C occurs when the sequence is transformed into ACB. As long as B and C constituted material from separate morphemes, the result is that C becomes an infix. A second possibility is that given a root A and two free morphemes B and C, through grammaticalization B and C might both become affixed to A. If C then, over time, lost its independent meaning, it might become associated with the root. At this point in the evolution of the language, the sequence ABC would arise with B as an infix.

6. Using a sample of 50 languages, Bybee (1985) arrived at the ordering statement in (16) by comparing the morpheme types in pairs and then extrapolating the overall order. That is, she and her associates examined the order of aspect and mood, the order of aspect and tense, and so on. The ordering distributions were quite strong in most cases. The weakest is the order of mood and person. In 18 of the languages in her sample, mood and person were overtly marked and occurred on the same side of the verb root. Of these 18, 13 followed the expected order (72%).

8

Morphological Typology

A basic typology of morphemes was presented in Chapter 7. The goal in that chapter was to describe the most common types of morphemes available to languages and some of the interactions among these classes of morphemes. It is also common, however, to type languages in terms of the dominant morphological strategies they employ because they can differ dramatically in this regard. To get a sense of just how radical the divergence can be, compare the Yay (Daic: China) sentence in (1a) to the Oneida (Almosan-Keresiouan: United States) sentence in (1b).

(1) a. mi^4 ran^1 tua^4 ηwa^1 lew^6
         not   see   CLASS   snake   CMPLT
         He did not see the snake.   (Example from Gedney 1991, xxx)
     b. yo-nuhs-a-tho:lé:
         3NEUT.PAT-room-epenthetic-be.cold.STAT
         The room is cold.   (Example from Michelson 1991, 133)

Yay and Oneida differ at many levels: the sounds they possess (e.g., Yay has tones,[1] indicated here by the superscripted numbers), the categories of words

127

(e.g., Yay has classifiers such as *tua^4*), and sentence structure. For present purposes, what is important to note is the composition of the words in the two languages. Whereas in the Yay data there is no affixation, and all words are monomorphemic, the Oneida sentence consists of a single word with multiple affixes. In fact, in this particular example, the word also contains two roots (the noun *nuhs* ["room"] and the stative verb *tho:lé:* ["be.cold"]).

The morphological differences between languages imbue them with a distinctive "feel." Not surprisingly, this has led linguists for the past two centuries to classify languages in terms of the amount and type of morphology that they utilize. The methods used to carry out this classification have changed over time, but the basic insight that morphology reveals important linguistic properties has not.

1.0. Languages as Morphological Types

Expanding on the morphological typology developed in the nineteenth century, Edward Sapir (1921) popularized the idea that languages vary morphologically on two parameters.[2] The first parameter is the **Index of Synthesis** (I have borrowed this terminology from Comrie 1989). It is used to label the amount of affixation that occurs in an individual language. The second parameter, the **Index of Fusion,** is used to label the ease with which individual morphemes can be segmented from others.

■   1.1. Index of Synthesis

It is best to conceive of the Index of Synthesis as a continuum. One end of the continuum is anchored by the ideal **isolating** language[3]—that is, a language in which every word is monomorphemic. The other end of the continuum is represented by the ideal **synthetic** language. That is, a language in which complete utterances are formed by affixing morphemes to a root.

The index is represented graphically in Figure 8.1. I have indicated where Yay, Oneida, and English might fall along this continuum, although their precise placement here is only impressionistic. In a more complete exposition, one could provide a quantificational basis for the relative positions on the continuum by counting the number of morphemes that occur per word in an

```
ISOLATING<--x----x----------------------x----->SYNTHETIC
          Yay  English              Oneida
```

Figure 8.1. Index of Synthesis

extended text sample from each of the languages. Greenberg (1954) outlines how such a measurement can be used in establishing relative degrees of synthesis.

Mandarin Chinese (Sinitic: China), like Yay, provides an example of a language that falls nearer to the isolating pole of the continuum:

(2) a. tā   zài   túshūguăn   kàn   bào
       he   at   library   read   newspaper
       He's at the library reading a newspaper.

    b. Xiăo   Huáng   kuài   yào   lái   le
       Little Huang   fast   will   come   ASP
       Little Huang is coming!

    c. tā   chī   le   yi   ge   yóutiáo
       he   ate   PFV   one   CLASS   fritter
       He ate one fritter.   (Data adapted from Li and Thompson 1981)

Notice how there is a one-to-one correspondence between morphemes and words in (2). Although this is considered the distinguishing characteristic of an isolating language, there is no such thing as a completely isolating language. Thus, even in Chinese there are a few inflectional affixes (such as the plural suffix *-men* in *péngyŏu-men* ["friends"]). There are also some derivational processes. For example, the prefix *kě-* combines with some verbs to create adjectives as in *kě-kào* ("dependable"), which is based on the verb root *kào* ("depend"). It is also true that Mandarin Chinese employs a great deal of compounding in the formations of its words. For example, the word *túshūguăn* ("library") in (2a) is actually composed of two morphemes, *túshū* ("book") and *guăn* ("tavern"). The notion of an isolating language, then, is a relative one. Chinese and Yay are considered isolating because they allow for far less polymorphemic words than other languages, not because they fully meet the one word-one morpheme ideal.

Certain other linguistic features are common (although not necessary) in isolating languages. First, they often have complex tonal systems. In Chinese, for instance, there are four phonemic tones. Hence, the same sequence of sounds can have four different unrelated meanings depending on which of the tones it carries:

(3) yī (high tone)   "clothes"
     yí (rising tone)   "to suspect"
     yǐ (falling then rising tone)   "chair"
     yì (falling tone)   "meaning"

(Adapted from Li and Thompson 1981)

The correlation between isolating languages and complex tonal systems may not reflect a deep property of language but instead be an areally based linguistic feature. Most highly isolating languages are spoken in southern Asia, and this is also where the most complex tonal systems are found—in languages such as Mandarin Chinese and Yay. Therefore, it is difficult to determine whether the correlation is meaningful as a cross-linguistic claim or whether it is just a remarkable areal trait.

Another frequent characteristic of isolating languages is the use of serial verbs, as in the following Yay sentence:

(4) may^{6}faay^4 koŋ^2 ma^1 rop^1 caw^3 hauɯ^3 ku^1
     bamboo   bend   come   stroke   head   give   I
     The bamboo bends down to stroke my head for me.

(From Gedney 1991, xxx)

As can be seen in (4), serial verb constructions are sequences of verbs or verb phrases in which there are no markers indicating the relationship between them. The verbs are simply placed next to one another. In this way, they are unlike an English construction such as "I love to fish," which also contains a sequence of verb forms, because the infinitive *to fish* is specially marked to reveal that it is subordinate to the verb *love*. Note further that serial verbs are often used just as prepositions are in English. Thus, where English employs the preposition *for,* Yay can utilize the verb *hauɯ*^{3} ("give").[4]

A final property that one finds in languages that fall toward the isolating end of the Index of Synthesis is that they have rigid word order. This is to be expected from a functional standpoint because such languages will not have case marking or complex verb marking to signal the relationship between a verb and its dependents. Without morphological marking of grammatical relations, a fixed word order is a convenient tool to indicate what noun phrase is serving as subject and which one is serving as object.

Languages that fall on the opposite end of the Index of Synthesis from isolating languages are called **synthetic.** Synthetic languages are characterized by a robust use of morphology in word building, as can be seen in the following Bare (Arawakan: Venezuela) clause:

(5) nu-khniñani   hme-muduka-na-ka   bĩ   babuka   Varela   abi

     1P-people   3P-kill-PFV-SEQ   you   around   Varela   with

     My people shot at you because of Varela   (Data from Aikhenwald 1995)

In the first two words of the Bare clause, there is extensive use of affixation. Rather than an independent pronoun, a prefix is used to indicate possession in *nukhniñani,* and several inflectional affixes appear on the verb. Not surprisingly, it is common for synthetic languages such as Bare to employ affixation to mark categories such as agreement, voice, tense, aspect, valence, mood, or all of these rather than marking them with derivational morphology or independent words.

Languages with extreme synthesis are called polysynthetic. Southern Tiwa (Tanoan: United States) serves as an example:

(6)   a.   Ti-khwian-mu-ban

        1S-dog-see-PST

        I saw the dog.

    b.   Men-mukhin-tuwi-ban

        2D-hat-buy-PST

        You two bought a hat.

    c.   In-khwian-wia-che-ban   seuanide-ba

        AGR-dog-give-PASS-PST   man-INST

        The man gave me the dog.

                       (Data from Allen, Frantz, Gardiner, and Perlmutter 1990)

Notice not only that words are composed of multiple morphemes but also that
a single word can contain two roots. This phenomenon, which was also
exhibited in (1b), is referred to as **noun incorporation.** It is similar to
compounding (cf. English *bird-watching*), but it is unique in several ways
(Baker 1988). For example, the compounding process in English that combines a noun root and a verb root usually results in a noun, whereas with noun
incorporation the result is a verb. Furthermore, in English compounds such
as *bird-watching,* the noun cannot refer to a specific bird. Therefore, the noun
in the compounds is said to be nonreferential. With noun incorporation,
however, it is often possible for the incorporated noun to refer to a specific
entity (NB, the gloss "the dog" in (6a) and (6c) is only appropriate if a specific
canine is intended).

Another common property of polysynthetic languages is that they tend to
have complicated agreement systems. Southern Tiwa is a case in point. The
agreement system is complex in two senses. On the one hand, information
about three different arguments of the verb can be indicated in the choice of
an agreement prefix.

(7)   'U-ide   **tow**-keuap-wia-ban
      child-A   1S:C:A-shoe-give-PST
      I gave the shoes to the child.

In (7), the prefix *tow-* indicates (a) that the subject of giving is first-person
singular, (b) that the object of giving is in class C (NB: the class of a Southern
Tiwa noun is based on its animacy and whether it is plural or singular), and
(c) that the indirect object of giving is in class A. In a sense, then, there is
agreement with three different elements. This is quite complex compared to
a language such as English in which verb agreement only occurs in the present
tense, and even then only reveals information about one element in the
sentence—the subject.

Because the information about all three elements occurs in a single
morpheme in Southern Tiwa, the form of this morpheme changes if any of the
elements changes.

(8)   'U-ide   **tam**-musa-wia-ban
      child-A   1S:B:A-cat-give-PST
      I gave the cats to the child.

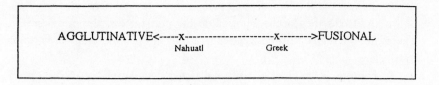

Figure 8.2. Index of Fusion

Because the object of giving is now from class B rather than class C as in (7), a different agreement prefix appears on the verb. Thus, Southern Tiwa is also complex in that it involves a large number of different forms to mark agreement. Indeed, there are more than 15 different prefixes that can be used just for when the subject of a clause is first-person singular!

Just as no language is perfectly isolating, there is no language that is completely synthetic. If such a language existed, all sentences would consist of a single word, and this word would contain a series of affixes in addition to one or more roots. Even in polysynthetic languages, however, sentences commonly consist of multiple words. Once again, then, we are reminded that the Index of Synthesis is a continuum used to map the relative amount of affixation utilized within a language.

■ **1.2. Index of Fusion**

Like the Index of Synthesis, the Index of Fusion is also best described as a continuum of language types. It is anchored on one end by the ideal **agglutinative** language and on the other by the ideal **fusional** language (Figure 8.2).

A language is agglutinative if the morphemes that occur in a word are easily segmentable. In other words, it is clear where one morpheme ends and the next begins. A comparison of the Michoacan Nahautl (Uto-Aztecan: Mexico) nouns in (9), for example, reveals that the constituent morphemes are readily identified:

(9)	no-kali	my house	no-pelo	my dog
	no-kali-mes	my houses	mo-pelo	your dog
	mo-kali	your house	mo-pelo-mes	your dogs
	i-kali	his house	i-pelo	his dog

(Data from Merrifield et al. 1982)

In (9), the roots *kali* ("house") and *pelo* ("dog") remain constant regardless of which affixes they occur with, as do the prefixes and the plural suffix. Therefore, the boundaries between the various morphemes in a word appear to be sharp.

In contrast, a language is fusional if the boundaries between its morphemes are hard to determine. The effect is as if the morphemes were blending, or fusing, together. Ancient Greek (Hellenic) provides an example of this sort of language:

(10) lu-ō   1S:PRES:ACT:IND (I am releasing)

      lu-ōmai 1S:PRES:ACT:SBJV (I should release)

      lu-omai 1S:PRES:PASS:IND (I am being released)

      lu-oimi 1S:PRES:ACT:OPT (I might release)

      lu-etai 3S:PRES:PASS:IND (He is being released)

These various Greek suffixes contain several bits of meaning: the person and number of the subject, the tense[5] (present tense in all these data), the voice (active, middle, or passive), and the mood (e.g., indicative or subjunctive). The suffixes cannot be further split into meaningful parts. Although there is no clear way to divide them into more than one morpheme, there are certain regularities (such as the presence of a back round vowel sound in first-person forms) that make it seem like segmentation should be possible. This is typical of fusional languages.

Again, it is useful to realize that no language is entirely agglutinative, nor is any language completely fusional. This latter option is almost inconceivable because, as Comrie (1989) points out, the language would have no segmentable or invariant morphemes. As such, the morphology would all be **suppletive.** Suppletive morphemes are units that bear no formal relationship to other morphemes but that are semantically equivalent to them in some sense. For example, the English plural marker *-en* (as in *oxen*) is a suppletive morpheme. Although it bears no formal similarity to the regular plural *-s*, the two mean precisely the same thing. If all the morphology of a language were suppletive, an incredibly vast number of lexical items would exist in the language. For example, there might be a first-person present tense verb *jufwuf,* which meant "I murmur." In a completely fusional language, in which no invariant morphemes occur, the corresponding second-person present tense verb would not have any obvious affinity to the first-person form. For the sake of our example, let's assume this second-person form is *blim* ("you murmur").

If one wished to place the event of murmuring in the past with a second-person subject, another unrelated form would be employed—for example, *quast* ("you murmured") and so on. This language would clearly be an abominably difficult one for anybody to learn, and nothing remotely like it exists. Hence, the end points on the Index of Fusion are ideal language types. Languages can approach the ideals to varying degrees, but they never actually manifest the ideal properties.

■ **1.3. The Relationship Between the Two Indices**

Strictly speaking, the Index of Fusion is irrelevant for isolating languages because these languages do not string together morphemes into a single word. There is a noticeable correlation, however, between the Index of Synthesis and the Index of Fusion with respect to synthetic languages: They tend to be agglutinative in nature. The correlation is observable in (5) through (9), which are all sentences from languages that are both agglutinative and synthetic. The frequency with which synthetic languages happen also to be agglutinative is expected from a intuitive point of view. Because synthetic languages tend to locate grammatical information in affixes, and such information (such as the person and number of verbal arguments, case, gender, tense, aspect, and the like) is relevant across a large number of roots, it is more efficient to keep the morphemes that signal this information constant than to have them vary depending on the presence of other affixes and roots.

This is easiest to demonstrate with a hypothetical example—the case of a language in which verbs are obligatorily marked for tense, voice, and the person of their subjects. For each of these grammatical categories, imagine there are the following three options:

(11)	*Tense*	*Voice*	*Person*
	Past	Active	1st
	Present	Passive	2nd
	Future	Middle	3rd

In a synthetic language that is characteristically agglutinative, each of these 9 options will be encoded by one morpheme: one for past tense, one for passive voice, one for third person, and so on. On the other hand, in a synthetic language that is purely fusional a different affix would be required for each possible combination. There would be one for past-active-first person, one for past-passive-first person, one for past-middle-first person, and so on. To capture all possible combinations, the language would require 27 separate affixes, which is three times the number needed in the case of the agglutinating language. Consequently, a synthetic language built on agglutinative morphology is highly economical. Of course, economy of linguistic forms is not the only pertinent factor in understanding language structure, which is precisely why all synthetic languages are not perfectly agglutinating in their morphology.[6]

■ 1.4. Historical Change in Morphological Type

Since the 1800s, linguists have suggested that languages tend to change their morphological type over time. Originally, this insight was wrapped up in an overtly ethnocentric perspective (see Chapter 2). Languages such as German, Greek, and Sanskrit were considered the quintessence of human speech. Not surprisingly, then, the typologists of this era believed that languages evolved to become more German-like (or Greek-like or Sanskrit-like). August Schleicher, for example, proposed that languages evolved toward increasing sophistication from isolating to agglutinative to fusional.

Although the teleological (i.e., moving toward a specific structure) and culture-bound view of linguistic change has been abandoned, the claim that languages do switch from one morphological type to another has found some empirical support. Crowley (1992) furnishes data from Melanesian Pidgin (unaffiliated: Solomon Island/Vanuatu) which suggest that the language is currently being transformed from an isolating language to an agglutinative one. As one piece of evidence, Crowley states that prepositions are now pronounced as prefixes to the noun phrases that follow them rather than as independent units.

(12) a. aus   bloŋ mi →   aus   blo-mi   "my house"
        house   of   me   house   of-me
     b. loŋ   aus →   l-aus   "at home"
        at   house   at-house

The forms to the left of the arrows presumably represent how these expressions are written in the language. Presumably, the written forms reflect a time at which the morphemes in question were clearly prepositions and had the more complete phonological form *bloŋ* ("of") and *loŋ* ("at"). At the right of the arrows is an approximation of the way in which these phrases are now pronounced. Note that the prepositions have become phonologically reduced—they have lost a final nasal—and they have developed a greater phonological dependence on the nouns that follow them, enough so that Crowley takes them to be affixes.

Phonological reduction is a common concomitant to morphological change. Furthermore, it commonly operates together with semantic reduction to create a novel morpheme that becomes more closely associated, both phonologically and semantically, with a neighboring word. This process can be represented graphically as in Diagram 8.1.

```
                        Semantic
                        and
                        Phonological Reduction
   isolating  ─────────────────────────────────▶  agglutinative
```

Diagram 8.1

Like the switch from isolating to agglutinative languages, the process whereby agglutinative languages become fusional is probably due to reduction. In this case, the frequent co-occurrence of two adjacent morphemes lends itself to reanalyzing the combination as a single unit. Once this occurs, the unit may fuse together phonological and semantic features of the erstwhile morphemes. This appears to be the case in the distant future prefixes of Paamese (Austronesian: Vanuatu), as in the following:

(13) a. *na-i-lesi-ø →   ni-lesi-ø   "I will see it."
        I-FUT-see-it   I:FUT-see-it
    b. *ko-i-lesi-nau →   ki-lesi-nau   "You will see me."
        you-FUT-see-me   you:FUT-see-me

                                                (Data from Crowley 1992)

Historically, the subject prefixes *na-* and *ko-* were independent of the future prefix *i-* (the asterisks in the data denote a reconstructed form). Over time, however, the morphemes fused so that the modern-day forms are instances of portmanteaux (recall that a portmanteau morpheme is a single indivisible unit that carries semantic information typically associated with two units). The picture of morphological change in (13) can now be amended to capture the transition from agglutinative to fusional language types (Diagram 8.2).

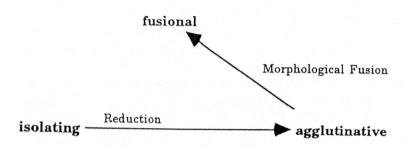

Diagram 8.2

Diagram 8.2 is precisely that proposed by Schleicher. It is incomplete, however. Whereas he believed that Diagram 8.2 represented the entire process of language evolution, it is now believed that fusional languages can become isolating. This occurred, for example, in the development of Modern English, which is largely isolating, from Old English, which had a much more robust morphological system of the fusional type. Thus, the potential change between morphological types is a cycle (Diagram 8.3).

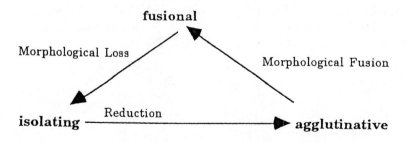

Diagram 8.3

This suggestion (which was proposed by Sapir 1921) also aids in understanding why languages never actually become ideal morphological types. The transition toward one type or another is not a development toward an ideal per se. Rather, it is a reflection of various smaller changes going on within the linguistic system. In some cases, the changes are phonological. In others, they may be partly semantic (as in the case of grammaticalization). In still others, the change may be the loss of certain kinds of morphology. Because all the kinds of changes can occur independently of one another, they may not be operating in tandem to produce an ideal language type. Instead, phonological reduction may be leading to agglutination in some parts of the language, whereas morphological fusion may be occurring elsewhere.

Although the hypothesis sketched in Diagram 8.3 has immense intuitive value and has enjoyed much popularity, two notes of caution are in order. First, the picture it paints is an overly simple one. Because ideal morphological types do not really exist, certain questions arise about just how fusional a language must be before it can be said to be altering its path toward becoming isolating or just how isolating a language must be before it can be said to be becoming agglutinative. One might even question whether Diagram 8.3 depicts what happens to entire languages or whether it depicts what happens to certain parts of the morphology of languages. Indeed, there is no conclusive evidence that any language has gone through a complete cycle such as that in Diagram 8.3. Most likely, this is due to the fact that it takes a great deal of time for a language to shift from one morphological type to another, and we simply lack historical records that go far enough back to reconstruct movement through the entire cycle. At any rate, it must be stressed that the model of change in Diagram 8.3 remains an unconfirmed hypothesis.

2.0. Types of Morphological Linkage Between Constituents

In the discussion of morphology so far (Chapter 7 and the previous sections of this chapter), I have focused on two types of classification: (a) the labeling of individual morphemes and (b) the categorization of languages on the basis of the Index of Synthesis and the Index of Fusion. As we look from language to language, however, we soon realize that these types of classification are not equipped to demarcate other key features of morphological marking. In this section, two further distinctions in the patterns of morphology are examined. The first is the traditional division between government and agreement. The second is a more recent proposal that distinguishes between head marking and dependent marking in languages.

■   **2.1. Government Versus Agreement**

In the following ancient Greek data, the choice of which case suffix is used on a noun is determined by the preposition (which is in bold type):

(14) a. **ana** skē:ptr-ō: (DAT) "upon a staff"
      b. **apo** tou hipp-ou (GEN)   "from a horse"
      c. **en** Spart-ē (DAT)   "in Sparta"
      d. **eis** basil-ea (ACC)   "to the king"

Notice that the prepositions carry no special morphology. They are monomorphemic and fixed in form regardless of the noun that follows them. This is a classic case of **government,** in which the syntactic relationship between two constituents is captured by obligatory marking on the dependent constituent. In the Greek example, the preposition is said to "govern" a particular case—for example, *ana* ("up") governs dative case.

A different situation arises in the Spanish (Italic: Latin America and Spain) data in the following:

(15) a. la elefanta negr-a   "the black elephant"
      b. las elefantas negr-as   "the black elephants"
      c. el gato negr-o   "the black cat"
      d. los gatos negr-os   "the black cats"

Unlike (14), the syntactically dependent constituents in (15) are placed in a form that corresponds to that of the head noun so that all three are in **agreement.** In (15a), the noun *elefanta* ("elephant") is feminine singular. Consequently, the feminine singular article *la* must be used, and the adjective must be formed with the feminine singular suffix. In the remaining data, the articles and adjective must similarly agree with the noun both in gender and in number.

The two types of morphological linkage—government and agreement—are similar in that the form of a dependent constituent depends on its head. The difference between them is that in government the morphological features that occur in the construction are only relevant to the dependent constituent and not to the head. Thus, in (14) the case of the nominals depends on the prepositions, but the feature of case is irrelevant to the form of the prepositions themselves. In contrast, in agreement, the morphological features that occur are relevant to head and dependent alike. Therefore, in (15a) through (15d) the reason that the articles and adjectives take on values for number and gender is because the head noun is itself specified for these features.

■ 2.2. Head Versus Dependent Marking

The notions of government and agreement are used in describing the nature of the morphological connection between constituents. If the morphological marking of a dependent is determined by a head, but does not reflect any semantic or grammatical features of the head, it is considered government (as in the Greek example in (14)). If the morphological marking does reflect such properties, it is a case of agreement (as in the Spanish example in (15)). These notions, however, do not easily permit linguists to describe differences in the location of morphological marking that arise among languages even in functionally analogous constructions.

For example, consider the following:

(16) a. a man's house (possessor marked)
     b. az   ember   h'az-a (possessee marked)
        the   man   house-3s

For these two possessive constructions, the terminology that has been introduced so far is not well suited to capture the relevant distinction between the English pattern (16a) and the Hungarian (Finno-Ugric: Hungary) pattern (16b). In terms of syntactic relations, these two examples are identical—a head noun is being modified by a possessor. One might describe (16a) as an instance of government because the dependent takes the genitive marker -*s* due to its relationship with the head noun. In (16b), however, it is not the possessor that is marked but the possessee. Because the dependent is not marked, the construction in (16b) is not an instance of government or agreement as these terms were defined previously.

Because the possessee is the head of the noun phrase, we say that Hungarian displays **head marking,** whereas English displays **dependent marking.**[7] These terms describe where in a given construction the syntactic dependence between a head and a modifier is morphologically indicated. Although the example in (16) exhibits this for possessive constructions in two languages, the terms can be applied to any construction involving a head and a dependent element.

TABLE 8.1. Nichol's Head-Modifier Pairs

Level	Head	Dependent
Phrase	Possessed noun	Possessor
	Noun	Modifying adjective
	Adposition	Object of adposition
Clause	Predicate	Arguments and adjuncts
	Auxiliary verb	Lexical ("main") verb
Sentence	Main-clause predicate	Subordinate clause

SOURCE: Adapted from Nichols (1986).

The notions of "head" and "dependent" are familiar by now—they proved to play a big role in much research on word order typology, and they were invoked in the discussion on government and agreement in the previous section. Ideally, there would be a list of heads and a list of dependents on which all linguists agreed, but as has been seen, this is far from being a reality. All claims about head marking and dependent marking, therefore, are inextricably tied to one's assumptions about the definition of a head (see Hudson 1987; Zwicky 1985; see also the papers in Corbett, Fraser, and McGlashan 1993 for examinations of this problem).

For present purposes, I adopt Nichols' (1986, 57) quasi-syntactic position that "the head is the [category] which governs . . . or otherwise determines the possibility of occurrence" of other categories. On the basis of the definition, she derives the head-modifier pairs given in Table 8.1.

The syntactic relation that holds between head and nonhead in these constructions is not always indicated morphologically. In Kobon (Trans-New Guinea: New Guinea), simply juxtaposing possessor and possessee (17) can create genitive constructions that are semantically comparable to the English and Hungarian discussed previously.[8]

(17)   Dumnab   ram
        Dumnab   house
        Dumnab's house

When the dependency is signaled morphologically, the marking may occur on either the head or the dependent, as was shown in (16). More exceptionally, marking may occur both on the head and on the dependent simultaneously.

This phenomenon, called **double-marking,** is exemplified by the following Turkish possessive phrase:

(18) ev-in   kapi-si
      house-GEN   door-3S
      the door of the house

In this example, a genitive marker is affixed to the possessor noun *ev* ("house"), and an agreement suffix is found on the head noun *kapi* ("door"). Both morphemes are necessary to form the construction properly.

Thus far, in the examples of possessive constructions it has been fairly clear whether a given phrase is head marked, dependent marked, or double marked. Yet, as shown in (19), it is not always completely clear to which constituent a morpheme is bound:

(19) asb-e-mard
      horse-LINKER-man
      the man's horse

As can be seen in the Persian (Indo-Iranian: Iran) data in (19),[9] the morpheme that marks the dependency relation cannot be assigned to either constituent. Therefore, it is referred to as a "linker." Croft (1990) points out that linkers have some common characteristics: (a) They are generally invariant in form, and (b) they are usually found within noun phrases.

In many instances, the presence of a dependency relation is the only bit of information that a morpheme is indicating. Like the English and Hungarian examples (16), Hebrew (Semitic: Israel) special possessives are of this kind.

(20) bayit   "house"
      bet sefer   "school" (book house)
      bet kafe   "cafe" (coffee house)
      bet holim   "hospital" (patients' house)
      bet keneset "synagogue" (assembly house)

The noun *bayit,* which means "house," undergoes a modification of the stem vowel (to *bet*) when it is used in this possessive construction. The examples in (20) would be considered an instance of head marking because it is the head noun that marks the possession.

In other cases, not only the presence of dependency but also the type of dependency is indicated by the morphology. In ancient Greek, for example, accusative case at the clause level signifies both that a nominal is dependent on a verb and that the dependency relation is as the direct object (as opposed to the indirect object, a benefactive, etc.):[10]

(21)   tuptei   ho   anēr   ton   paid-**a**
       strikes   the   man   the   boy-ACC
       The man strikes the boy.

As was discussed in the previous section, the morphology is marking the government of the direct object by the verb.

Morphology used to mark syntactic dependency also frequently serves as a means to index information about gender, number, person, and the like. Because it is cross-referencing this information, it is a type of agreement. In Kinyarwanda (Niger-Congo: Rwanda), a head-marking pattern arises because the dependency of a subject is indicated by the presence of a verbal prefix (in bold print). In addition to the dependency relation, the prefix indexes the person, the number, and the noun class of the subject as shown in the following:

(22)   Umugore   **y**-oohere-je-ho   isoko   umubooyi
       C1.woman   C1-sent-ASP-LOC   market   cook
       The woman sent the cook to the market.   (Data from Kimenyi 1980)

■ **2.3. Implications for Universals**

To this point, I have been interested in cataloging the kinds of head and dependent marking that are commonly encountered in the languages of the world. Instead of focusing on individual constructions, it is possible to classify languages in terms of the dominant strategy used in signaling dependency relations. Using a database of 60 languages, Nichols (1986) discovered that languages fall into the following four major types:

1. Head marking—the predominate strategy of indicating dependency is to mark the head (e.g., Blackfoot and Lakhota).
2. Dependent marking—the predominate strategy of indicating dependency is to mark the dependent (e.g., Greek).

3. Double marking—a significant number of constructions mark both head and dependent, thereby making it impractical to place the language in the head-marking or dependent-marking categories (e.g., Aleut and Arabic).

4. Split marking—they display roughly equivalent numbers of head-marking and dependent-marking patterns (e.g., Bantu languages, in which the clause level is head marked and the phrase level is dependent marked).

Several remarks should be made in regard to these four types. First, languages of the first three types are probably never entirely consistent. That is, even a language that is overwhelmingly dependent marking will still undoubtedly have scattered instances of head marking. Thus, the four categories listed above represent tendencies and not discrete sets. Another conclusion reached by Nichols is that the first two types are the most common. Third, Nichols found that the distribution of head marking and dependent marking in split marking languages was not random, but instead followed two fundamental principles.

Nichols (1986, 75) writes, "Two broad types of splitting principles can be identified: those distinguishing different kinds of constituents . . . and those dealing with the particular categories and relations indexed." As for the first principle, the Figure 8.3 ranks the types of constituents that Nichols surveyed in order of their propensity to be head marked.[11]

On the basis of the findings presented in Figure 8.3, Nichols (1986, 75) offers the following two implicational universals:

— If a language has major, salient, head-marking morphology anywhere, it will have it at the clause level.

— If a language has dependent-marking morphology at the clause level, it will have it at the phrase level.

The other broad splitting principle that was determined by Nichols—that certain grammatical categories tend to follow a head-marking or dependent-marking pattern—is less clearly articulated. Nichols (77-8) simply notes that grammatical categories, such as person, number, and gender, are commonly marked on heads even in dependent-marking languages. On the other hand, clausal adjuncts (such as temporal, locational, and manner expressions) are rarely marked on the head and are usually themselves case marked or flagged by adpositions.

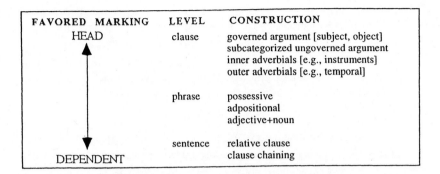

Figure 8.3. Correlation Between Marking Type and Construction Type

■ **2.4. Head Marking and Constituent Order**

Nichols (1986, pp. 81ff) proposes that there is a correlation between the pattern of marking that a language uses to indicate dependency and the basic word order: "Head-marking morphology favors verb-initial order, while dependent-marking morphology disfavors it." As a potential functional explanation for this correlation, she suggests that languages tend to establish the core grammatical relations in a clause as early in the clause as possible. Thus, if a language is verb initial, morphology will occur on the verb (a head-marking pattern) that references the core grammatical relations. On the contrary, if the language is not verb initial, the grammatical relations will be marked on the noun arguments (a dependent-marking pattern).

3.0. Summary

In this chapter, I have introduced the core terminology used in researching patterns in the morphological structure of languages, and I have reviewed the two primary typologies that are used to classify languages. The first, based on the work of Sapir (1921), classifies languages in terms of how many morphemes they employ within words (Index of Synthesis) and how easily segmentable these morphemes are (Index of Fusion). The second categorizes languages on the basis of whether dependency relations are indicated on heads or dependents. These two schemes are designed to capture very different properties of language; therefore, there is no direct relationship between them.

I have avoided introducing much statistical information on the distribution of language types as defined by the two typological schemes. This is because of the extreme genetic and areal effects on the morphological structure of languages. For example, it was noted in Section 1.1 that the bulk of highly isolating languages are clustered in South East Asia. To this, one might also add that these languages tend to be members of the Austric or Sino-Tibetan language families. Similarly, Indo-European languages are largely dependent marking. North America contains a large number of head-marking languages. Because of such facts, it is a difficult task to construct a sample and test distributions of morphological types to determine what is typical of language per se. Rather, as is implied in Section 2.2, the more compelling distributions of morphological types are found by examining particular constructions within languages. Here, one finds intriguing correlations such as the fact that head marking is preferred across languages at the clause level (see Table 8.1).

4.0. Key Terms

Agglutinative	Index of Fusion
Agreement	Index of Synthesis
Dependent marking	Isolating (analytic)
Double marking	Noun incorporation
Fusional	Split marking
Government	Suppletive morpheme
Head marking	Synthetic

Notes

1. A tone is a distinctive pitch associated with a syllable.
2. Great liberties have been taken in presenting Sapir's (1921) model of morphological types. Where convenient, terminology has been altered, added, or dropped. Moreover, the

description here is a simplified form of Sapir's ideas. Despite the changes, I believe the spirit of Sapir's original proposal has been maintained.

3. Isolating languages are also commonly referred to as **analytic** languages.

4. It is an intriguing fact that the verb form meaning "give" is commonly employed in serial constructions to mark benefactives.

5. What has traditionally been called "tense" in ancient Greek might be better described as aspect (for a discussion, see Fanning 1990).

6. One reviewer of this chapter provided a scenario in which the benefits of fusion might outweigh its inefficiency. If a suffix were to trigger a phonological change in the stem to which it attached, the stem modification would make the presence of the affix easier to detect. This could be highly beneficial if the affix were of a particularly relevant category. As a consequence, one might expect a set of common stems, probably a small set, to develop such fusional tendencies (or to maintain them) in the context of this affix.

7. Nichols (1986) provides the basis for this section. Most data and terminology are taken from this source.

8. The example is taken from Davies (1981, 57).

9. The Persian data are taken from Mace (1962) and are discussed in Croft (1990).

10. The use of accusative case is not quite as restrictive as the discussion here implies. Accusative case is used to mark certain kinds of adjuncts as well.

11. Some of the terms from the chart may be unfamiliar to readers with a limited background in linguistics. Most of them are explained at some point in the book; therefore, rather than exemplify each pattern, I simply direct the reader's attention to the index and glossary for assistance in identifying the various constructions.

PART

IV

Encoding Relational
and Semantic Properties
of Nominals

9

Case and Agreement Systems

The notions of case and agreement have played a role in many of the discussions in previous chapters. However, there has not been much said about how these systems operate in language or how complicated they may get. In this chapter, I discuss such issues in more depth. In the first section, the interaction of case and agreement is examined. In Section 2.0, the question of just how much case and agreement is found in languages is addressed. To keep the discussion to a manageable size, I restrict attention to agreement between verbs and noun phrases and the role of case at the clause level.

1.0. Marking of Grammatical Relations

It has been pointed out several times in previous chapters that case marking, agreement, and constituent order can all function at the clause level to indicate the relationship that a noun phrase bears to a verb. For instance, in Chapter 8, Section 2.2, the use of case affixes to mark verbal arguments was labeled as a type of dependent marking, whereas the use of agreement affixes on the verb was identified as the parallel head-marking device, and the use of constituent order was an example of no marking (i.e., neither the head verb nor the nominal dependents were morphologically marked to reflect their syntactic association). Indeed, it is most likely true that all natural languages use at least one of these relation-marking strategies to identify the nominals that have unique grammatical relations (such as subject and object) or unique semantic relations (such as agent and patient) or both.

All languages, rather than relying exclusively on constituent order, case, or agreement to encode such relations, utilize elements of two or three of the strategies (1).

(1) umugabo   y-ataaye   umwaana   mu   maazi
     C1.man   C1-threw   child   in   water

The man has thrown the child into the water.

It is clear in the Kinyarwanda (Niger-Congo: Rwanda) sentence in (1) that *umugabo* ("man") is the subject of the clause because Kinyarwanda places subjects preverbally and a subject agreement prefix obligatorily appears on the verb. The direct object, *umwaana* ("child") is typical in occurring postverbally. Similarly, we know that *maazi* ("water") is a locative expression because it is flagged by the preposition *mu* (Note: Adpositions are frequently considered to be a type of case marker). In Kinyarwanda, then, all three marking strategies are employed: Subjects are encoded via constituent order and agreement, objects by constituent order, and other nominals by prepositions.

Given that languages have various mechanisms at their disposal to identify the grammatical and semantic relationships that nominals bear to the clause, the question arises as to whether the usage of these mechanisms follows any typical or universal patterns. Some answers to this query are provided in the following sections.

■ 1.1. Case and Agreement Hierarchies

Although languages may utilize multiple marking strategies, the use of these strategies is not haphazard but follows some basic principles. First, even languages that make use of all the types of relation marking generally have one strategy that dominates, particularly in the marking of core relations (subject, direct object, and indirect object). Certain constructions or subsystems in the language, however, stray from the dominant strategy. Thus, English nearly always uses constituent order to demarcate subject and object but additionally uses case when pronouns are involved (e.g., *she* for subjects and *her* for objects).

Another observable principle is that case and agreement typically operate according to a hierarchy of relations. The agreement hierarchy is provided in Figure 9.1. This hierarchy predicts that if verb agreement is employed to signal the grammatical relation of any one nominal, it will be with the subject. If there is agreement with only two nominals, they will be subject and object, and so on. Although the hierarchy is not an absolute, it does capture the typical situation. Therefore, we expect only rarely to come across languages in which, for example, an indirect object agrees with the verb but a subject does not. It should be noted that as one moves to the right on the hierarchy, the frequency with which one finds agreement falls off drastically. That is, subject agreement is extremely common, object agreement much less common, indirect object agreement fairly uncommon, and agreement with other nominals quite rare.

Interestingly, the hierarchy that indicates the correlation between grammatical relation and case operates in the opposite direction (Figure 9.2). On the basis of this hierarchy, one does not expect to find many languages that mark subjects, but not any other relations, with case, or any languages in which subjects and indirect objects are marked with case but not direct objects, etc.

The two hierarchies, then, naturally fit together (Figure 9.3) When languages use both case and agreement, they tend to parcel out the work so that the grammatical relations of nominals are not doubly marked. Therefore, wherever agreement stops along the hierarchy for a given language, case picks up with little overlap. This is the case, for example, in Turkish (Turkic: Turkey):

---

subject > direct object > indirect object > other

Figure 9.1. The Agreement Hierarchy

---

other > indirect object > direct object > subject

Figure 9.2. The Case Hierarchy

---

subject > direct object > indirect object > other

AGREEMENT<————>

<————————>CASE

Figure 9.3. Relationship Between Case and Agreement

(2) a. Ben bu   makale-**yi**   yarın   bitir-eceğ-*im*
         I   this   article-ACC   tomorrow   finish-FUT-1S
         I shall finish this article tomorrow.
     b. Hasan   çocuğ-**a**   elma-**yı**   ver-di
         Hasan   child-DAT   apple-ACC   give-PST
         Hasan gave the apple to the child.
     c. Kitap-lar   masa-**dan**   yer-**e**   düş-tü
         book-P   table-ABL   floor-DAT   fall-PST
         The books fell from the table to the floor.   (Data from Kornfilt 1987)

In Turkish, verb agreement only occurs with subjects. Consequently, in (2a) the prefix *-im* marks the presence of a first-person singular subject,[1] and whereas the subject is caseless, other nominals are marked by case suffixes (in bold type).

Although languages are similar in that they typically devote morphosyntax to the marking of relations in these ways, they differ, sometimes greatly, in the types of relations that are central to their clause structure. The linguist's job would be straightforward if "subjects" and "objects" in all languages were basically the same as in English, but they are not. In the following section, weexamine some common ways in which languages differ with regard to which grammatical relations they choose to encode in their morphology and syntax.

■ 1.2. S, A, and P

To discuss how languages can differ from English in the grammatical relations they mark at the clause level, it is necessary to introduce some terminology. Consider the following sentences in (3):

(3) a. John crushed the can.
     b. Bill disappeared.

In the pair of sentences given in (3), the first sentence is transitive (i.e., has a direct object), and the second sentence is intransitive (i.e., does not have a direct object). Regardless of whether the sentence is transitive or intransitive, there is no doubt that the nominals *John* and *Bill* are subjects. In fact, for speakers of English it is difficult to see how *John* and *Bill* could be treated in any other way than straightforwardly as the subjects of their respective sentences.

Languages do differ, however, in the treatment of nominals that are equivalent to *John* and *Bill*. In some languages, *Bill* in (3b) is treated in the morphosyntax more like the direct object (*the can*) of (3a) than the subject (*John*). This is true, for instance, in Lakhota (Almosan-Keresiouan: United States and Canada):[2]

(4) a. a-**ma**-ya-phe
        LOC-1-2-hit
        You hit me.

    b. **ma**-haske
      1-tall
      I am tall.

In the first Lakhota sentence, verb agreement is employed to index the subject (*ya*- marks second person) and the object (*ma*- marks first person). A startling occurrence happens in (4b). Instead of subject agreement appearing on the verb, the lone participant is referred to with the object agreement prefix.

    Clearly, some new terminology is needed to allow us to describe what is happening. After all, to call "I" in (4b) a subject masks the fact that it is signaled by object agreement; to call "I" an object, however, misses the fact that the sentence parallels (3b). Hence, I introduce some labels that have become fairly standard in overviews of case and agreement systems[3] (Diagram 9.1).

S—the nominal that corresponds to the subject of an English intransitive clause.

A—the nominal that corresponds to the subject of an English transitive clause.

P—the nominal that corresponds to the object of an English transitive clause.

Diagram 9.1

We can use these terms to describe transitive and intransitive clauses regardless of how nominals are indexed.

(5) a. Juan-ø   aywa-n
       Juan-CM   go-3S
       He(S) goes.
    b. Juan-ø   maqa-ma-n
       Juan-CM   hit-1S-3S
       Juan(A) hit me(P).   (Adapted from Weber 1981)
    c. Juan-ø   Pedro-ta   maqa-n-ø
       Juan-CM   Pedro-CM   hit-3S-3S
       Juan(A) hits Pedro(P).

(6) a. W-as-ø   w-ekér-ula
         MSC-child-CM   MSC-run-PRES
         The boy(S) runs.

     b. Inssu-cca   j-as-ø   j-écc-ula
         father-CM   FEM-child-CM   FEM-praise-PRES
         Father(A) praises the girl(P). (Data adapted from Ebeling as cited in
            Blake 1994)

The Quechua (Equatorial-Tucanoan: Peru) data in (5) are reminiscent of
the English pattern of core marking: S and A are treated alike in the morphosyntax. Specifically, they both are marked on the verb with a suffix that occurs
immediately after the root, and they have no overt case marking (indicated in
the data by CM). P, on the other hand, is case marked, and the agreement suffix
that indexes it occurs outside the agreement suffix for A. When S and A are
encoded the same way, the system is frequently referred to as **nominative-
accusative.** On the other hand, the Avar (Caucasian: Russia) sentences in (6)
are like the Lakhota data given previously: S and P are treated alike. This can
be determined by comparing the case-marking and agreement patterns of (6a)
and (6b). The S and P nominals have no case but do evince verb agreement.
Alternatively, the A nominal does have a case suffix, but it does not agree with
the verb. When S and P are grouped together in this manner, the system is
frequently referred to as **ergative-absolutive.**

It is common to find ergative-absolutive systems, especially in case
marking and agreement. Much less common is constituent order that follows
this pattern, but it does exist as the Makusi (Carib: Brazil) data show in the
following:

(7) a. pemonkon-yami   witi-'pi
         man-P   go-PST
         The men(S) went.

     b. tuna   ekaranmapo-'pi   uuri-ya
         water   ask.for-PST   I-ERG
         I(A) asked for water(P).

In (7), S and P are preverbal, whereas A is postverbal. In terms of basic
constituent order, Makusi is using an ergative-absolutive system.

When considering the logically possible groupings of S, A, and P,
there are three other systems that might occur in addition to nominative-

accusative and ergative-absolutive (see Kibrik 1985 for a more in-depth examination of this topic). All the potential types are listed in (8) along with a general indication of how commonly they arise in the languages of the world.

Possible Groupings of S, A, and P

(8)	Grouping	Label	Frequency
	[A, S] [P]	Nominative-accusative	Common
	[A] [S, P]	Ergative-absolutive	Common
	[A] [S] [P]	Tripartite	Very rare
	[S] [A, P]	Accusative focus	Unattested
	[A, S, P]	Neutral	Unattested

In a **tripartite** system, S, A, and P all receive unique morphosyntactic treatment. Compare the following transitive (9a) and intransitive (9b) clauses from Wangkumara (Pama-Nyungan: Australia):

(9) a. Kana-ulu   kalkana   titi-nana
        man-ERG   hit   dog-ACC(FEM)
        The man(A) hit the bitch(P).
     b. Kana-ia   paluna
        man-NOM   died
        The man(S) died.   (Data from Mallinson and Blake 1981)

As these data show, A, S, and P all take distinct case suffixes.[4] A true tripartite system—that is, one in which A, S, and P are consistently treated uniquely—is extremely rare. It is more common, although still quite rare, for a language to use a tripartite system for a certain subset of the noun phrases in the language, such as pronouns.

In an **accusative-focus** system, the sole verbal argument in an intransitive clause is treated distinctly from the two arguments of a transitive clause. This system would, of course, put a heavy burden on the users of the language who employed it because there would be no means to distinguish between subjects and objects in transitive clauses other than context. Not surprisingly, no full accusative-focus systems are known to exist, although Comrie (1989) notes that some Iranian languages use this system for certain classes of nouns.

In a **neutral** system, there is no morphosyntactic differentiation between S, A, and P. Like accusative-focus systems, it is highly unlikely that a true neutral system would develop in a language because there would be no linguistic means to differentiate between subjects and objects in transitive clauses.

Of the five possible ways of handling S, A, and P, only two are at all common. Why should this be? Like many other typological patterns we have previously encountered, the relative frequency of the different case-agreement systems requires an explanation. Specifically, we need to address the following question: Why should systems reflecting accusativity or ergativity be most common, tripartite extremely rare, and the other options nonexistent? There seems to be a reasonable functional explanation for this distribution.

Recall that a major function of case, agreement, word order, or all three is to identify semantic or grammatical relations. On the basis of this observation, we might set up the following principle (adopted from Gerdts 1990; see also Kibrik 1991):

(10) *Relational visibility:* The relation of a nominal must be recoverable
from the morphosyntax of a language.

This principle accounts for why accusative-focus and neutral systems never develop into the dominant strategy for signaling core grammatical relations. Because the A and P are indistinguishable, their grammatical relations cannot be recovered from the morphosyntax.

In the discussion of the case and agreement hierarchies earlier in the chapter, it was noted that languages tend not to allow multiple marking of the same nominal. For example, if the case marking makes it clear what the direct object is, generally there will not also be object agreement. It is likely that this follows from the following broad functional principle (also from Gerdts 1990):

(11) *Relational economy:* Systems of relational marking tend to avoid
redundancy. That is, nominals tend not to be multiply identified, and
unneeded morphosyntactic distinctions are avoided.

In both nominative-accusative and ergative-absolutive systems, A and P are distinguished from one another. That is, in transitive clauses the principle of visibility holds. Because S never co-occurs with A or P, there is no need to offer S unique marking to meet the requirements of relational visibility. True to the principle of relational economy, S is simply marked as either A or P depending on the language.

A tripartite system also meets the principle of relational visibility because A and P are distinguishable from their respective marking(s). Tripartite systems, however, violate the principle of economy. Because S cannot be confused with A or P, it is not economical to give it its own marking. Rather, a language will either group S and A (nominative-accusative) or group S and P (ergative-absolutive).

Both these principles govern tendencies and not absolutes. They are designed to capture the most common scenario. Quite obviously, case, agreement, and word order can also be used to indicate information other than grammatical relations (e.g., discourse notions such as topicality or semantic notions such as animacy or definiteness). For this reason, the principles can be violated in certain constructions. Furthermore, the system employed by a language can change over time. In the course of the transitions, violations to the principles may also arise.

■   1.3. Split Case and Agreement Systems

Up to this point, I have intentionally simplified the discussion of case and agreement systems, although it may not seem that way! We have been assuming that languages are largely nominative-accusative, consistently ergative-absolutive, etc. In reality, a single language often uses two or more of these systems depending on the type of construction that is involved. Such splits, as they are often called, typically result from the following: the semantic content of the verb, the tense and aspect of the verb, or the semantic-pragmatic content of the noun.

To understand how the semantic content of the verb might influence the choice of a marking system, it is useful to ask the following questions: What is similar about S and A that a language would opt to treat them in the same way? and What is it about S and P that a language would treat them in the same way? Both of these questions are addressed in turn.

It is very common for verbs to represent an event that typically includes a participant who is an agent (12).

(12) a. **Phil** killed Bill.

b. **Phil** was running.

As in the English sentences in (12), agents are almost always either S or A in active clauses.[5] A nominative-accusative system capitalizes on this semantic similarity by treating S and A alike.

The lexicons of all languages, however, also include many verbs that describe a change of state (13).

(13) a. mgel-i   movk'ali
       wolf-NOM   1.kill.3
       I killed the wolf.
     b. mgel-i   mok'vda
       wolf-NOM   3.died
       The wolf died.   (Data from Harris 1982)

In these examples from Georgian (South Caucasian: Georgia), *mgel* ("wolf") is changing from a state of life to a state of death. Although the nominal is a P in (13a) and an S in (13b), it receives the same case marking (i.e., it is following the ergative-absolutive pattern). It is unusual to ascribe the property of changing state to A (try it in English by thinking of as many verbs as you can). Hence, ergative-absolutive systems seem to be focusing on the nominal that is undergoing a change of state. I will refer to this nominal as the patient.

Notice that intransitive clauses can either depict S as an agent or patient depending on the semantic content of the verb. Some languages adjust their relation-marking systems to capture this semantic difference. If the intransitive verb has an agent as its sole argument, they mark S according to the nominative-accusative system. If the intransitive verb has a patient, they mark S according to the ergative-absolutive system. This phenomenon is referred to as **split intransitivity.** The Eastern Pomo (Hokan: United States) data in (14) exemplify split intransitivity in the form of the personal pronouns (in bold type).

(14) a. Xá:su:là   **wí**   ko:kʰóya
       rattlesnake   1S   bit
       A rattlesnake bit me(P)
     b. **Há:**   mí:pal   šá:ka
       1S   him   killed
       I(A) killed him.
     c. **Wí**   ḍa:lálma
       1S   sick
       I(S) got sick.
     d. **Há:**   xá:qákki
       1S   bathe
       I(S) bathed.   (Data from McLendon 1978)

The two transitive clauses in (14a) and (14b) exhibit the usual form of the first-person singular pronouns for A and P. With an intransitive verb whose subject is nonvolitional, the S takes the same personal pronoun as the P does in (14a). In contrast, the S of a verb indicating a volitional activity takes the same personal pronoun as an A. Thus, the intransitive verbs are split in the manner that their subjects are marked.

One question that may have entered your mind is what split-intransitive languages do with intransitive verbs that can have either a volitional (with an agent) or nonvolitional (with a patient) reading (cf. the English verb *cough,* which denotes an activity that can be carried out on purpose or an activity that happens involuntarily). Some languages seem to place these verbs in one pattern and keep them there regardless of semantics. Other languages such as Eastern Pomo are fluid and alter the marking to match the semantics (15).

(15) a. Wí   će:xélka
        1S   slip
        I(P) am slipping. (accidentally)
     b. Há: će:xélka
        1S   slip
        I(A) am sliding. (deliberately)

The splits in the case-agreement systems examined so far have occurred on the basis of verbal semantics. Sometimes splits occur along the lines of tense and aspect (this phenomenon is usually placed under the rubric of **split ergativity**). These splits are so consistent cross-linguistically that we can propose the following universal:[6]

(16) If a language has split ergativity based on tense or aspect, the ergative-absolutive pattern is found either in the past tense or in the perfect aspect.

An example of split ergativity comes from Georgian (17):

(17) a. Student-i   midis (present)
        student-CM   goes
        The student goes.
     b. Student-i   ceril-s   cers (present)
        student-CM   letter-CM   writes
        The student writes the letter.

   c. Student-i   mivida (perfect)
      student-CM   went
      The student went.

   d. Student-ma   ceril-i   dacera (perfect)
      student-CM   letter-CM wrote
      The student wrote the letter.

In the present tense (17a and 17b), Georgian follows a nominative-accusative pattern. Thus, the same case suffix *-i* is found on the subjects of the respective clauses. In the perfect (17c and 17d), there is a switch to ergative-absolutive. Now it is the P of the transitive clause, rather than the A, on which the *-i* is located.

    A division of marking on the basis of tense or aspect may at first appear odd. There is good reason, however, to believe that this split occurs due to the same type of verbal semantics that we examined previously with split intransitivity. Normally, past tense and perfect aspect are used to depict completed events that lead to other events (either directly causing them or indirectly affecting them due to being temporally contiguous). If each event is conceptualized as a state in time, then the passing of one event means there is a change in state. As discovered previously, focusing on a change in state is characteristic of ergative-absolutive marking.

    Although verbal categories often affect the type of marking used in language, it is also common to find nominal properties having an effect. For example, Dyirbal (Pama-Nyungan: Australia) is mostly ergative-absolutive in its marking (18a and 18b), but it uses a nominative accusative pattern when first- and second-person pronouns are employed (18c-18f):

(18) a. ŋuma   banaga-ɲu
       father   return-PST
       Father returned.

     b. yabu   ŋuma-ŋgu buṛa-n
       mother   father-ERG see-PST
       Father saw mother.

     c. ŋana   banaga-ɲu
       1P   return-PST
       We returned.

     d. ɲura   banaga-ɲu
       2P   return-PST
       You returned.

e. ɲura   ŋana-na   buɾa-n
   2P   1P-CM   see-PST
   You saw us.

f. ŋana   ɲura-na   buɾa-n
   1P   2P-CM   see-PST
   We saw you.   (Data from Dixon 1979)

In addition to splits based on whether the referent is pronominal or not, languages base splits on definiteness and animacy. Once again, there is a pattern behind all these splits. I return to this topic in Chapter 13.

2.0. Complexity of Case and Agreement Systems

In the previous section, the interaction between case and agreement (and to some extent word order) was examined. In this section, the two types of marking are examined independently to answer the question, just how complex does agreement (or case) get?

In the context of case and agreement, the question of complexity is a vague one because the systems can be complex in many different ways. By complexity, one might intend the overall number of distinct forms that occur in the system, or one might mean the different kinds of semantic information that the system encodes. Still further, one might take complexity to be the number of instances of agreement (or case) that co-occur in a single clause. Rather than attempting to explore all these possibilities, this section provides some examples of robust agreement and case systems to give some sense of just how intricate such systems can be. Along the way, I offer some general comments on the types of information that are commonly marked in these systems.

■ 2.1. Verb Agreement

In Section 1.1, the agreement hierarchy was introduced. It was noted that agreement does not commonly extend beyond subjects and objects. When there is agreement with other nominal types, it is often of a special kind. For

example, in some languages, the presence of four arguments can be indexed
on the verb but only if there is no overt noun phrase in the sentence (19).

(19) Y-a-kí-mú-bá-hé-er-eye
He-PST-it-him-them-give-BEN-ASP
He gave it to him for them.   (Data from Kimenyi 1980)

The Kinyarwanda sentence in (19) identifies four participants involved in the
action of giving with prefixes on the verb; the subject *y-* ("he"), the object *ki-*
("it"), the indirect object *mu-* ("him"), and the benefactive *ba-* ("them"). Three
of these prefixes, however, are not *agreement* in the usual sense of the word.
The direct object, indirect object, and benefactive prefixes can only be used
if there is no noun phrase in the sentence that corresponds to them. Thus, if
the noun phrase *abaana* ("children") were to be placed after the verb as the
benefactive nominal, the prefix *ba-* would not appear. Therefore, the prefix
does not cross-reference a nominal but serves as a substitute for it. For this
reason, it is not a canonical instance of agreement.

A few languages do allow for agreement with four nominals but only in
causative constructions. This is the situation in Abaza (Northwest Caucasian:
Russia and Turkey):

(20) alə́gaζʷ   ácʸkʷəncʷakʷa   llá   aphʷə́pa   y-gʸ-y-z-d-m-l-r-ətxd
     boys   old.man   dog   girl   3S-NEG-3P-POT-3S.HUM-NEG-3S.FEM-CAUS-
                                                   gave
The old man couldn't make the boys give the girl her dog back.
                                                  (Adapted from Allen 1956)

Unlike the Kinyarwanda (19), the Abaza sentence permits the agreement
prefixes to co-occur with overt noun phrases. Hence, this represents an
instance of agreement.

To my knowledge, no language that permits agreement with five nominals
simultaneously has ever been reported. The reason for this fact may be partly
due to processing constraints. It may simply be too complex for humans to
process that much agreement within a clause. More likely, however, the limits
on agreement arise for more mundane reasons. In any language, it is not very
common for speakers and writers to include five nominals within a single
clause. Consequently, there is little pressure on languages to develop agreement systems to cross-reference this many nominals.

In addition to the number of arguments that can be referenced on a verb, agreement systems also vary in the types of information that the agreement indicates. It is quite common for languages to possess agreement that operates in terms of person or number or both. In the Abaza data (20), for example, all the agreement prefixes indicate third person and singular number. In addition, they can mark whether a nominal is human (d- is third singular human, whereas y- is third singular nonhuman) and the gender of a nominal (l- is third singular *feminine*). In other languages, animacy, rather than humanness, may be indicated by agreement.

The Kinyarwanda sentence in (19) introduces yet another type of semantic information that can play a role in agreement—noun classes. In Bantu languages such as Kinyarwanda, nouns all are assigned to a class. Nouns such as *umugore* ("woman"), *umugabo* ("man"), and *umuuntu* ("person") are in Class 1, whereas *igitabo* ("book") and *igaari* ("bicycle") are Class 5.[7] When an agreement prefix is employed, it must correspond to the class of the nominal that it is cross-referencing.

Finally, the definiteness of a nominal may determine, in part, whether it triggers agreement or what form the agreement takes (21).

(21) a. Kassa   borsa-w-in   wässädä-**w**
       Kassa   wallet-the-OBJ   took-it
       Kassa took the wallet.

     b. Kassa   borsa   wässädä
       Kassa   wallet   took.
       Kassa took a wallet.   (Data from Givón 1976)

Abkhaz (Northwest Caucasian: Turkey), represented in (21), uses an agreement system that is sensitive to the definiteness of direct objects. If they are definite, an agreement suffix is used (21a); otherwise, no suffix appears (21b).

■ 2.2. Case Systems

The number of cases found in languages ranges from 0 to as many as 53 (this system being reported by Comrie 1981 for Tabassaran [Northeast Caucasian: Russia]). Despite the potential variance suggested by these figures, the organization of case systems tends to follow certain restrictions.

When languages develop case systems containing more than 8 distinct cases, almost invariably it is because they express different notions of location—such as "to," "from," "at," and so on—with case inflections. In Finnish (Finno-Ugric: Finland), for example, which has 15 cases, 9 of them are geared toward expressing types of location (Blake 1994):

(22) -na   "at"
      -ssa   "in"
      -lla   "to"
      -tta   "of/among"
      -sta   "from" (inside)
      -lta   "from" (outside)
      -ksi   "through"
      -Vn   "into" (NB: V indicates vowel. The particular vowel
                     varies for this suffix.)
      -lle   "towards"

A second observation, due to Blake (1994), about the organization of case systems is that they generally adhere to the following hierarchy:

(23) Nominative > accusative-ergative > genitive > dative > locative >
       ablative-instrumental > others

This hierarchy is to be understood as follows: If a case on the hierarchy is found in a language, this language also tends to have any cases to the left—for example, if a language has dative case, it will also have genitive, accusative (or ergative), and nominative.

A four-case system, as just described, is fairly common. It is found, for instance, in ancient Greek (Hellenic):

(24) log-os "word"   (nominative)
      log-on   (accusative)
      log-ou   (genitive)
      log-ō   (dative)

For contrast, compare the paradigm in (25), which comes from Tamil (Dravidian: India and Sri Lanka):[8]

(25) maram   "tree"   (nominative)
      maratt-ai   "tree" (direct object)   (accusative)

maratt-uṭaiya	"of the tree"	(genitive)
maratt-ukku	"to the tree"	(dative)
maratt-il	"at the tree"	(locative)
maratt-iliruntu	"from the tree"	(ablative)
maratt-āl	"using the tree"	(instrumental)
maratt-ōtu	"together with the tree"	(sociative)

(Data from Steever 1987)

Although the Tamil case system is more robust than Greek, it still bears out the predictions of the hierarchy in (23).

Case systems are not only designed to reflect semantic roles and grammatical relations. They also can indicate animacy, humanness, and definiteness. One common scenario is for languages to place direct objects in the accusative if they are definite (or animate or human, depending on the language) and leave them unmarked or in an oblique case (i.e., a case other than nominative, accusative, ergative, or absolutive) if they are indefinite. Recall that these semantic categories were also significant for agreement systems.

3.0. Summary

Case and agreement provide two basic mechanisms for indicating the grammatical and semantic relationships that hold among the elements of clause. In this chapter, some basic observations about these systems were provided. It was noted that when case and agreement co-occur in language, they are characteristically employed in concert in a maximally economical fashion. Although all languages appear to employ some combination of case, agreement, and constituent order to identify core grammatical relations, it was demonstrated that the organization of this marking system can differ in some fundamental ways—for example, along nominative-accusative or ergative-absolute lines.

Such systems can be quite intricate. Languages need not be consistently ordered in one way; rather, they can split their marking systems in various fashions, according to different components of grammar, verb semantics, verbal categories such as tense and aspect, or nominal categories such as definiteness and animacy. Indeed, the role of animacy and definiteness in the morphosyntax of clauses can be quite profound—far beyond what I have indicated. Consequently, I turn to this topic in Chapter 10.

4.0. Key Terms

Accusative-focus	Split ergativity
Ergative-absolutive	Split intransitivity
Neutral	Tripartite
Nominative-accusative	

Notes

1. Verbs do not agree with third-person singular subjects and only agree in specific circumstances with third-person plural subjects. Thus, no subject agreement is found in (2b) and (2c).

2. Data are taken from Rosen (1984). In fact, Lakhota does not always follow the pattern of agreement exhibited in (4). Rather, the language is an example of a language with split intransitivity, which is explained later in the chapter.

3. Dixon (1972) was the first to propose labels of this sort. The label A was chosen because subjects of transitive clauses are prototypically semantic agents. The label P was chosen because objects of transitive clauses are prototypically semantic patients. In essence, however, these labels are syntactic. The surface subject of a transitive clause does not have to be a semantic agent: In "John suffered the humiliation," *John* is not an agent but an experiencer.

4. In many languages, an ergative case affix often marks an additional function such as instrumental (as in Tibetan) or possessive (as in Eskimo). Also, in some instances, the ergative case is employed only when necessary for disambiguation.

5. Indeed, one of the functions of passive voice is to permit a nonagentive nominal to occur as an A.

6. Stephen Levinsohn (personal communication, 1990) brought this universal to my attention.

7. There are 16 different noun classes in Kinyarwanda.

8. I have provided glosses for the various forms as an aid to readers who might not be familiar with the labels given to the various cases. These glosses, however, should not be taken too literally.

10

Animacy, Definiteness, and Gender

In Chapter 9, it was noted that although the marking of grammatical relations is a central function of case, word order, and agreement, this is not the only type of information that they are utilized to depict. In many languages, morphology and syntax can also be exploited to underscore the degree of animacy, the definiteness, the person (first, second, or third), or the gender of noun phrases.[1] This, for example, is true of Mixe (Penutian: Mexico):

(1) a. Tə   paat   ha   həyuhk   t-wopy
         PST   Peter   ART   animal   3-hit
         Peter hit the animal.
      b. Tə   paat   ha   hɔɔʔy   t-wopy
         PST   Peter   ART   person   3-hit
         Peter hit the man.

c. Tə   mehc   ha   hɔɔʔy   s-wopy
   PST   you   ART   person   2-hit
   You hit this person.

d. Tə   əhc   ha   hɔɔʔy   n-wopy
   PST   I   ART   person   1-hit
   I hit the person.

e. Tə   əhc   mehc   n-coky
   PST   I   you   1-want
   I wanted you.

(2) a. Tə   paat   ha   həyuhk   w-[y]opy-ə
       PST   Peter   ART   animal   3-hit-OH
       The animal hit Peter.

    b. Tə   paat   ha   hɔɔʔy   w-[y]opy-ə
       PST   Peter   ART   man   3-hit-OH
       The man hit Peter.

    c. Tə   mehc   ha   hɔɔʔy   m-wopy
       PST   you   ART   person   2-hit
       The person hit you.

    d. Tə   əhc   ha   hɔɔʔy   š-wopy
       PST   I   ART   person   1-hit
       The person hit me.

    e. Tə   əhc   mehc   š-wopy
       PST   I   you   1-want
       You want me.   (Data from Lyon 1967)

At first glance, the data in (1) and (2) appear to exhibit a pattern of verb agreement that is somewhat arbitrary, particularly if one expects to find agreement based on notions such as subject and object. If we focus solely on the data in (1), we might analyze the basic constituent order as being subject-object-verb (SOV) and claim that verbs agree with subjects. The data in (2), however, violate these generalizations. In (2e), like all the examples in (2), the word order is OSV, and the agreement is with the object. Moreover, in (2a) and (2b) the suffix -ə arises on the verb; this marker, however, occurs in no other clause in the data.

Foley and Van Valin (1985) propose that properties of the nominals other than their grammatical relations are determining the operation of Mixe agreement. To adequately describe what is occurring in the Mixe data, they argue one must first realize that both constituent order and agreement are sensitive to the relative "animacy" of the participants in the clause. In simple transitive clauses, the verb agrees with the nominal that possesses the higher animacy, and this nominal is positioned first. In Mixe, humans are rated as being more animate than animals (cf. (1a) and (2a)), proper nouns more animate than common nouns (cf. (1b) and (2b)), both first and second person more animate than common nouns (cf. (1c) and (1d) to (2c) and (2d)), and first-person pronouns more animate than second-person pronouns (cf. (1e) and (2e)). The only complication to this straightforward pattern is that in the case of a transitive clause with two third-person noun phrases, an additional suffix (marked in (2a) and (2b) as OH for "object higher") appears when the Animacy Hierarchy triggers agreement with the object nominal.

1.0. Animacy Hierarchy

By setting up an animacy hierarchy for Mixe, it is possible to state simply that the more animate nominal is placed before the less animate nominal, and the verb agrees with the nominal of higher animacy. Similar phenomena (which are reviewed below) arise in a host of other languages. Hence, it has been proposed (see, e.g., Silverstein 1976) that there is a universal **Animacy Hierarchy** of the sort given in Figure 10.1.

Those categories that are higher (i.e., further left) on the hierarchy often are grammatically distinguished from those that are lower (i.e., further right) and, in general, they tend to be treated as more central to clause structure. Thus, in the Mixe discussed previously, the more animate element was cross-referenced on the verb.

Several comments need to be made at this juncture with respect to the Animacy Hierarchy. First, the title "Animacy Hierarchy" is somewhat of a misnomer because animacy, taken in its usual and narrower sense, is only one of the parameters that are reflected. Three other parameters are also relevant. First, the hierarchy is structured by a **sociocentric orientation** (see Hanks 1990 for a discussion). Inter alia, this captures the notion that speakers and writers tend to place most importance on themselves and those listening to them (i.e., those who generally are referred to in the second person). Hence, although the entities referred to by human animate noun phrases are just as

1 & 2 person > 3 person pronoun > proper name/kin term > human NP >
animate NP > inanimate NP

Figure 10.1. The Animacy Hierarchy

animate as the referents of first- and second-person pronouns, the latter are granted a certain priority in the construction of discourse.

Second, the hierarchy assigns primacy to nominals with which speakers and writers are familiar or have **empathy**.[2] During the formation of a discourse, the participants are aware of themselves and of each other. Thus, those involved with the immediate speech act (first and second persons) will again be ranked highest on this parameter. Third-person pronouns represent an entity that both speaker and hearer are able to uniquely identify in their minds, and so here too there must be a certain awareness or empathy toward such entities. Similarly, proper names require more familiarity among interlocutors and, therefore, involve greater empathy than do other noun phrases referring to humans.

Finally, **definiteness** plays a role in the structuring of the hierarchy. Pronouns and proper names are always definite. When one uses the pronoun *he,* for instance, it cannot properly refer to an indefinite entity such as *a doctor.* Rather, it either refers to a nominal that was previously introduced into a discourse (e.g., "I need to see *a doctor$_i$* about my back, *he$_i$* will be able to relieve some of the pain"), or it refers to a specific individual known from context. Because human noun phrases are more likely to be central to discourse than nonhuman noun phrases, they are also more likely to be definite. The same is true of animate (as opposed to inanimate) nominals.

The Animacy Hierarchy, then, is not based on a unitary notion. Rather, it evinces the interaction of at least three separate semantic features that affect the way that information is packaged in language. The description of these features has been necessarily brief, but I return to one of them—definiteness—below. There is reason to believe that the significance of sociocentric orientation, empathy, and definiteness extends beyond language to the way humans process information generally. If this is the case, then the universality of the hierarchy (which is discussed further in Section 1.2) is rooted in general properties of human cognition rather than specific properties of the language capacity.

A final point in regard to the Animacy Hierarchy that must be clarified is that the first category on the hierarchy (first and second person) cannot be further broken down on a universal basis. Individual languages, however, often select one or the other member of this category as bearing a higher degree of animacy. As shown previously, Mixe places first person before second. Other languages may treat first and second person equivalently, and still others may place second person before first person.

■ 1.1. Reflexes of Animacy in Morphology and Syntax

The particular ways in which animacy is reflected in morphology and syntax differ from language to language, but certain realms of grammar are more likely to make formal distinctions based on distinctions drawn from the Animacy Hierarchy. One such area is verbal agreement, which was exemplified in (1) for Mixe. In those data, the notion of animacy driving the agreement was fairly complex, involving most of the potential divisions on the hierarchy. Cross-linguistically, it does not appear that this degree of complexity is very common. Instead, when verb agreement is driven by animacy, languages usually base the system on fewer distinctions. In Tangut (Tibeto-Burman: extinct),[3] for example, the agreement operates according to a "1 > 2 > other" hierarchy. Thus, in (3a) the verb of the first clause, *thInga,* is marked for object agreement because the object is first person (i.e., highest on the hierarchy), whereas the verb of the second clause is marked for subject agreement because the subject (which is second person) ranks higher than the object (which is third person). The same pattern can be seen in a comparison of (3b) and (3c), although here the priority of second person over common nouns and proper names is exemplified.

(3) a. ni tɪn nga ɪn   ldɪə   thɪ-nga   ku   that tsɪ   viəthɪ-na
        2S if   1S   ACC indeed   chase-1   then 3S   also chase-2
        If indeed you are chasing me, then chase her too.

     b. ni   pha   ngimbɪn   ndɪsiei-na
        2S   other   wife   choose-2
        Choose another wife!

     c. mei-swen   manə   na   khe-na
        Mei-swen   formerly   2S   hate-2
        Mei-swen formerly hated you.   (Data from DeLancey 1981)

It has been pointed out repeatedly in previous chapters that constituent order and case are functionally equivalent to agreement in that each can be used to signal grammatical relations. Therefore, one would expect these phenomena to be affected by animacy considerations as well. They are. In Mixe ((1) and (2)), the linear order of subject and object was sensitive to animacy. Animacy effects on constituent order are also found in languages for the relative positioning of one verbal object with another as the Sesotho (Niger-Congo: Lesotho) data demonstrate (4):

(4) a. ke-phehétsé   ngoaná   lijó
       1S-cooked   child   food
       I cooked the child food.
    b. *ke-phehétsé   lijó   ngoaná
       1S-cooked   food   child
       I cooked the child food.
    c. ke-bítselítsé   morena   baná
       1S-called   chief   children
       I called the chief for the children, or I called the children for the chief.
    d. ke-bítselítsé   baná   morena
       1S-called   children   chief
       I called the chief for the children, or I called the children for the chief.

(Data from Morolong and Hyman 1977)

Note that the order of postverbal objects must be human nominals before nonhuman (4a). The opposite order is ungrammatical (4b). If the objects are both human, either order is possible (4c and 4d).

Similarly, case marking can be sensitive to animacy. According to Mohanan (1982), direct objects in Malayalam (Dravidian: India) are put in the accusative case when they are animate (5a), but they are put in the nominative if they are inanimate (5b).

(5) a. awaĺ   awane   kaṇṭu
       she.NOM   him.ACC   saw
       She saw him.
    b. awaĺ   pusṭakam   kaṇṭu
       she.NOM   book.NOM   saw
       She saw the book.

Mohanan argues that inanimate noun phrases still have direct object properties in sentences such as (5b).[4] Hence, the switch in case marking does not alter the fact that the sentences are simple transitive clauses. Rather, the case alternation seems to be solely driven by animacy considerations.

In some languages, however, the transitivity of a clause is altered to accommodate animacy. A much discussed example of this phenomenon comes from Navaho (Athabaskan: United States).[5] The determination of whether a clause is placed in the active voice (and as a result is transitive) or in the passive (where the clause is intransitive) is largely determined by animacy.

(6) a. hastiin   łịị   yi-ztał
         man   horse   AGT-kick
         The man kicked the horse.

     b. hastiin   łịị   bi-ztał
         man   horse   PAT-kick
         The man was kicked by the horse.

     c. shi-łịị   sá   bi-isxị
         my-horse   old.age   PAT-killed
         My horse was killed by old age.   (Data adapted from Witherspoon 1977)

In (6a), the agent nominal *hastiin* ("man") is serving as subject, and the prefix *yi-* is used, whereas a passive clause (6b) is characterized by the use of the prefix *bi-*. In the final sentence, in which the agent of the clause is less animate than the patient, the passive must be employed, as one can observe from the appearance of *bi-*.

To this point, only examples in which animacy has a bearing on the marking of nominals in clause structure have been presented. It has also been observed (e.g., Croft 1990; Ingram 1978) that nominal classes are sometimes organized on the basis of animacy. For example, in languages with noun classes it is not uncommon to discover a particular class devoted primarily to noun phrases depicting humans (or, in other cases, animate nouns). This is quite typical of Bantu languages, as the following Kinyarwanda (Niger-Congo: Rwanda) data attest:

(7) Class I Nouns

Noun	Meaning	Noun	Meaning
umuntu	"person"	umwaarimu	"teacher"

Noun	Meaning	Noun	Meaning
umukoobwa	"girl"	umubaaji	"carpenter"
umugore	"woman"	umudaandaza	"merchant"
umuhuungu	"boy"	umusore	"bachelor"
umugabo	"man"	umuvoomyi	"water carrier"
umwaami	"king"	umuvyeeyi	"parent"

The Class I nouns of Kinyarwanda are a clear instance of nominal classification founded solely on an animacy category, but it is not common to run across such transparent examples. The manifestation of animacy in the formation of noun classes is obscured by the fact that many other kinds of semantic notions may underlie noun class distinctions including gender, physical shape, size, or material (see Allan 1977).

As in noun classes, the influence of animacy distinctions can be observed in the organization of pronoun systems. For example, consider the paradigm for Shoshone (Uto-Aztecan: United States) personal pronouns (8):

(8)	Pronoun		Nominative	Objective
	1S		nü	nia
	D	INCL	tangku	tahi
		EXCL	nungku	nuhi
	P	INCL	tammü	tammi
		EXCL	nümmü	nümmi
	2S		ü	ümmi
	D		mungku	muhi
	P		mümmü	mümmi
	3 S			ma	(Data from Dayley 1989)

In this language, first- and second-person pronominals make several distinctions that are not found for third person: They have both dual and plural forms that are unique from their respective singular forms, and they have complete sets of pronouns for both nominative and objective cases.

Although there are several further examples that could be presented to show how animacy apparently influences the organization of pronoun systems, it is not clear that the Animacy Hierarchy is really all that relevant, at least not from a typological perspective. In a study by Forchheimer (1953), of the over 60 pronominal systems that were examined, most of the languages exhibited paradigms of personal pronouns for which no animacy effects were observable. Indeed, only 11 could be said to reflect any of the animacy distinctions. Moreover, the data from some of the languages in his study seem to be inaccurate such that the overall number of pronoun systems that manifest the Animacy Hierarchy is even smaller.[6] Finally, he lists two pronoun systems that contradict the predictions of the Animacy Hierarchy. The first is English, in which there are distinct singular and plural forms for third person (*he-she-it* vs. *they*) but not for second person (*you*). The second is Arabic (Semitic: Middle East and North Africa), which has a singular-dual-plural distinction for second and third person but only a two-way division (singular-plural) for first person.

This raises a challenging question: In exactly what sense is the Animacy Hierarchy a universal? It is clear that animacy plays a role in the shape of many languages, but the influence on specific languages varies dramatically. Furthermore, there are some subsystems, such as pronouns, for which one might expect to find animacy effects, but the overall evidence is less than compelling. I turn to this issue in the following section.

■   **1.2. Animacy Hierarchy as a Universal**

One reason that the Animacy Hierarchy is assumed to reveal a significant property of the human mind in organizing language is because of its ubiquitous appearance in the languages of the world. By the same account, it is also considered a universal. Of course, by calling the hierarchy a "universal," no one means that each division on the hierarchy must have an effect on the grammar of every language. Instead, the realization of the Animacy Hierarchy is language specific.

What, then, does the claim of universality entail? There are two essential claims involved. First, each division on the hierarchy must be motivated by some language. That is, one only wants to posit a division where it improves the grammatical description of a language (or languages). In actual practice, this requirement for ascribing a universal status to the hierarchy has been met many times over as each division on the hierarchy has been discovered in multiple languages.

Second, for the Animacy Hierarchy to be a universal, its observed effects must arise outside of a single language family or a single linguistic area. Otherwise, rather than being universal in any sense, it would be a genetic or areal trait. As such, it would still be of interest, but one could account for it as an accident of linguistic history instead of a reflection of some deep linguistic property. Again, the Animacy Hierarchy meets this requirement for universality. Nichols (1992) reports that nominal classification based on animacy (or gender—she conflates the two) appeared in 27% of the languages in her 174-language sample. These languages arise in a number of language families and are not restricted to any single geographic area.[7]

Finally, for the Animacy Hierarchy to be an absolute universal, it also must be true that the number of exceptions to its claims be statistically insignificant. I have not come across any research that demonstrates this fact satisfactorily. The exceptions to the hierarchy found in the literature, however, are amazingly sparse, which provides at least the impression that the Animacy Hierarchy also meets this requirement for universal status.

2.0. Definiteness and Gender

There are two further semantic properties of nouns that can govern the manner in which they are treated in the morphology and syntax of languages: definiteness and gender. The significance of definiteness was introduced in Chapter 9 in example (21). There, it was shown that object agreement in Abkhaz is sensitive to whether or not the object is definite. A similar effect is found in case marking in some languages. In Hebrew (Semitic: Israel), only definite objects are flagged by the clitic *et-* (9).

(9) a. ha-ish   koteb   dabar
         ART-man   write   word
         The man is writing a word.
     b. ha-ish   shomer   et-ha-torah
         ART-man   observe   DEF-ART-law
         The man is observing the law.

Definiteness and animacy often interact. Comrie (1989) presents Hindi (Indo-Iranian: India) as a revealing case study. In the language, direct objects that are human are almost always flagged by the postposition *ko* regardless of whether they are definite. Only in rare cases will human referents appear without *ko,* and when they do, they are indefinite. Definite nonhuman nominals also typically take *ko.* However, indefinite nonhuman nominals never do.

Thus, neither the human-nonhuman nor the definite-indefinite distinction is sufficient to determine the distribution of *ko*. Rather, the interaction of the two semantic categories is required (10).

(10)   *Definite*   *Indefinite*

    Human   *ko* (required)   *ko* (almost always)

    Nonhuman   *ko* (typical)   —

The interchange between animacy and definiteness should not come as a surprise. Recall that one of the parameters on which the Animacy Hierarchy is based is definiteness.

The sex or **gender**[8] of a nominal is another property of nominals that can influence the grammar of a language (see Corbett 1991). Pronouns, for example, often reflect gender distinctions, such as the third-person singular set in English (*he, she,* and *it*). Noun classes are commonly sensitive to gender as well—for example, in French, female entities tend to be marked by feminine gender and male entities by masculine gender.

In addition to lexical classification, the morphosyntax of languages can reflect gender distinctions. In Russian (Balto-Slavic: Russia), for example, verbs display gender agreement in the past tense:

(11) a. babuška   čitala
       grandmother.FEM   read.FEM
       Grandmother was reading.

   b. čelovek   čital
       man.MSC   read.MSC
       The man was reading.

   c. okno   otkrylos
       window.NEUT   open.itself.NEUT
       The window opened.   (Data from Moravcsik 1978)

In this particular case, the influence of gender is indirect because the verb is actually agreeing with noun classes (which are labeled "feminine," "masculine," and "neuter") rather than the sex of the nominal referents per se. Nevertheless, the importance of gender is apparent.

3.0. Summary

It should now be clear that inherent properties of nominals can be more crucial to understanding the morphology and syntax of languages than purely grammatical concepts such as subject and object. This is indisputable. Furthermore, the idea that animacy is rooted in basic conceptual distinctions made by humans as they process knowledge provides an exciting link to research on other cognitive systems.

The current understanding of animacy, however, is still in its infancy. In particular, there is a lack of work based on representative samples of the world's languages so that statistical generalizations about the frequency of various types of animacy-based marking are unavailable. In some cases, such as pronominal systems, it is still unclear whether animacy even plays a role.

4.0. Key Terms

Animacy Hierarchy	Gender
Definiteness	Sociocentric orientation
Empathy	

Notes

1. The work of Bernard Comrie has been pioneering in underscoring the significance of animacy for comprehending the morphosyntax of natural language. Although he has explored the importance of these semantic categories since the mid-1970s, Comrie (1989) provides a convenient overview of his ideas on animacy.

2. I am using the term *empathy* in a broad way here. See Silverstein (1976), Delancey (1981), Kuno (1987), and Chafe (1976, 1987, 1994) for more complete discussions. Each of these authors is careful to make a distinction between the perspective taken by a speaker when relating a proposition and the status of information (whether it is given or new). I conflate these logically independent concepts here.

3. The example is drawn from Croft (1990).

4. See Bhat (1991), however, who suggests that the notion of grammatical relation is irrelevant in Malayalam case marking.

5. See Comrie (1989) and Croft (1990).

6. For example, Forchheimer (1953) lists Burmese (Tibeto-Burman: Burma) as having a three-way distinction in pronouns between person (first, second, and third) and a distinction in number (singular vs. plural) but lacking a third-person plural pronoun. In this way, first and second person possess greater morphological marking than third person, which could be traced to the Animacy Hierarchy. In Cooke's (1968) review of pronominal reference in Burmese, however, there do indeed appear to be unique third-person singular and plural pronouns. Furthermore, he reveals that there are a vast number of forms for first, second and third person, rather than the limited set in Forchheimer's data. The abundant forms are employed to mark degrees of politeness and formality. Consequently, it is unclear that this system is even susceptible to an analysis in which the total number of first- and second-person forms are compared with third person to determine whether they receive the same degree of morphological marking.

7. Nichols does note, however, that animacy marking languages do cluster in four broad areas: Africa, the Near East, Europe, and northern Australia. A large number are also found in North America, but the overall density of these languages is too low to be significant for Nichols.

8. The term *gender* is used ambiguously in linguistics. Sometimes it refers to the actual sex of a nominal referent (i.e., whether it is male, female, not capable of classification/neuter or all three). At other times, it is used synonymously with "noun class." I will use the term in the former sense.

11

Valence

The term *valence* was borrowed into linguistics by the French linguist Lucien Tesnière (1959). Originally, it was used in chemistry where it denoted the capacity of an element to bond with other chemical elements. Similarly, in linguistics the term refers to the number of arguments that can combine with a verb. To understand how the nomenclature of valence is applied to language, consider the following English examples:

(1) a. I am sleeping.
   b. I touched the Mona Lisa.
   c. I gave the million dollars to a waitress.

In (1a), the valence of the verb is "1" because only a single argument is required. Any additional noun phrases or prepositional phrases that might be added to the sentence (e.g., "I am sleeping **in typology class**") are considered to be "adjuncts" because their presence is optional. Adjuncts do not get included in the valence of a verb;[1] therefore, *sleep* remains monovalent even

183

when the prepositional phrase *in the typology class* co-occurs. In the same vein, *touch* (2b) has a valence of two, and *give* has a valence of three.

Often, there is confusion between the notion of valence and transitivity. Properly speaking, transitivity has to do with the presence or absence of grammatical objects. A verb with a direct object is called **transitive**. A verb with a direct object and an indirect object is called **ditransitive** (literally, "doubly transitive").[2] A verb without a direct object is **intransitive** (literally, "not transitive"). There is no direct correlation between transitivity and valence, so it is not always true that transitive verbs have a valence of two, ditransitive verbs a valence of three, and intransitive verbs a valence of one. For instance, the verb *place* has a valence of three because one must specify the person doing the placing, the thing being placed, and the location of the placing (2a). If any of these arguments are omitted, the resultant clause is ill formed (2b-2d).

(2) a. The instructor placed my exam before me.
  b. *Placed my exam before me.
  c. *The instructor placed before me.
  d. *The instructor placed my exam.

Although the verb has a valence of three, it is a transitive verb and not a ditransitive one. This is because it takes a direct object and not both a direct and an indirect object.

Verbs dealing with meteorological conditions do not fit comfortably into the classification scheme of valence. In many languages, such verbs are not accompanied by an overt subject argument or, if they are, the subject argument is cognate—that is, it is based on verb's lexical root. This can be observed in the following sentence from Even (Manchu-Tungusic: Russia) in which the parentheses indicate optionality:

(3) (Imanra)   iman-ra-n
     snow.NOM   snow-nonFUT-3S
     It is snowing.   (Data from Malchukov 1995)

Other verbs that follow this pattern in Even include *udan-* ("rain") and *dolbo-* ("get dark"). These verbs might be said to have a valence of zero.

In other languages, these verbs only appear with a **dummy** subject—that is, a pronominal subject that has no actual reference, as in "*it* rained."

Although the subject is a dummy in these cases, it is still obligatory so that meteorological verbs in English have a valence of one, and they are simply taken as a special class of intransitive predicates.[3]

1.0. Valence-Changing Devices

The core valence of a verb can generally be determined by observing the distribution of its arguments when the verb is in its basic form. By a basic form, I mean the form of a verb when it appears in simple active declarative sentences (such as those shown previously). The morphosyntax of a language, however, is capable of altering this core valence, either by increasing it or by decreasing it. What is most interesting from a typological perspective is how languages go about changing valence in different ways.

Some valence-changing mechanisms are morphological. This means that decreases or increases in valence are signaled by affixes on either the predicate (verbal morphology) or on its arguments (case). In other instances, analytical means are employed for changing valency. That is, words and word order are utilized as the primary approaches to valence changing rather than affixes. Not surprisingly, morphological and analytical devices can also occur in tandem.

Finally, the alterations on a verb's valence can become lexicalized over time. When this occurs, a new verb has been created in the language, albeit often an irregular one. Examples of each of these mechanisms are examined in the following section.

■ 1.1. Valence-Decreasing Devices

The valence of a verb is decreased when the number of required arguments associated with a particular verbal root is lowered. Of the many ways to decrease the valence of a verb, passive constructions are perhaps the most common (4 and 5), although they are not universal.[4]

(4) a. The thugs will mug Bugs.
     b. Bugs will be mugged (by the thugs).

(5) a. X-at-in-bok   (liạn)
        TNS-2-1-call   I
        I called you.
     b. X-at-bok-e'   (lạat)   (in-ban)
        TNS-2-call-PASS   you   1-by
        You were called by me.   (Data from Berinstein 1990)

As represented in the English and K'ekchi (Penutian: Guatemala) sentences, passives (4b and 5b) serve to reduce the valence of a transitive clause by promoting the logical object (i.e., the nominal that would be the direct object in transitive clauses (4a and 5a) to the subject relation.[5] Alternatively, the logical subject is demoted such that it does not receive the marking of a core grammatical relation. The resultant clause is, therefore, intransitive. Most commonly, passive constructions are found in nominative-accusative languages. They can be primarily analytic (like the English) or primarily morphological (like the K'ekchi). They also vary as to whether the agent nominal is expressed. In both the examples above, the presence of the agent nominal is optional. Some languages, however, disallow expression of agents in passive clauses.

Passives can also be lexicalized over time. In ancient Greek (Hellenic), many morphologically passive forms became fixed; they did not have any corresponding active.

(6) phobeomai   "be afraid"
     erchomai   "come"

Once a form has become lexicalized, it may no longer be proper to analyze it as being synchronically related to nonlexicalized forms. This is certainly true in the Greek examples. Historically, *phobeomai* was the morphological passive of "cause fear" and *erchomai* the morphological passive of "bring." The forms, however, became frozen and ceased to appear in an active forms. Therefore, although they are etymologically related to passives, it is best to propose that they are stored in the lexicon as simple intransitive verbs.

Commonly, ergative-absolutive languages such as Iñupiaq (Inuit: Greenland and Canada) employ a similar detransitivizing construction called **antipassive.** Rather than demoting the subject of a transitive clause, antipassive demotes the object (7b).

(7) a. Aŋuti-m   umiaq   qiñiġ-aa   tirraġ-mi
         man-ERG   boat   see-3.3   beach-at
         The man sees the boat at the beach.
     b. Aŋun   umiaġ-mik   qiñiq-tuq   tirraġ-mi
         man   boat-MOD   see-3   beach-at
         The man sees a boat at the beach.   (Data from Seiler 1978)

There are two clues that *umiaq* ("boat") (the absolutive object in 7a) has been
demoted in (7b). First, the verb agreement indicates that the clause in (7b) is
intransitive. Second, the case marking is different in the two clauses. In the
transitive clause in (7a), *aŋuti-m* has an ergative case suffix, but in the
antipassive construction it is treated as an absolutive. The Iñupiaq data reveal
another interesting fact about antipassive constructions. Often, they are employed just in case the object is indefinite (as in (7b)). That is, the construction
is driven according to the dictates of the Animacy Hierarchy (see Cooreman
1994 for a cross-linguistic overview of other functions of the antipassive
construction).

Silverstein (1976) proposes that antipassive constructions only occur in
ergative languages and, furthermore, that antipassive and passive do not both
arise in the same language. Both these claims, however, have been called into
question (e.g., Heath 1976).

A third valence-decreasing device is noun incorporation. Here, the direct
object is incorporated into the verb stem resulting in detransitivization (8):

(8) Ti-pi-sheuw-we
     1S.ABS-deer-hunt-PRES
     I'm hunting for deer.   (Data from Allen, Gardiner, and Frantz 1984)

Like antipassives, noun incorporation such as that found in the Southern Tiwa
(Tanoan: United States) example is often sensitive to whether the object to be
incorporated is definite. Although the precise details can be complicated (see
Mithun 1986), it is generally true that incorporation is most common when
the object is indefinite.

Among valence-decreasing devices, one should also include derivational
morphology. Languages frequently contain nominalizing affixes (e.g., *destroying* and *destruction* are nominalizations of *destroy*). In many languages,
the valence of the verb is reduced when these affixes are employed. Hence,
in English, *destruction* has a valence of zero. To specify its semantic argu-

ments, one must place them in genitive constructions ("the army's *destruction of the city*").

Other major devices for reducing valence are reflexive and reciprocal constructions.

(9) a. ni   kwə́ləš θ-ám ʔš-əs   kwθə   swə́yʔqe?
         AUX   shoot-1.OBJ-3.ERG   DET   man
         The man shot me.

     b. ni   kwə́ləš θ-ət   kwθə   swə́yʔqe?
         AUX   shoot-self   DET   man
         The man shot himself.   (Data adapted from Gerdts 1989)

A comparison of a basic transitive clause in Halkomalem (Almosan-Keresiouan: Canada) with a reflexive clause reveals differences in the system of verb agreement. In (9a), both the ergative and the absolutive nominals are cross-referenced on the verb. When the reflexive suffix appears on the verb, however, it is no longer possible to use the ergative agreement suffix. That is, the clause is intransitive.

Interestingly, languages that employ an analytic approach to reflexivization do not usually appear to decrease verb valence in reflexive constructions. Thus, in the English equivalents to (9b), all the evidence suggests that the reflexive clause remains transitive and the verb maintains a valence of two. Although there is a general correlation between morphological reflexives and valence reduction versus analytical reflexives and valence maintenance, Gerdts (1989) provides convincing evidence that the correlation is not exact.

Predicates with reflexive meanings can also be lexicalized. For example, "to shave" and "to dress" in English are interpreted as reflexive unless accompanied by an overt object (e.g., "I shaved the dog" and "I dressed my son").

Finally, there is a less common valence-decreasing device called **anticausative.** In this construction, a transitive verb with causative semantics (i.e., X causes Y to Z) is marked with a suffix that detransitivizes it, and the agent of the construction is left unexpressed (10b). Such a construction occurs in many Bantu languages, such as Swahili (Niger-Congo: East Africa). The tradition in Bantu studies has been to call the anticausative marker a stative suffix, and therefore it is glossed STAT in (10).

(10) a. i-me-vunj-ika
          it-PERF-break-STAT
          It is broken.

b. i-me-poto-ka
   it-PERF-twist-STAT
   It is twisted.   (Data from Wald 1987)

Crucially, the detransitivizing suffix in (10) is distinct from a passive (which
also promotes a logical object and demotes or eliminates the agent), and this
is why it is considered an anticausative. Perhaps the reason why such constructions are fairly rare cross-linguistically is because it is so easy for
languages simply to employ passive morphology for the same effect (see
Haspelmath 1990).[6]

■ **1.2. Valence-Transposing Devices**

In certain grammatical constructions, there is no change in the overall
verbal valence, but the arguments have altered their respective grammatical
relations. One such construction is subject-object reversal. The following data
are from Kutenai (Almosan-Keresiouan: North America):

(11) a. wu:kat-i   paɫkiy-s   titqat'
        see-IND   woman-OBV   man
        The man saw the woman.
     b. wu:kat-aps-i   titqat'   paɫkiy
        see-S/O.REV-IND man-OBV   woman.
        The man saw the woman. (or, The woman was seen by the man.)
                                                        (Data from Dryer 1994)

Both the subject and object of (11a) remain core arguments in (11b)—that is,
the clauses are both transitive. Thus, although (11b) might best be translated
by a passive clause in English, there is no reason to believe it is a passive in
Kutenai (see Dryer 1994 for details). For this reason, there is also no reason
to say that the valency has been decreased. Rather, the two nominals have
exchanged grammatical relations while maintaining their semantic properties.

A phenomenon called **dative shift** also seemingly realigns the grammatical relations of a clause without altering valency. Indonesian (Austronesian:
Indonesia) exemplifies the construction. A verb with a valence of three can
appear with its arguments in a typical ditransitive pattern—that is, with a
direct object and an indirect object (the nominal *Ali* in (12a), which is flagged
by the preposition *kepada*)—or it can appear with double objects. Notice that
both *Ali* and *surat* occur in (12b) without case marking or an accompanying

preposition. For this reason, they both appear to have the morphosyntax of direct objects—hence the label "double objects."[7]

(12) a. Saja mem-bawa   surat   itu   kepada   Ali
      I   TRANS-bring   letter the   to   Ali
      I brought the letter to Ali.
   b. Saja mem-bawa-kan   Ali   surat   itu
      I   TRANS-bring-BEN Ali   letter the
      I brought Ali the letter.   (Data from Chung 1976)

English is an example of a language that has dative shift constructions (compare the English glosses of the Indonesian in (12)), but requires no verbal morphology to signal the shift. In this way, the language might be said to employ a purely analytic method of valence transposition. English also lexicalizes, in a limited fashion, the distinction between the typical ditransitive construction and the typical double object construction. The verb *promise* tends only to be used with double objects (therefore, some speakers find "Mary never promised the money to you" unacceptable), whereas the verb *donate* generally is used as a typical ditransitive ("?I donated him my favorite baseball cards").

■ **1.3. Valence-Increasing Devices**

There are two basic ways that languages increase verb valence: the promotion of nonrequired arguments to object status and causatives. Each is described in this section.

In many languages, it is possible to replace the logical object of a transitive construction with another nominal (13).

(13) a. Ha   punu'   si   Miguel i   babui para guahu
      3S   kill   PNoun Miguel the pig   for   me
      Miguel killed the pig for me.
   b. Ha   puni'-i yu'   si   Miguel nu   i   babui
      3S   kill-for me   PNoun Miguel OBL the pig
      Miguel killed the pig for me.   (Data from Gibson 1980)

The Chamorro (Austronesian: Mariana Islands) example in (13a) is a simple transitive clause. Notice that the direct object, *babui* ("pig"), is not governed by a preposition, and it precedes the benefactive nominal. The sentence in (13b) remains transitive, but the benefactive nominal has usurped those properties that are assigned to the direct object in (13a), and *babui* now appears flagged by the preposition *nu*. In this configuration, both *yu'* and *babui* are obligatory. Thus, the valence of the verb has increased by one. Note further that this alteration in verbal valence is signaled by a verb suffix.

In some languages, it is similarly possible to promote an adjunct of an intransitive verb to object status, thereby increasing the valency by one. This occurs in Sierra Popoluca (Penutian: Mexico):

(14) a. te:ñ
   He stood up.
b. i-tye:ñ-ka
   OBJ-3S.stood.up-INST
   He stood up by means of it.   (Data from Elson 1956)

The object agreement prefix on the verb indicates that the clause in (14b) is transitive. A suffix is employed to encode the promotion of the instrumental adjunct to object status.

Constructions such as those in (13b) and (14b), in which an increase in verb valence is marked by a verbal affix, are often referred to as **applied constructions** or **applicatives.** These examples were instances of a nominal taking on direct object properties, although in other cases the applied construction assigns the properties of an indirect object to the promoted nominal.

Another common way to increase the valence of a verb is by using **causative** constructions. A causative is a linguistic device by which the relationship between two events is explicitly captured within a single clause. The topic of causatives is a complicated one; therefore, I return to it again in the following section. For now, let it suffice to provide some representative examples.

Some languages, such as Tigrinya (Semitic: Ethiopia), produce causatives via verbal morphology:

(15) a. Bärĥe   mäšĥaf   rə'iyu
   Berhe   book   see.PST.3S
   Berhe saw the book.
b. Məsgənna   nə-Bärĥe   mäšĥaf   'a-r'iyu-wo
   Mesghenna   ANIM-Berhe   book   CAUS-see.PST.3S-OBJ
   Mesghenna showed Berhe the book.   (Data from Palmer 1994)

Example (15a) is an instance of a simple transitive sentence for which the verb valence is two. The addition of the causative prefix in (15b) increases the valence to three.

It is not uncommon for languages to have lexicalized the causative semantics of verbs. This means that rather than deriving a causative verb from a verb root, two separate roots develop in the language, one that indicates the causative version of the other. English, for instance, has the pairs *see-show, die-kill, lie-lay, sit-seat, remember-remind,* and so on.

Languages also form causatives analytically. Again, English is an excellent example:

(16) He caused/compelled/forced me to do it.

Constructions such as this in which multiple verb forms (e.g., *compelled + to do*) are used to indicate causation are frequently referred to as **periphrastic** causatives.

As has been seen from the English causative data, a given language may have more than one means by which to create causatives. The various types, however, are often used to represent different types of causation. This is one of the issues we return to in Chapter 12.

2.0. Causatives

Because I include lexical causatives as a type of causative construction, it is safe to say that every language in the world has causative constructions. It also comes as no surprise that languages that are morphologically isolating tend to use analytical causatives, whereas those languages that are agglutinating tend to employ morphological causatives.

Another typologically significant aspect of causatives is the grammatical relation of the causee. Comrie (1976b, 1985a) observes that the grammatical relation of the causee tends to be predictable based on the type of valence increase that is occurring (e.g., is a verb with a valence of one being increased to two, is a transitive verb with a valence of two being increased to three, etc.). If the causative is built on an intransitive structure, then the causee tends to have direct object properties. If the causative is built on a transitive structure, subject > direct object > indirect object > oblique

Figure 11.1. The Causee Accessibility Hierarchy

the causee will be treated as an indirect object, and if the causative is built on a ditransitive clause, the causee will be treated as an oblique. In other words, Comrie argues that the causee will take the highest available position on the hierarchy in Figure 11.1.

The hierarchy in Figure 11.1 should seem familiar. It has already been shown relevant for case assignment and agreement. Thus, to the degree Comrie's (1976b) claim is correct, the hierarchy here provides additional evidence for the relevance of grammatical relations to human language. Some counterexamples, however, have been raised against his analysis (see Song 1991a).

The nature of causatives becomes most fascinating when languages are examined that have more than one means to signal causation. One quickly discovers that the choice between a morphological, analytical, or lexical causative is not completely arbitrary. Instead, the form that a causative construction takes can capture (sometimes subtle) variations in meaning.

■ **2.1. Direct Versus Indirect Causation**

The human mind has the capacity to conceptualize the relationship between two events, A and B, in many ways. A and B may be entirely unconnected in space and time and be believed to have no connection whatsoever (17).

(17) A. Bob ate burnt toast this morning.
B. John Kennedy was assassinated in 1963.

Alternatively, there may be some perceived association between the two events. When one event is thought to bring about the occurrence of a second event, it is called causation. Every language possesses many ways to capture causation. Two clauses might simply be juxtaposed (18a), leaving the causation implicit; a temporal connector that leads to a causative interpretation might be utilized (18b); or a special connector dedicated explicitly to capturing the causation (18c) might be employed.

(18) a. I laughed. She left.
   b. As soon as I laughed, she left.
   c. Because I laughed, she left.

In all these examples, two clauses are combined; in addition to these possibilities, however, languages develop one or more constructions specifically geared toward encoding causative semantics within a single clause. English has adopted a set of causative verbs for this purpose.

(19) a. Bugsy caused her to leave.
   b. Rocco made her leave.
   c. Baby Face had her leave.
   d. Al let her leave.

Although all the examples in (19) depict causation, their meanings are clearly not identical. Therefore, it is important to recognize different causative types.[8] The basic semantic distinction is between **direct causation** and **indirect causation**. As the names imply, direct causation refers to a situation in which the actions of the causer have immediate impact on the actions of the causee, and indirect causation refers to a situation in which the causation is further removed. The division is not categorical but permits shades of directness.

The difference between direct and indirect causation may be clarified by comparing the English lexicalized causative *kill* and the corresponding causative construction *cause to die*. For example, you are sitting on a bench at a busy intersection and have the misfortune of witnessing a terrible accident. A small girl chases a basketball that she has been dribbling into the street after it caroms off her foot. At just that moment, a speeding car zips around the corner striking the girl. It is far more likely that you yell out "I think he killed her" than "I think he caused her to die." If both utterances are causatives, why would one be so obviously preferred? The analytical causative construction *cause to die* implies indirect causation, but in this scenario there is no doubt that the driver's actions directly brought about the girl's death, even if there was no intention to do so. Therefore, to use *cause to die* is misleading. It fails to capture the nature of the causation. Rather, it is much more suited to a

Type of Causative	Form	Causation
LEXICAL	(X - "smaller")	More direct
MORPHOLOGICAL	(Y-Z)	
ANALYTIC	(Y Z - "larger")	Less direct

Figure 11.2. Haiman's Iconicity Pyramid

situation in which the causee is not even cognizant that his actions are leading to death, as in (20).

(20) By dumping their raw sewage into the river, the factory may have caused hundreds of innocent people to die.

Notice that the verb *kill* is still possible in (20). The rhetorical effect of using *kill,* however, would be to strengthen the claim of negligence.

Haiman (1983) has proposed a useful typological principle that makes predictions about which of two or more competing causative types will be used to describe direct causation. In general, if a language has more than one formal kind of causative, the "smaller" one (i.e., the one that is more structurally integrated) will be used for (conceptually) more direct causation, whereas the "larger" one will be used for less direct causation. This principle is captured graphically in Figure 11.2, in which its consequences for the three types of causatives are drawn out.

In lexical causatives, cause and effect are bound up in a single lexical unit (X). The close formal connection correlates with close semantic connection; thus, the form is said to be iconic with respect to the meaning. In morphological causatives, the effect is typically a verb (Y) and the causation indicated by an affix (Z). The formal separation correlates with an increase in separation between the conception of cause and effect. Finally, in analytic causatives the cause and effect are expressed as separate verbs. There is a greater formal division and, hence, a greater conceptual distance between the cause and its result.

The predictions of Haiman's Iconicity Pyramid (Figure 11.2) can be seen in a comparison of English lexical versus analytical causatives. To say "John seated Mary at the table" reflects a conscious and deliberate act on the part of John. He has a great deal of control in instigating and completing the action. Conversely, in a clause such as "John caused Mary to sit at the table," it is no longer certain that John consciously or deliberately effected the event of Mary's sitting. His degree of control is more remote, which correlates with the greater formal distance between the causative verb (*cause*) and the event verb (*sit*).

As shown in the following, Korean (Korean: Korea) offers a contrast between morphological and analytical causatives:

(21) a. emeni-nun   ai-eykey   os-ul   ip-key   ha-ess-ta
           mother-TOP   child-DAT   clothes-ACC wear-COMP   do-PST-IND
           The mother had the child put on the clothes.

       b. emeni-nun   ai-eykey   os-ul   ip-hi-ess-ta
           mother-TOP   child-DAT   clothes-ACC wear-CAUS-PST-IND
           The mother put the clothes on the child.   (Data from Shibitani 1973)

In the analytic structure (22a), the gloss reflects an indirect causation by *emeninun* ("mother") versus the morphological causative (22b) that attributes direct causation.

One note of caution must be presented about the chart in Figure 11.2. The Iconicity Pyramid is not designed to compare a causative construction in one language with a causative construction in a second language. It makes claims only about those languages that themselves have more than one means of expressing causation.

■ **2.2. Indicating the Degree of Control Retained by the Causee**

A second semantic difference that often distinguishes causative types is the degree of control retained by the causee. The discussion returns to (19b) and (19d), which are repeated here for convenience, to exemplify this difference:

(19) b. Rocco made her leave.

       d. Al let her leave.

There is little doubt that the causer, *Rocco,* retains nearly all the control of the situation in (19b). In (19d), however, the causee plays a part in determining whether to carry out the act of departure, albeit within the context of the causer's greater control.

In some languages, the degree of control held by the causee may be expressed by choosing different case endings. This is the situation in Hungarian (Finno-Ugric: Hungary):

(22) a. Én   köhög-tet-te-m   a   gyerek-kel
     I   cough-CAUS-PST-1S   the   child-INST
     I got the child to cough (e.g., by asking).

   b. Én   köhög-tet-te-m   a   gyerek-et
     I   cough-CAUS-PST-1S   the   child-ACC
     I made the child cough.   (Data from Hetzron as cited in Comrie 1989)

As the Hungarian data show, it is common for a causee with little control to appear in a core case (such as accusative in (22b))[9] and a causee with greater control to appear in an oblique case (such as instrumental in (22a)). Typically, the oblique case that is used is also the case used to express an agent nominal in passive constructions. The relationship between case and degree of control is captured in Figure 11.3.

Once again, care must be taken to recognize that this case hierarchy is not meant for comparisons of causative constructions from two different languages. We would not want to conclude, for instance, that a causative construction in some language X that places the causee in nominative case depicts more causee control than the Hungarian construction in (22a), which employs an oblique case for expression of the causee.

■ 2.3. Permission Versus Causation

A final semantic consideration that effects the form of causatives is whether they indicate permission, requests, or true causation. In many languages, there is no morphosyntactic distinction between causation and permission, but there is in others. In English, the difference is most directly captured lexically. That is, the choice of the verb indicates permission (*allow, let, permit,* etc.), requests (*ask*), and causation (*make, cause,* and *force*). There are also, however, structural properties that correspond to these lexical differences.

Case	Causee's Degree of Control
NOMINATIVE	High
OBLIQUE	Less
ACCUSATIVE	None

Figure 11.3. Case and the Causee

(23) a. I asked that he (NOM) leave.
     b. I asked him (ACC) to leave.
     c. I made him (ACC) leave.

With verbs of request, it is often possible to frame the particular request as a finite clause. This leaves the causee in nominative case and interrupts any tight cohesion between the verb of request (*ask*) and the content of the request (*leave*). By both Haiman's Iconicity Pyramid and the case hierarchy in Figure 11.3, one would expect the causee to have a great deal of control in this situation. Indeed, this is the case: In (23a), the causee clearly retains the right to refuse the request. In (23b), in which the causee is in accusative case and the verb *leave* is structurally more integrated with *ask,* the request is more direct, although only slightly. Strictly causative verbs (23c) never place the causee in nominative case, and they often allow maximal integration between the causative verb and the verb indicating what is being caused. In this case, the event being caused (*leave*) is neither a finite verb [as in (23a)] or an infinitive (23b). It is a bare form that is fully dependent on the verb of causation (*made*). This parallels the decreasing amount of control that the causee possesses.

3.0. Summary

Valency, the basic theme of this chapter, is concerned with the grammatical association between a predicate and its arguments. (I have only discussed the relationship between verbs and their dependents, although the notion of valency is easily extended to other kinds of predicates [such as nouns and adjectives] as well). Specifically, valency is the number of required arguments that a verb takes.

A verb's valence is not fixed. When a verb occurs in its basic form—that is, as the head of a simple declarative clause—it will manifest what might be called its core valency. This core valency can be manipulated in a number of ways, however. By way of morphology, word order, or other devices, languages can decrease or increase valency or they can realign the grammatical relations that are assigned to a verb's arguments.

The motivations for such valence-altering mechanisms differ from construction to construction. In the previous sections, only a few were noted. For instance, it was observed in Section 1.1 that the impetus behind antipassive structures can be to treat indefinite nominals as something other than an object of the verb. As such, the antipassive can be viewed as a construction that has become grammaticized to signal certain semantic information about a noun phrase. In the next three chapters, I turn away from examining how grammatical and semantic information about noun phrases is represented in language and discuss verbal categories such as tense, mood, and negation.

4.0. Key Terms

Anticausative	Dummy
Antipassive	Indirect causation
Applicative (applied construction)	Intransitive
Causative	Periphrastic
Dative shift	Transitive
Direct causation	Valence
Ditransitive	

Notes

1. The distinction between verbal adjuncts and arguments is actually much more complicated than this. For a much more comprehensive explication, see Whaley (1993).

2. The use of the word *ditransitive* is common, but as language purists like to point out, *bitransitive* is more etymologically sound. Because the word transitive is of Latin origin, it is more consistent to use the Latin prefix *bi-* than the Greek *di-*.

3. Foley and Van Valin (1984) propose the term *atransitive* for verbs such as weather predicates, but this confuses the distinction between transitivity and valency.

4. For example, Van Valin (1985) reports that Lakhota (Almosan-Keresiouan: United States and Canada) has no passive structures equivalent to those in (4) and (5). Keenan (1985a) also lists Enga (Austronesian: Papua New Guinea), Tamang (Tibeto-Burman: Nepal), Isthmus Zapotec (Oto-Manguean: Mexico), and Yidiŋ (Pama-Nyungan: Australia)

5. I use the notion "subject" very loosely in this depiction of passive because ergative-absolutive languages can also have passives.

6. When languages use passive morphology in this manner, it is often referred to *middle passive* or *mediopassive*. It should also be noted that many languages also use the same morphology for middle passive and reflexives—for example, ancient Greek (Rijksbaron 1984), Albanian (Hubbard 1980), and Huastec (Constable 1989).

7. The precise grammatical relations that they hold is a matter of controversy, but it is irrelevant here. What is important is that, despite the variation in the morphological and syntactic properties of *Ali,* the valence of the verb is unaffected by the appearance of the verbal suffix *-kan.* In both (10a) and (10b), both postverbal nominals are required by the verb; therefore, the valence is unaffected.

8. See Talmy (1976) for a thorough discussion of the linguistic encoding of various types of semantic causatives.

9. Comrie (1989) notes that not all speakers accept (22b).

PART

Verbal Categories

12

Tense and Aspect

Part of what it means to be conscious is to have a sense of the passage of time. Time, however, is a great mystery, in large part because it cannot be directly experienced. We only sense that it exists because we have the capacity to remember and note changes from our immediate sense impressions. If we had absolutely no recollection of the past, we would find ourselves to be caught at a single moment endlessly. There would be no inclination of the future because the concept of change would be unimaginable. Needless to say, the notion of time forms a crucial part of our understanding of reality.

It is no accident that language is particularly complicated with regard to describing this mystery of time. In addition to an enormous array of contextual clues, languages have special sets of adverbs and time expressions dedicated just to the task of locating events in time. Perhaps most complex of all, however, are the verbal categories of tense and aspect.

Tense is a grammatical expression of the relationship between two points in time. That is, given two events, one that occurs at time T1 and another that occurs at time T2, tense is used to describe whether T1 came before T2, overlapped with T2, or came after T2. Present and past are the most commonly expressed tenses. **Aspect,** on the other hand, is employed to focus on the internal temporal makeup of a situation. It can be utilized to conceptualize an event as extended in time (with a beginning, middle, and end) or as a single point with no internal divisions. Compare the following sentences in (1), which differ with respect to aspect:

(1)   a. I *read* a great novel yesterday.
      b. I was reading a great novel yesterday.

The two sentences in (1) do not differ with regard to tense; both depict that the event of reading (T1) occurred before the time of speech (T2). They do differ, however, in terms of aspect: (1a) treats the event as an unanalyzable whole, whereas (1b) frames the event as being extended in time.

There is a third and closely related grammatical category, **mood,** that also manifests a speaker's perspective on how an event relates to time. Mood is the linguistic expression of **modality,** which is a semantic notion about the reality of a situation—that is, whether the event does or does not actually occur, or its possibility of occurring. The following data in (2) differ with regard to modality:

(2)   Patricia *did/can/may* read a book in French.

By use of the auxiliary *did,* a speaker is asserting that the reading actually occurred at some point in the past. *Can,* however, makes no claims about the reality of reading. The choice of this auxiliary allows a speaker to state the possibility that the event could occur due to Patricia's capacity for grasping the French written word without any further commitment as to whether Patricia actually has or will read. The auxiliary verb *may,* for its part, mostly reflects the likelihood, which is neither strong nor weak, that Patricia will engage in the act of reading. In English, modal auxiliary verbs, such as *can* and *may,* are used to express modality.[1]

Keep in mind that the use of tense, aspect, and mood are not direct reflections of temporal reality. They are grammatical devices that are used to relay a particular perspective on this reality. Not surprisingly, the three categories interact in complex and multifaceted ways. For this reason, although native speakers use these categories effortlessly, it is very rare to find a thorough description of tense, aspect, or modality in reference grammars or language texts.

Tense and aspect are typically so closely bound in linguistic expression that it is impossible to analyze one fully apart from the other. It is somewhat easier to demarcate modality. Therefore, I leave a more complete discussion of modality to Chapter 13. In the present chapter, I examine the issues that must be addressed most commonly when describing tense and aspect systems.

1.0. Tense

Tense is considered to be a type of **deixis.** Deictic elements anchor an utterance to its immediate context. For example, consider the word *here:*

(3) I have had all kinds of difficulties *here.*

To interpret what *here* means, the word must be enmeshed in a particular context. Notice how different the referent of "here" becomes when another sentence is placed before it:

(4) a. I hate Paris. I've had all kinds of difficulties here.
     b. See step two in my design plan. I've had all kinds of difficulties here.

Thus, *here* shifts its denotation depending on context.

There are many types of deictic expressions: personal pronouns, time expressions such as *now* and *yesterday,* demonstratives such as *this* and *that,* and so on. Similarly, the category of tense is deictic because to interpret it one must have a context. The temporal reference of "I was tired" changes dramatically if I am telling a story about what I said last week or indicating a fact about my physical state earlier today.

A timeline (Figure 12.1) is often helpful in sorting out the deictic nature of tense. Recall that tense, as a grammatical category, is a mechanism used to indicate that a point in time follows, precedes, or is simultaneous with a reference point. Commonly, the reference point is the time at which the sentence is being uttered—that is, "now." The diagram exhibits the times that tense might refer to if this is the case. Because the "now" of speech constantly is in flux, so too is the objective reference of tense.

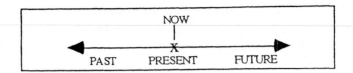

Figure 12.1. The Nature of Tense

In addition to past, present, and future time periods, languages also allow the option of specifying "at all times," as in (5a), or at "an unspecified time," as in (5b).

(5) a. Michael dunks *everyday.*
     b. He dunks *whenever he feels like it.*

■ **1.1. Strategies for Tense**

Although all languages have means by which to indicate time reference and temporal relations, they differ widely in the morphosyntactic devices they employ to accomplish it. In some cases, there is no special tense morphology. Instead, time expressions and other grammatical categories such as modality are used. This strategy is the true for Burmese (Tibeto-Burman: Burma):

(6) a. săneineí-taìñ   myeʔ   hpyaʔ-te
        Saturday-every   grass   cut-REAL
        (he) cuts the grass every Saturday
     b. da-caúñmoú   mă-la-ta
        that-because   not-come-REAL
        because of that (they) didn't come
     c. măneʔhpañ   sá-me
        tomorrow   begin-IRR
        (we) will begin tomorrow   (Data from Okell as cited in Comrie 1985b)

In Burmese, there is no specific morpheme (or morphemes) that is dedicated to marking past, present, or future tense. Rather, time adverbials are used in conjunction with modal affixes. The use of a realis affix (roughly, this affix is used to assert that an event actually occurs) suggests a past event. Time adverbials, such as *săneineí* ("Saturday"), can further clarify the temporal reference. Likewise, an irrealis affix (meaning that the event does not occur in real time) is used for future time or events that had or will have a possibility of occurring. Once again, adverbs can make the precise temporal nature of the event clearer.

Many languages do, of course, have special tense morphology. The way in which they section off the time line (shown previously), however, can vary greatly. Lithuanian (Balto-Slavic: Lithuania) is an example of a language with a tripartite system:

(7) a. dirb-au
       work-1S.PST
       I worked/was working
    b. dirb-u
       work-1S.PRES
       I work/am working.
    c. dirb-s-iu
       work-FUT-1S
       I will work/be working.

                    (Data from Senn as cited in Chung and Timberlake 1985)

The Lithuanian example, although not common from a cross-linguistic perspective, reflects the notion of tense presented in Figure 11.1. There is distinct morphology for past, present, and future. It is possible, however, to make finer distinctions than those allowed under the tripartite system. In languages with finer-grained distinctions, tense categories can be used to indicate degrees of remoteness in time, as in KiVunjo-Chaga (Niger-Congo: Tanzania). With respect to future time reference, three different verb prefixes may be employed.

(8) a. Mana   n-a-**i**-enda
       child   FOC-SUB-TM-go
       The child is [definitely] going/leaving [soon].
    b Msulri n-a-**ici**-zrezra
       nobleman   FOC-SUB-TM-speak
       The nobleman will [definitely] speak [sometime in the future].
    c. Mana   n-a-**e**-enda
       child   FOC-SUB-TM-go
       The child will [perhaps] go/leave [sometime in the future].

                    (Adapted from Moshi 1994—tone is indicated in her data)

The prefix in (8a) can actually also be employed for an event that occurs simultaneously to the speech event—that is, it can indicate present tense. Hence, Moshi (1994) proposes that this suffix marks immediate events that definitely are occurring or will occur. It can be applied as a future marker only when the occurrence of the future event is imminent. The prefix in (8b) is employed when the event being referred to is not imminent but the speaker still wishes to aver the certainty of its occurrence. The final prefix marks future events that may or may not happen. Such complex semantics are typical in cases in which languages have multiple markers for future tense.

Kivunjo-Chaga also has two prefixes to indicate past tense (9):

(9)   a. Kite   n-ki-**a**-lya   nyama
         dog   FOC-SUB-TM-eat   meat
         The dog [as recently as today] ate meat.
      b. Kite   n-ki-**le**-lya   nyama
         dog   FOC-SUB-TM-eat   meat
         The dog [before today] ate meat.

As past events, the contrast in this case does not revolve around the certainty that the event will occur. Rather, the emphasis is on the relevance to the present moment. As Moshi (1994, 137) writes, "The discourse function of the **a** time marker is to emphasize the relevance of the past event to the immediate context of situation."

Tense systems based on degrees of remoteness can get fairly intricate. For example, Bamileke-Dschang (Niger-Congo: West Africa) has a five-way contrast in both the past and the future (10):

(10) *Past*   *Future*   *Time Frame*
      àá 'taŋ̂   a'a tang   Immediate
      à áà n̂táŋ̂   àà'pìŋ'ŋ́táŋ   Today
      à kè táŋ'ŋ̂   àà 'lù' z̀ ú táŋ   1 Day away
      à lè táŋ'ŋ̂   à'á láʔé 'táŋ   2 or more days
      à lè láŋ n'táŋ   à'á fú 'táŋ   1 Year or more
                                            (Adapted from Comrie 1985b)

The data in (10) show the tense-marking system for the verb "bargain." As can be observed, this particular system employs particles rather than affixes to describe time. The labels that appear on the chart should not be taken too literally. They are helpful heuristic devices in that they allow us to see the relative impact of choosing one particle over another. They are not, however, selected on any strict categorical basis. An event that occurred just yesterday might be framed with several of these particles depending on the speaker's perspective on the event, the modality of the sentence, the context, and so on.

Bamileke is somewhat special in allowing such fine distinctions in types of future reference. Even languages that are similar to Bamileke in having robust tense distinctions usually follow a more common asymmetrical pattern. That is, the past time frame is carved up into more units than the future.

In addition to tripartite and multiunit tense distinctions, some languages also function in accordance with a two-way split. Most commonly, the split is between past events and nonpast events (as in Dutch and German). Less commonly, one finds a division rooted in a nonfuture-future distinction.

■ 1.2. Absolute Versus Relative Tense

To this point, all the tense categories we have discussed have been instances of **absolute tense.** That is, they have depicted a single event that was temporally defined with regard to a single reference point (the time of the utterance). Languages also have ways to relate **relative tense.** Consider the following situation: At 1:00 p.m., Tom is lying down on the couch. At 1:01 p.m., he turns on the TV with the remote and begins to watch a football game. If I want to describe what has happened, I might say the following:

(11) Lying on the couch, Tom watched the game.

There is no tense indicated on the participle *lying.* How, then, does one know that Tom's lying on the couch is not a future event that is to happen after he finishes watching the game? There is no chance of this interpretation because participles are understood to have tense relative to the action described by the main verb. Figure 12.2 recasts the sentence on a time line.

The verb *watch* is placed in an absolute tense that is determined on the basis of the speech time. The time reference of the verb *lie,* on the other hand, is a relative tense. Its time reference is based on the verb *watch.* The phenomenon of relative tense is ubiquitous when dealing with nonfinite verb forms (i.e., those that cannot be marked for absolute tense). Relative tense, however, is also relevant to finite verbs. The following is a particularly interesting case from the standard variety of English:

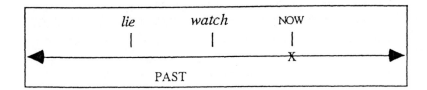

Figure 12.2. The Nature of Relative Tense

(12) a. The teacher said that **Theodore was an excellent student.**

In cases of reported speech (in bold type), the verb of the subordinate clause gets its tense from the main verb. In (12), the verb *was* is past tense because *said* is in past tense. If *says* were used instead, then present tense would also be used in the reported speech giving *is*.

This section has by no means touched on all the many issues surrounding the category of tense. Tense is so fully tied to the category of aspect, however, that little more can be said without first addressing the nature of aspect.

2.0. Aspect

Aspect, as explained above, is a mechanism that permits a speaker to conceptualize a temporal quality of an event in different ways. The major aspectual division is between **perfective** and **imperfective**.[2] The primary focus of this distinction is on the terminal boundaries of the events involved. An event is cast as perfective if it is viewed as temporally bounded. Conversely, imperfective is employed to make reference to the internal temporal structure of an event. It is not cast as being bounded. The distinction is exemplified by the Mende (Niger-Congo: Benin) data as shown in the following: •

(13) a. Musa   lo   hei-**ni**
          Musa   FOC   sit-PFV
          Musa sits/is seated.

b. Musa lo hei-**ma**

Musa FOC sit-IMPF

Musa is (in the process of) sitting.

(Data from Shawn Boylan, personal communication, 1988)

In (13a), *sitting* is in the perfective, being expressed as a point in time that has no temporal extension. In (13b), in which the imperfective is used, the focus is on the internal structure of *sitting* and, thus, the event is taken to be a process.

Another major category of aspect that is often in opposition to perfective and imperfective is the **perfect**.[3] The similarity with the term perfective can lead to confusion so more and more often linguists use the label **anterior** in its place. Anterior aspect is used to signal a past event that has enduring relevance to a set reference time. Often, this reference time is the moment of speech (14).

(14) a. I **have** already **done** the dishes, so now I don't have to.

b. The Republicans **have taken** a majority of the seats in both houses of congress.

In English, anterior aspect is marked by use of the auxiliary *have* in conjunction with a past participle. When the auxiliary verb is in present tense, the anterior notes that the event depicted carries implications for the moment of speech. The implication may be made explicit (14a), but it need not be. If it is not, context usually suffices to make it clear. Hence, the implication of (14b) might be that a Democratic president will have a harder time passing legislation.

The point of reference for which an anterior verb has relevance may also be another event, as in (15).

(15) By the time John came, I **had cleaned** the entire house.

Like English, it is common for languages to form the perfect by use of an auxiliary verb in combination with a participle (or other verbal form). Some languages, however, construct anterior aspect by use of verbal affixes. This is true, for example, in ancient Greek (Hellenic) (16):

(16) tas poleis autōn par-ēi-rētai

the cities their LOC-ANT-take

He has taken away their cities (and still holds them).

Another common formal distinction made by language is between imperfective and **stative** aspect. Whereas the imperfective is employed for dynamic events, the stative is utilized to mark states of existence. The following examples are drawn from Mende:

(17) a. mahei   ha-**ma**
         chief   die-IMPF
         The chief is dying.

     b. mahei   ha-**ngo**
         chief   die-STAT
         The chief is dead.

Tense and aspect are easily confused because they both specify the temporal characteristics of an event. Consequently, one frequently finds aspectual morphology seemingly functioning as a tense marker. In Mixtec (Oto-Mangean: Mexico), the perfective is frequently employed in clauses conceptualizing past events (18a), whereas the imperfective is used for events contemporaneous with the act of speech (18b).

(18) a. iku   ǹ   ku?wi   nì?
         yesterday   PRV   sick   1S
         I was sick yesterday.

     b. té?néni   nì?   čìxi   nì?
         IMPF.hurt   1S   stomach   1S
         My stomach hurts.   (Data from Bickford 1988)

Although the aspectual system appears to encode absolute tense in these data, there is reason not to analyze them as tense markers. In particular, the distribution of aspect in texts reveals that perfective forms are used to plot the main story line, whereas imperfective forms are used for background information regardless of whether this information is past or present (19).

(19) iku   ká?wi   wí?í   ini   ya^n sá   ǹ   nenta   rè?
      yesterday   IMPF.worry   much   inside   3.FEM   while   PERF   arrive   3.MSC
      Yesterday, she was very worried when he arrived.

The categories of tense and aspect frequently co-occur in the clause structure of languages, being marked by separate morphemes or by separate words. Therefore, they are not only logically distinct, they can also be linguistically differentiated. The following example from Turkish (Turkic: Turkey) is an instance of unique tense (past) and aspect (progressive) suffixes appearing together:

(20)   Gel-iyor-du-m
come-PROG-PST-1S
I was coming.   (Data from Watters 1993)

When tense and aspect markers do arise together in a language, their order is not random. The aspect marker nearly always occurs closer to the verb (Bybee 1985; Foley and Van Valin 1984).[4] This ordering is iconic in that aspect indicates information specifically about the nature of the verb, whereas tense has an entire proposition in its scope. That is, although tense is commonly a verbal category, it is really supplying information about the entire sentence, specifically where the proposition indicated by the sentence is located in time. Because aspect is semantically more tightly associated with the verb, it is formally closer as well.

Up to this point, I have introduced just a few of the major aspectual distinctions that are to be found in language. There are others.

(21) a. I **read** a great novel yesterday.
b. I **was reading** . . .
c. I **began to read** . . .
d. I **finished reading** . . .

Although the tense of the sentences in (21) make it clear that they all occurred in the past, the differences in aspect allow us to conceptualize the event of reading in various ways. Example (21a), which treats the event as a point without any constituent parts, is perfective; (21b), which treats the event as extended in time, is imperfective. These two oppositions were introduced above. Example (21c), which highlights the beginning of the event, is often called **inceptive.** Example (21d), which highlights the end of the event, is usually called **completive.** Note, however, that the expression of inceptive and completive aspect is accomplished here through the creation of a verb + infinitive construction. The aspect is not expressed by a grammatical category (as in (21a) and (21b)).

The choice of aspect profoundly alters the way in which we interpret the event being described. For example, unless the context dictates otherwise, we are prone to interpret (21a) to mean that the entire novel was read in one day. Similarly, (21d) makes it clear that the end of the novel was reached, but the implication is that it had been begun at an earlier date. Example (21c) explicitly indicates that the novel was started yesterday, but strongly implies that it was not finished. Finally, (21b) is open to many possible readings, a likely one being that a middle portion of the novel was enjoyed.

These nuances are part of the core meaning of the various aspects. It is not the case that every time a past tense verb in English is placed in the perfective one must take the event to have been completed (cf. "I wallpapered yesterday," which does not require that the task of wallpapering was completed). How then do such connotations arise? It is due to a number of things, but primary among them is the **lexical aspect** of verbs (also referred to as **Aktionsart**) and the sentence constituents that are used with the verb. The influence of these elements on aspect is examined in the following two sections.

■ 2.1. Aspect Versus Aktionsart

Every verb has its own Aktionsart—that is, an inherent aspect that speakers assume the verb to convey unless otherwise indicated. For example, the verb *to read* is **durative.** This means that the action described by the verb necessarily lasts for a certain period of time. Compare this with a verb such as *to sneeze,* which is **punctual** because the event it describes is not extended in time but happens instantaneously.

The shades of meaning that we typically associate with aspectual categories, such as perfective and imperfective, vary depending on the Aktionsart of the verb (22).

(22) a. The light blinked.

     b. The light was blinking.

In (22a) and (22b), the effect of using perfective and imperfective aspect with durative verbs was partly to demarcate completion versus noncompletion. With punctual verbs as in (22), the effect is somewhat different. The perfective form describes a single blink in (22a). The imperfective, on the other hand, encodes an **iterative** (repetition of a single action) situation.

Languages appear to form the same Aktionsart classes in their lexicons. At the coarsest level, there are four such classes (Dowty 1979; Foley and Van Valin 1984; Vendler 1967): states, achievements, accomplishments, and activities. **States,** as the name implies, are predicates that denote properties (e.g., *to be yellow* and *to be broken*) or nondynamic circumstances (*to see* and *to exist*). **Activities** are dynamic events (e.g., *to cry, to sneeze,* and *to run*). **Achievements** are predicates that indicate a change of state (*to yellow* or *to break*—as in "the window broke") or dynamic circumstances (*to notice* and *to smell*). **Accomplishments** are predicates that involve causation (*to show* or *to break*—as in "John broke the window").

States and activities are conceptually simpler than achievements. Thus, note that an achievement verb can often be paraphrased to subsume a state or activity predicate: "the window broke" might be paraphrased as "something occurred such that the window became broken." In some sense, the achievement *to break* can be said to entail the state *be broken.* Similarly, accomplishments entail achievements. The sentence, "John broke the window," could be paraphrased as "John did something such that the window broke," again an indication that an accomplishment is conceptually more complex than an achievement.[5] In English, the four verb classes are usually lexically differentiated, but Van Valin (1993b) notes that in some languages derivational morphology is employed to capture the conceptual relationship between states, achievements, and accomplishments.

(23)

State	*Achievement*	*Accomplishment*
ʔaknu:-y ("A is underground")	ta:knu:-y ("A goes underground")	ma:knu-y ("B buries A")
lakčahu-y ("A is closed")	talakčahu-y ("A closes")	ma:lakčuhu-y ("B closes A")
paša-y ("A is different")	tapaša-y ("A changes")	ma:paša-y ("B changes A")

(Data from Watters 1988 as cited in Van Valin 1993b)

These data from Tepehua (Penutian: Mexico) demonstrate how three of the four Aktionsart classes can be derived from a common root rather than lexicalized as different verbs as in English.

Regardless of how the four classes are evinced in a language, they tend to have certain aspectual categories associated with them. For example, states resist being placed in the imperfective because they are nondynamic. Therefore, in American English it is awkward to say "the banana is being yellow" or "I was seeing the movie." States, as nondynamic verbs, cannot be punctual because the essence of punctuality is a dynamic event that happens almost instantaneously. Activities verbs, however, can be punctual (*to flash* or *to sneeze*), and because achievements and accomplishments can be built on the conceptually simpler class of activities, one also predicts these classes to contain punctual verbs. This prediction is borne out: "the twig snapped" (punctual achievement) and "I snapped the twig in half" (punctual accomplishment).

■   **2.2. Nonverbal Effects on Aspect**

Verbal categories and Aktionsart are not the only linguistic elements relevant to aspect. Changes in aspect can also be encoded by adverbial expressions, prepositional phrases, and nominals. Consider the aspect manifested in the following sentences headed by the verb *to flash:*

(24) a. The beacon flashed.
      b. The beacon flashed five times in a row.   (Data from Talmy 1987)

As noted previously, *flash* is an activity verb that, because it expresses a rapidly completed event, is punctual when it occurs in the past perfective (24a). This single punctual event, however, becomes iterative when accompanied by an expression such as "five times in a row" (24b). The effect is similar to placing the verb in the progressive ("the beacon was flashing"), although the iteration has an explicit endpoint in (24b).

Another much cited instance of the significance of nominal features for aspect can be observed in transitive clauses. The verb's aspect can be affected by whether the direct object refers to a specific entity (25a) or not (25b).

(25) a. The boy scout troop ate the pizza.
      b. The boy scout troop ate pizza.

When the article precedes *pizza* in (25a), the verb has a completive sense: The eating had a definite endpoint. In (25b), there is no such implication.

3.0. Summary

In this chapter, I have described some of the typical mechanisms that are employed within language to express time reference, the temporal relationship between events, and the temporal contours of an event. Frequently, languages develop grammatical categories—tense and aspect—to carry out this function.

The semantic relationship between tense and aspect is tight. When both categories exist in a language, the combinations of specific tense morphemes and specific aspect morphemes can encode subtle distinctions. Where either one of the verbal categories is absent from a language, the remaining one can be extended to cover some of the same functional ground.

In addition to the grammatical categories of tense and aspect, other features of language play a role in determining how time reference in sentences is understood. One particularly prominent feature in this regard—Aktionsart—was discussed in Section 2.0. Another crucial feature, the category of mood, is discussed in Chapter 13.

4.0. Key Terms

Absolute tense	Iterative
Achievements	Lexical aspect
Accomplishments	Modality
Activities	Mood
Aktionsart	Perfect (anterior)
Aspect	Perfective
Atelic	Punctual
Completive	Relative tense
Deixis	States
Durative	Stative
Imperfective	Telic
Inceptive	Tense

Notes

———

1. Particularly within the tradition of Indo-European linguistics, the term mood has been restricted to verbal inflectional systems. I will use it in a slightly broader sense that groups inflectional mood, modal auxiliary verbs, and modal particles together.

2. The category of imperfective is also referred to as **continuous** or **progressive** in the liteature. It is not always clear what, if any, difference scholars take the difference between them to be. In research on aspect systems, there has been an effort to make the distinction between the three clear. Comrie (1976a), for example, proposes that continuous refers to imperfectivity not based on habitually and progressive to be a combination of continuous meaning and nonstative meaning. Bybee et al. (1994) offer a useful discussion of aspect definitions.

3. Bybee (1985) takes perfect-anterior to be a tense rather than an aspect category on the basis of its semantics. It functions more to locate an event in time than to depict the internal temporal structure. As Bybee notes, however, perfect-anterior morphemes often co-occur with tense markers in languages (such as ancient Greek) so that there is not the paradigmatic contrast one usually finds with members of the same category.

4. In Bybee's (1985) sample, tense affixes never occurred closer to the verb stem than aspect affixes.

5. It is possible that the four-way distinction outlined here is based on three main semantic properties: telicity, stativity, and causation. **Telic** events are those with a built-in endpoint, **atelic** are those with no inherent end point (*read* or *swim*), and **stative** are nonevents (*be red* or *appear tall*). The feature of causation operates in the same way as the system outlined here.

13

Mood and Negation

Mood is a grammatical category through which speakers of a language can indicate whether they believe that an event or state actually occurs, does not occur, or has the potential to occur (1). This conceptual domain is called **modality**.

(1) a. ja-ŋani-yug
        3.REAL-talk-AUX
        He is talking.

      b. ŋiɲjag   ŋani-yug
        PROHIB   talk-AUX
        He doesn't/can't/will not talk.

      c. (y)a-ŋani-yug
        IRR-talk-AUX
        He might talk.   (Data from Merlan 1981)

As the sentences from Mangarayi (Australian: Australia) reveal, the actuality of the event of talking, or more precisely the speaker's estimation of the actuality, can be determined on the basis of prefixes or preverbal particles. In (1a), the utilization of a third-person realis prefix relays the fact that the talking did occur. In contrast, the prohibitive particle in (1b) indicates the nonoccurrence of the event (NB, negation interacts with other modal categories, but it does not constitute a mood category itself—further discussion of this fact is provided in Section 2.0). In (1c), an irrealis marker denotes a future possibility that the talking will happen.

It was noted in passing in Chapter 12 that mood often works in consort with tense and aspect in languages to capture the temporal nature of a linguistic utterance. Although this is certainly true, there is a strong sense in which mood differs from the other two categories. Aspect describes the temporal contours of an event as it occurs in time; tense depicts where in time the event occurs relative to the moment of speech or some other event. Modality, on the other hand, is ontologically more basic. It is concerned about the truth value of statements, revealing a speaker's attitudes and assumptions regarding the reality of what he or she is describing.

In this chapter, I introduce some of the distinctions that linguists make when describing modality. One caveat is in order: Because modality is reflected in languages in such different ways, it is nearly impossible to give it a simple characterization that is then applicable to all languages. The discussion below only touches on the mere basics of this complex topic.

1.0. Traditional Categories of Mood

Traditionally, grammarians and linguists have categorized sentences into major types based on what mood is employed. Those sentences that directly assert the truth of some proposition (2) are said to be in the **indicative** mood (2).

(2) I shot the sheriff, but I did not shoot the deputy.

Both the clauses in (2) are indicative despite the fact that the first is affirmative and the second is negative. This is because they are both assertions about the truth value of the propositions they describe.

Cross-linguistically, verbs in declarative sentences tend to bear no special formal marking. In a similar vein, for many languages (e.g., most within the Indo-European language family), there is also no special verbal morphology used in forming questions. Therefore, the category of indicative in these languages is extended to include the questions such as that in the following:

(3) Why were you carrying a gun?

Note that most questions presuppose a proposition with a positive truth value. For example, the question in (3) assumes "you were carrying a gun." In this way, they bear some similarity to **declarative** sentences (i.e., statements) such as that in (2).

In some languages, the morphology of questions is distinct from that of declarative sentences. In these languages, in which a unified category of indicative modality seems unwarranted, a separate mood category, **interrogative,** is needed, as in Japanese (Japanese-Ryukyuan: Japan):

(4) a. Kore wa   hon   desu **yo**
        this   TOP   book   is   DECL
        This is a book.
     b. Kore wa   hon   desu **ka**
        this   TOP   book   is   INTER
        Is this a book?   (Data from Kuno 1973)

Another traditional category of mood is **subjunctive.** The range of uses for the subjunctive differs a great deal from language to language, but commonly it is used to express an attitude of uncertainty on the part of the speaker (5a) or a hypothetical situation (5b).

(5) a. epilath-ōmetha   tēs   oikade   hodou
        forget-1P.SBJV   the   homeward   road
        We may have forgotten the way home.
     b. an   de   tis   anth-ist-ētai
        PTL   PTL   any   against-stand-3S.SBJV
        If anyone opposes us . . .

In these ancient Greek (Hellenic) sentences, the subjunctive mood is identifiable from the set of subject agreement markers that are employed. Had the sentences been indicative, a different agreement marker would have been used. In (5a), the subjunctive is used in an independent clause. Example (5b), however, is more representative of typical subjunctive use from a cross-linguistic perspective in that it is employed within a dependent clause.

Commands are said to be in the **imperative** mood. Not uncommonly, imperatives are encoded by using a verb form that is morphologically deficient. That is, the imperative verb is missing morphology that occurs in other moods.[1] The nature of an imperative is to issue a command to a listener. Consequently, imperative clauses are usually understood to have second-person subjects. In English, this fact is obscured because overt subjects are not permitted in imperatives and the agreement morphology for second person happens to be zero marking. In other languages, however, the second-person subject is overtly reflected in the verb agreement. The following Burushaski (Isolate: India and Pakistan) forms demonstrate this fact:

(6) a. et-i
         do-2S
         Do (something)!
     b. et-in
         do-2P
         (You two) do (something)!   (Data from Lorimer 1935)

If a language does not restrict the subjects of commands in this way, the mood is often said to be **optative** rather than imperative.

(7) a. hïwá:t-e:-č
         run-VOL-2P
         Run!
     b. hïwá:t-e:-nì:š
         run-VOL-3S
         Let him run!
     c. hïwá:t-e:-màš
         run-VOL-1P
         Let us run!   (Data adapted from Freedland 1951)

These data, from Sierra Miwok (Penutian: United States), exhibit commands being formed using the volitional suffix -e:. In (7a), the subject is second person, so the mood is straightforwardly imperative. In (7b) and (7c), however, the subject reference is to third singular and first plural, respectively. On this basis, the mood might be said to be optative rather than imperative.

This is an unfortunate use of the term *optative*, however, because there are languages, such as ancient Greek, that have a morphologically distinct optative category and allow non-second-person agreement in commands (8).

(8)	*Optative*		*Imperative*	
1S	didask-oimi	"I hope to teach"		
2S	didask-ois	"You hope to teach"	didask-ou	"Teach!"
3S	didask-oi	"He hopes to teach"	didask-stho	"Let him teach"
1P	didask-oimen	"We hope to teach"		
2P	didask-oite	"You (plural) hope to teach"	didask-esthe	"(You all) teach!"
3P	didask-oien	"They hope to teach"	didask-esthon	"Let them teach"

On the basis of morphological form, it is best to analyze Greek as having an optative and an imperative mood with the latter permitting both second- and third-person subjects. The core function of the optative is to express desires, whereas the imperative is employed to issue commands or exhortations. Because of languages such as Greek, it is probably best, for those languages that lack a distinct optative category, to posit a single imperative mood, even if non-second-person forms can be used as subjects.

■ 1.1. Deontic Versus Epistemic Modality

In addition to demarcating the major categories of mood, it is also necessary to make a distinction between deontic and epistemic modalities. In short, **deontic modality** deals with obligation or desire, whereas **epistemic modality** deals with degrees of possibility. The following are examples of deontic modality:

(9)   a. John **must** come tomorrow.
     b. Gas stations **should** keep their restrooms clean.
     c. We really **ought** to water the plants.

The sentences in (9) are revealing the speakers' beliefs about obligations that various individuals have. The same English auxiliaries can be used in the expression of epistemic modality (10).

(10) a. He **must** have arrived here earlier today.

    b. My guess is that it **should** rain tomorrow around 6:00 p.m.

    c. She left ten minutes ago. She **ought** to be there soon.

Although the formal expression of epistemic modality in (10) is the same as that described previously, the sense of these expressions has shifted. For example, (10a) differs from (9a) by not imposing any obligation on the subject of the sentence. Rather, it designates the degree of certainty that the speaker expresses about the actuality of the event.

As you might imagine, determining whether deontic or epistemic modality is involved in a proposition can be a difficult enterprise. Frequently, the interpretation given to a modal auxiliary (or affix or particle, depending on the language) rests on a complex bundle of factors including tense, aspect, intonation, context, and nonverbal cues. In (10a), for instance, the fact that the event being described is cast in perfect tense (as indicated by the use of the auxiliary *have* + a past participle) is what makes it epistemic rather than deontic.

■ 1.2. Evidentials

One of the primary considerations involved in epistemic modality is the degree of certainty that speakers wish to convey. Their decisions about how to express their level of certainty are based on all kinds of information. Therefore, to say "it must have rained last night" is to indicate confidence, although not complete confidence, that rain did actually fall. When we hear this sentence, we naturally assume the speaker has reliable evidence such as the fact that there are puddles in the street.

Some languages develop a special set of markers, called **evidentials,** which more explicitly convey the quality of information on which an assertion is based. Generally, evidentials are not treated as a type of mood category, but they do bear an obvious affinity to epistemic modality (see Palmer 1986 for a discussion). The following Tuyuca (Equatorial-Tucanoan: Brazil and Columbia) sentences exemplify evidential marking:

(11) a. díiga   apé-**wi**

       soccer   play-VISUAL   He played soccer (I saw him).

    b. díiga   apé-**ti**

       soccer   play-nonVISUAL He played soccer (I heard him playing).

    c. díiga   apé-**yi**
        soccer   play-APPARENT   He played soccer (I have evidence though I
        didn't actually witness the game in any way).
    d. díiga   apé-**yigɨ**
        soccer   play-SECONDHAND   He played soccer (Someone told me).
    e. díiga   apé-**hĩyi**
        soccer   play-ASSUMED   He played soccer (It seems reasonable
        that he did).   (Adapted from Barnes as cited in Palmer 1986)

These sentences can all be translated in the same way. The choice of a verbal suffix, however, serves as an indication of the quality of the information. Consequently, the evidential system is a way of relaying information very much like epistemic modality.

■ 1.3. Realis Versus Irrealis

In the preceding sections, you have been introduced to several kinds of moods and a major division between types of modality. Languages, however, vary considerably as to how much of their morphology and syntax they devote to making all of these distinctions explicit. To adequately describe some languages, one would need to untangle complex verbal morphology or sets of auxiliaries to explicitly describe the various moods and modalities. In other languages, various mood distinctions are collapsed. In such languages, there is frequently a morphosyntactic division between realis and irrealis modality.

Simply stated, **realis** is a description of situations that are or were real. **Irrealis** marking depicts situations that were not or are not yet a reality, only possibilities. Certain of the mood categories naturally conflate under the rubric of realis and irrealis. Subjunctive, optative, and imperative moods, for example, all relate propositions that have not actually occurred yet—that is, the propositions are not "real." Consequently, some languages treat these notionally distinct moods identically in their morphology. Palauan (Austronesian: Palau) is one such case.

(12) a. Mo-lim   a   kҽrum
       2S(HYP)-drink   the   medicine
       Drink your medicine!
   b. Ku-rael   ҽl   mo   ҽr   a   blik
       1S(HYP)-travel   LINKER   go   LOC the   house
       I'd better go home.

    c. Do-męngur ęr   tiang
       1P(HYP)-eat LOC here
       Let's eat here.   (Data from Josephs 1975)

In each of these sentences, a hypothetical (equivalent to irrealis) person prefix is employed. The typical interpretation when a second person is subject is a command (12a). First-person subjects give rise to a sense of obligation (12b), and third-person subjects create an exhortation.

Even in languages in which imperatives, subjunctives, optatives, or all three comprise separate morphological categories, the uses of the categories often encroach on each other's semantic territory. Thus, subjunctives can have the force of imperatives or vice versa. There is also a clear overlap in the meaning of irrealis moods and the future tense because again all are used to capture events that have not yet happened. Some languages capitalize on this similarity and simply use a single morphological category.

(13) a. Ma-khúži   kte
       1S-sick   FUT
       I will be sick.
    b. Yí-kta   iyéčheča
       go-FUT   perhaps
       It is likely that he will go/He ought to go.
    c. He   ithácha-kta čhí
       that chief-FUT   want
       That one wants to be chief.
        (Data from Boas and Deloria as cited in Chung and Timberlake 1985)

What has been called the future tense marker in Lakhota (Almosan-Keresiouan: United States and Canada) actually marks both simple futures (13a) or irrealis modality (13b and 13c).

2.0. Negation

The **negative** is a grammatical category employed to deny the actuality of an event or some portion thereof. Negation, however, can occur in any of the traditional mood categories (e.g., "Don't do that!" is a negative imperative), and a negative sentence can be uttered with complete certainty or with some doubt. Thus, like evidentials, negation is not generally treated as a type of mood but as a unique category that is related. When examining the means by which languages form negative sentences, one must distinguish between the standard negation strategy (i.e., the basic way in which languages negate clauses) from secondary modifications (i.e., other features that accompany the standard negation device rather than accomplishing negation by selves). Inga (Equatorial-Tucanoan: Columbia) provides a clear example of the difference:[2]

(14) a. Rircanchi-mi

we.went-AFFIRM

We went.

b. **Mana**   rircanchi*chu*

NEG   we.went

We didn't go.

c. Rircanchi*chu*?

Did we go?

The negative clause in (14b) is signaled by the presence of the particle *mana* and the suffix *-chu*. Rather than considering both to form the primary negation strategy, we relegate *-chu* to secondary status because it appears in non-negative sentences such as (14c). Instead of describing this suffix as a negative marker, it is more accurate to say that it marks nondeclarative sentences and, as such, it must accompany the primary negation strategy.

This is not to say that languages never distribute negation over a clause. The move to label verbal affixation as a secondary strategy was not motivated by the fact that it appears in a distinct structural position apart from the negative word *mana*. Rather, it was because the suffix *-chu* could be demonstrated to have a broader function than sentence negation. Indeed, there are many languages in which the primary negation strategy involves multiple elements. Standard French (Italic: France) furnishes a familiar example. Sentence negation is accomplished using a combination of negative particles—for example, *ne . . . pas* (15):

(15)   Pierre   **ne**   parle   **pas**   français

Pierre   NEG   speak.3S   NEG   French

Pierre does not speak French.

Double marking such as this is not common, but neither is it rare. In a 345-language sample, Dryer (1988b) found 20 languages that obligatorily used multiple elements to mark negation and several others that did so optionally. He suggests that there is a simple semantic explanation for this fact: "Negative morphemes carry a large communicative load in the sense that they carry an important part of the message. If a hearer fails to hear the negative morpheme in a sentence, they will have fundamentally misunderstood the sentence" (102). Therefore, although the double marking of negation is not economical, it still occasionally develops in languages to assist in the accurate identification of negative sentences.

■ 2.1. Standard Negation Strategies

There are three basic standard strategies that languages employ to negate sentences: (a) a negative particle, (b) a negative auxiliary, or (c) a negative affix (Dahl 1979). In the first case, the negative marker may be invariant, as in English, or there may be a variety of negative forms (16), as in Mandarin Chinese (Sinitic: China).

(16) a. Tā   **bu**   hē   jiǔ
         3S   NEG   drink   wine
         He/she does not drink wine.

     b. Tā   **méi**   kāi   mén
         3S   NEG   open   door
         He/she didn't open the door.

     c. **Bié**   dòng
         NEG   move
         Don't move!   (Data from Li and Thompson 1981)

The choice of which negative is used in Mandarin is, in part, determined by which verb is used in the clause. Verbs denoting states take one negative particle (16a), whereas verbs denoting accomplishments take a different one (16b). As Li and Thompson (1981, 417) write, "*méi* negates the completion of an event." The mood of the sentence, however, can also determine which alternate appears (16c).

The second standard negative strategy, using an auxiliary verb, is found in Evenki (Manchu-Tungusic: Russia):

(17) a. Bi   dukuwūn-ma   duku-cā-w
      I   letter-OBJ   write-PST-1S
      I wrote a letter.
   b. Bi   dukuwūn-**ma**   ə-cə̄-w   duku-ra
      I   letter-OBJ   NEG-PST-1S   write-PART
      I didn't write a letter.

(Data from J. Payne 1985b)

In Evenki, the negative (17b) takes the form of a finite verb—it is inflected for tense and subject agreement—and the event that is being negated is put in a subordinate form.

Finally, negative affixes can be used as the primary means to indicate negated sentences. This is true in Maasai (Nilotic: Kenya):

(18)   **m**-a-rany
       NEG-1S-sing
       I do not sing.   (Data from Tucker and Mpaayei 1955)

Cross-linguistically, there is a tendency for languages with affixal negation to use prefixes (Bybee 1985).[3] This is a somewhat unexpected property given the overall suffixing preference that exists in language (see Chapter 7). The prefixing preference for negation, however, is likely tied to the fact that negative auxiliaries and particles, which are generally the historical sources of negation, tend to be preverbal. Verb-subject-object (VSO) languages always place the negative preverbally, and SVO languages nearly always do (Dryer 1988b).

The morphological character of a language largely determines the type of negative strategy employed. Highly agglutinative languages commonly use negative affixes, whereas fusional languages do so far more infrequently. Negative particles are fairly widespread, but they are extremely common in languages that fall on the isolating end of the Index of Fusion.

■ 2.2. Secondary Modifications

There is a host of kinds of secondary modifications of negative structures. In this section, we examine the most common of these. The first is a change in word order. This may involve minor constituents, as in some English negatives in which the subject and auxiliary are transposed (19), or it may involve the reordering of basic constituents (20) as in Dewoin (Niger-Congo: Liberia).

(19) Never have I seen such strange behavior.

(20)   *S*   *V*   *O*   *S*   *O*   *V*
    a. ɔ   pi   sayé   b.   ɔ se   sayé   pi
        he   cook   meat   heNEG   meat   cook
        He cooked meat.   He didn't cook meat.

(Data from Marchese 1986)

In other languages, there is a neutralization of tense and aspect distinctions in negative sentences (21).

(21) a. giž-ö
       write-3S.nonPST
       He writes.
    b. giž-as
       write-3S.FUT
       He will write.
    c. o-z   giž
       NEG-3S   write
       He doesn't-won't write.   (Data from Payne 1985b)

The Komi (Finno-Ugric: Russia) clauses in (21a) and (21b) reveal a contrast between nonpast and future tense. In the negative, however, the tense distinction is not made, leaving the meaning ambiguous between a present and future reading.[4]

Changes in case marking are yet another secondary modification of negatives that is found in natural language. Russian (Balto-Slavic: Russia) is much discussed in this regard. Generally, direct objects in Russian appear in accusative case, although in a negative sentence they may also appear in the genitive (see Neidle 1988).

■ 2.3. Scope and Constituent Negation

We have limited our attention so far to examples of negation of a simple sentence. However, the interpretation of negative sentences is greatly complicated when they have more complex morphosyntax (22).

(22) a. John deliberately didn't touch Bob.
     b. John didn't deliberately touch Bob.

Notice that these two English sentences mean radically different things. In (22a), John does not touch Bob and his restraint is premeditated. On the contrary, in (22b) John does touch Bob, but the contact is accidental. This divergence in meaning arises because the negative has different **scope** in the two sentences. In (22a), it has scope over the verb phrase *touch Bob*. In (22b), it has scope over *deliberately touch Bob*. The operation of scope is a complicated topic and one that I will not delve into here. For present purposes, suffice it to say that at the clause level negatives tend to minimally have scope over everything that occurs after them, although in certain circumstances and languages this principle does not hold.

Dryer (1988b) and Bybee (1985) both suggest that the predilection for negatives to be preverbal is a reflection of their scope properties. Again with regard to the clause level, negatives almost invariably have the verb in their scope and, therefore, if scope tends to be determined in a rightward manner, it stands to reason that there should be a corresponding preference to place negatives preverbally.

3.0. Summary

The concern of this chapter has been to determine some of the mechanisms that arise in language to express speakers' attitudes about the propositions they are relaying: obligation, necessity, certainty, etc. A significant fact about these mechanisms, one that I have left implicit throughout most of the discussion, is that languages rarely develop a single system to express modal notions. Although many languages do have a set of grammatical morphemes (such as a set of modal auxiliaries or verbal inflections) that bear much of the burden in expressing mood, these morphemes crucially interact with other facets of the grammar (such as tense, evidentials, negation, etc.) to reflect modality. For this reason, mood is one of the more difficult aspects of human language to compare cross-linguistically.

4.0. Key Terms

Declarative	Irrealis
Deontic modality	Negative
Epistemic modality	Optative
Evidentials	Realis
Imperative	Scope
Indicative	Subjunctive
Interrogative	

Notes

1. Sadock and Zwicky (1985) found this strategy used in about half of the languages that they surveyed for imperative marking.

2. This example was provided by Stephen Levinsohn. Similar data are reported in Cole (1982).

3. Dahl (1979), using a 240-language sample, arrives at the opposite conclusion. As Dahl himself admits, however, the sample was heavily biased toward verb final, suffix-dominated languages.

4. It is not true, however, that Komi makes no tense distinctions in negative sentences. A different auxiliary is used for past tense.

14

Morphosyntax of
Speech Acts

There is no question that language is put to use for many different purposes.
It is used for developing and destroying relationships, for establishing group
solidarity, for thinking, for affirming and determining social position, for
education, for aesthetic reasons, and just for fun. At the core of each of these
functions is the truism that language operates as a medium through which we
can interact with one another. For verbal communication to expedite human
interchange, it must, at a minimum, provide ways to present information, to
glean information, and to manipulate behavior. When speakers engage in these
linguistic pursuits, they are said to be committing a **speech act**. Given how
basic such communicative needs are, it comes as little surprise that languages
conventionalize certain constructions to perform each of them. That is, a
package of grammatical devices (morphemes, word order, intonation, etc.)
evolves to meet these fundamental requirements of communication.

The grammatical structure that is routinely assigned to presenting bits of information and making assertions about the world is a **declarative** sentence, that used for the gathering of verbal information is the **interrogative** sentence, and **imperative** sentences are the conventional mechanisms by which we regulate the actions of those around us.

It was shown in Chapter 13 that many languages often use special morphology to mark moods that correlate to these sentence types. There is, however, a difference between moods and sentence types. Mood is a grammatical category (such as tense, gender, or person) that may or may not find overt expression in a given language. Even when it is expressed, its uses are multifaceted and intricate. Conversely, the three sentence types—declarative, interrogative, and imperative—are universal.

It should also be pointed out that a sentence type can be put to uses other than the one to which it is conventionally assigned (1).

(1)   a. Do you know how to work this TV?
      b. It's a bit chilly in here with your window open.

Example (1a) is an interrogative sentence. Typically, one uses the combination of grammatical features found in it to elicit a yes or no response, thereby learning some fact about the world. In most situations, however, it is likely that this particular sentence would be uttered in an attempt to get the hearer to turn the TV on or to assist in turning it on; that is, the point of the question is not simply to learn about the extent of the listener's technological know-how but also to benefit from this know-how. Therefore, the sentence is being used as a (polite) command—something like, "please help turn on this TV for me." Likewise, (1b) more often than not would be used to get the hearer to shut a window and not as a proclamation of useful information. When there is a mismatch between the form of a sentence and its actual use, we say that the utterance is an **indirect speech act.**

In addition to the three major types of speech acts, there are also many minor ones: greetings, leave-takings, exclamations, and so on. To understand how to use a particular language properly, one must be familiar with the sentence type used for each of these. For the remainder of this chapter, however, we will restrict our attention to the major speech acts.

1.0. Encoding Declaratives

Declarative sentences tend to be the most "neutral" of all sentence types. They are least likely to require special morphology and tend to have the fewest restrictions on what verbal categories can be used. It is for these reasons that declarative sentences generally form the basis of generalizations about the normal word order of a language. Perhaps most significantly, the intonation contour of declaratives is usually relatively level. Although rises or declines in pitch do occur in declaratives (i.e., the intonation is not completely level), pitch variations are less rapid and dramatic than in interrogative and imperative sentences.

All these features are, of course, broad generalizations. There are probably exceptions to all of them. For example, Cashibo (Ge-Pano: Peru) employs a set of auxiliary verbs for declarative sentences that are distinct from those used in other sentence types. These auxiliaries form a system of evidentials (see Chapter 13). Indeed, it may be the case that the most common kind of language requiring special marking for declaratives is one with evidentials.

2.0. Encoding Imperatives

In their research on speech acts, Sadock and Zwicky (1985, 172) report that a common way to indicate imperative sentences, probably the most common, is to "employ an entirely affixless verbal base." For instance, tense and aspect markers are often omitted in the formation of imperative sentences, as in Danish (Germanic: Denmark) (2).

(2) kobe   "to buy"   hoppe   "to hop"
     kobta "bought"   hoppede   "hopped"
     kob   "buy!"   hop   "hop!"

(Data from Sadock and Zwicky 1985)

The Danish imperatives neutralize the tense distinction by occurring in a bare form. Languages also eliminate tense in imperatives by employing the infinitive, as in Armenian (Armenian: Middle East) (3).

(3) Lṙ-el
     be.silent-INF
     Shut up!   (Data from Kozintseva 1995)

Another common characteristic of imperatives is the omission of a subject nominal. Often, a concomitant is suppressing agreement marking. Thus, in English the verb must appear in its uninflected form (4).

(4) a. *is/*are/*am quick about it!
     b. Be quick about it!

In those languages that omit the subject but still mark imperative verbs with agreement, it is most common to find the verb indicating a second-person singular subject (although see Chapter 11 for examples where this is not the case).

(5) bi-hiwa   phaní-ute
     2S-go   house-DIR
     Go home!   (Data from Aikhenwald 1995)

The Bare (Equatorial-Tucanoan: Columbia) imperative in (5) is recognizable in two ways. The verb is not marked for tense or mood, and there is no overt subject. Verb agreement, however, still arises. This verb agreement is always second person.

Several other features of imperatives should be noted. First, some languages form positive imperatives differently from negative imperatives, or **prohibitives.** This is, for instance, true of Bare (6):

(6) ba-bi-kiyate-'da-ka
     NEG-2S-fear-ASP-NEG
     Don't be afraid!

Note that the prohibitive in (6) indicates aspect (with the suffix -'da in this example), a possibility apparently not open to positive imperatives. About half of the languages surveyed in Sadock and Zwicky (1985) used a special negative marker for prohibitives that was not used in other sentence types. This is also true of the Bare prohibitive in (6). The normal means by which to signal negation is the use of the negative particle *hena* in combination with a verbal suffix *-wa*.

Second, verbs which denote actions that are not potentially under the control of the subject are highly dispreferred in imperatives (7).

(7) a. Run!/Duck!/Watch it!
    b. Slip!/Melt!/Be smelly!

The commands in (7b) are formed of verbs that denote nonvolitional events. Therefore, to will someone to carry out such an act is pragmatically odd. With special contexts, however, such imperatives are possible. For instance, one could imagine an impatient cook standing over a pot of hard chocolate saying "Melt!" Of course, this would be a case of an indirect speech act. The cook is not really trying to alter the behavior of the chocolate. He is expressing a desire, "I wish this chocolate would melt quickly."

Another feature of imperatives is that they are generally restricted to main clauses.

(8) a. After you run, shower!
    b. *After run!, you will shower.
    c. *After run!, shower!

Although imperatives (marked here by the exclamation point) may comprise the main clause of a complex sentence (8a), they cannot be placed in the dependent clause (8b and 8c).

Finally, imperative sentences are normally associated with a rapidly descending pitch.

3.0. Encoding Interrogatives

Normally, languages make a distinction between two types of interrogative sentences: polar and content. **Polar interrogatives** (also called **yes-no**

questions) are those that are framed in such as way as to make "yes" or "no" the minimally expected answer (9).

(9) a. Would you care to dance?
  b. Did you see the game on TV last night?
  c. Can I use your phone?

Content interrogatives are those in which a particular piece of information is requested rather than the truth value of a proposition. They always involve a question word or expression (10).

(10) a. Who will stop the rain?
  b. Where have all the good times gone?
  c. What's love got to do with it?

■ **3.1. Polar Questions**

In the majority of languages, polar questions use rising intonation at the end of a sentence that is in marked contrast to the intonation of a declarative sentence. This feature of polar interrogatives—to prosodically mark the end of the sentence—is so pervasive cross-linguistically that Greenberg proposed the following universal for it:

(11) Greenberg's Universal 9: When a yes-no question is differentiated
    from the corresponding assertion by an intonation pattern, the
    distinctive intonational feature of these patterns is reckoned from
    the end of the sentence rather than from the beginning.

Given the ubiquity of sentence final intonation as a marker for polar questions, it should come as little surprise that, in some languages, intonation alone is the primary means by which to determine whether an utterance is declarative or polar. This occurs in Papiamentu (Creole: Caribbean), in which a polar expression is realized entirely by intonation, including a rising pitch on the final syllable (Kouwenberg and Murray 1994). It is also true of Fijian (Dixon 1988), Palauan (Josephs 1975), and Hixkaryana (Derbyshire 1985). As you may have observed, the languages in which intonation is the primary polar strategy are areally and genetically quite distinct.

A syntactic mechanism for marking questions is **inversion,** which is a rearrangement of words from the pattern manifested in declarative clauses.

The English sentences in (9) are all built on this strategy. Rather than subjects being placed before the auxiliary as in declaratives (e.g., "I can use your phone"), the auxiliary is sentence initial. Unlike intonation, the concentration of this device in European languages suggests it is largely a genetic trait or perhaps an areal one.

A common way to form a yes-no question is with a question particle that occurs either at the beginning (12a) or at the end of the sentence (12b).

(12) a. ha=tovah   hā'ārets
    QUES-good   ART-land
    Is the land good?

   b. Ta   nom.yg   üze-j   baj-na   uu
    You book-ACC see-IMPF be-PRES QUES
    Are you reading the book?   (Data from Binnick 1979)

Biblical Hebrew (Semitic) creates yes-no questions by placing the particle *ha* sentence initially (12a). Because the particle is a clitic, it bonds phonologically with the word that follows it. Mongolian (Mongolian: Mongolia) mirrors Hebrew in setting the question particle word finally (12b). Question particles are not restricted to sentence boundaries; they may also occur in a fixed position somewhere in the middle of a sentence or even have variable position. Cross-linguistically, however, it is the sentence-initial and sentence-final question particles that frequently occur. There is a general correlation between basic constituent order and the position of a question particle: In object-verb (OV) languages, it is much more common to have sentence final particles. There is a weak correlation between VO languages and sentence-initial particles; this correlation, however, falls short of statistical significance in more conservative sampling techniques (e.g., Dryer 1992).

Polar questions may also be generated by employing verbal affixation. The following examples are from Greenlandic Eskimo (Inuit: Greenland):

(13) a. Piniar-a
    hunt-3S.QUES
    Is he hunting?

   b. Igav-a
    cook-3S.QUES
    Does he cook?   (Data from Sadock and Zwicky 1985)

In this particular case, the question affixes could be assigned the status of mood markers because they are in paradigmatic opposition with person markers used for indicative and imperative clauses.

All languages utilize yes-no questions for a variety of communicative purposes. Of course, the conventional use is to determine the truth value of a given proposition. Speakers, however, often have a bias as to what they want or what they believe the answer to be. This bias can be instantiated into yes-no questions in various ways. In English, the addition of the negative particle serves to reveal that the speaker expects an affirmative response (14).

(14) a. Don't you just love his new shirt?
     b. Isn't the grammar teacher hard?

In a similar vein, many languages allow polar questions to be used as "tags" on statements (15); hence, they are called **tag questions.**

(15) a. Dartmouth College is in New Hampshire, isn't it?
     b. You're going, aren't you?
     c. She's not going to eat that, is she?

Tag questions, although they take the form of an interrogative sentence, are rarely used to gather information. A speaker uses them to receive confirmation of his or her own beliefs (14a), to persuade ((15b) in some contexts), or to express amazement (15c).

■ 3.2. Content Questions

Recall that, unlike polar questions, content questions are not used to determine the truth value of a proposition but rather to fill in pieces of information about a larger proposition that are unknown. The type of information which is desired on the part of the speaker is indicated through question words (16).

(16) a. **Where** did that little green man say he was from?
     b. **Who** is going to clean up this mess?
     c. **What** is Ms. Smith buying at K-Mart?

As can be observed from the sentences in (16), the production of content questions in English parallels the formation of polar questions; both invert the subject and an auxiliary verb (16a and 16c). It is not the case, however, that content questions are merely yes-no interrogatives with a question word tacked onto the front. Note that when the question word is the subject of the clause, inversion does not occur (16b). Moreover, the intonation pattern of content questions differs: They do not require rapidly rising intonation at the end of the sentence like polar questions do. Typically, languages are similar to English in using slightly or completely different strategies for content questions.

The question word of content interrogatives is often placed in a sentence focus position. This is either sentence initially, as in English, following a focused constituent, or preverbally. Hungarian (Finno-Ugric: Hungary) exhibits two of these options. A question word can be placed sentence initially (17a) or just before the verb (17b).[1]

(17) a. **Ki**   hívta   fel   János-t
      who   called   up   John-ACC
      Who called up John?

    b. János-t   **ki**   hívta   fel
      John-ACC   who   called   up
      Who called up John?   (Data from Kiss 1994)

Alternatively, the question word in some languages appears in the same position as it would in a declarative sentence, as in Mandarin Chinese (Sinitic: China). When this occurs, the question word is said to remain **in situ**.

(18) a. tā   xiàwǔ   lái
      3S   afternoon   come
      S/He will come in the afternoon.

     a'. tā   **shénme**   **shíhou**   lái
       3S   what   time   come
       When will s/he come.

    b. wǒ   qǐng   nǐmen   chī fan
      I   invite   2P   eat food
      I invited you all to eat.

     b'. wǒ   qǐng   **shéi**   chī   fan
       I   invite   whom   eat   food
       Whom did I invite to eat?

    c. nǐ   qù
      you   go
      You will go.

     c'. **shéi**   qù
       who   go
       Who will go?

                         (Data from Li and Thompson 1981)

The number of question words that a language may have at its disposal varies considerably. English has many (*who, whom, what, when, where, why, how, which, whose,* and complex expressions built on each of them). The minimum number of question words reported by Sadock and Zwicky (1985) is three (Yokuts [Penutian: United States]), but regardless of the number, most languages at least make a distinction between human and nonhuman question words (e.g., *who* or *what*).

It is also highly typical for question words to be used as indefinite pronouns in a language. Sometimes the overlap is slight, as in Fijian, in which only one of the question words is used indefinitely: *vica* ("how many, some") (Dixon 1988). In Chinese, on the other hand, at least four of the question words do double duty as indefinite pronouns. Finally, in some languages indefinite pronouns can be derived from question words in a fairly productive way. This is, for example, true in English (*whoever, whatever, wherever, whenever,* etc.).

To conclude this section on content interrogatives, I raise one final point of variation between languages—how languages form **multiple interrogatives.** A multiple interrogative is a question in which more than a single bit of information is desired, so two or more question words are employed. Some English examples are given in (19).[2]

(19) a. Who did what to whom?
       b. Where did the snake bite whom?

Recall, though, that English content interrogatives generally require that the question word be placed sentence initially. In these examples, in which there are two or more question words, only one of them arises in the expected position. The rest remain in situ.

Other languages, such as Polish (Balto-Slavic: Poland) and Hungarian (Finno-Ugric: Hungary), differ from English in that all the question words of a multiple interrogative tend be fronted.[3] Some Hungarian data are furnished in (20).

(20) a. Ki   milyen   könyv-et   olvasott   el?
          who   what   book-ACC   read   PREVERB
          What book did who read?
      b. Ki-nek   miért   segített-él?
          who-DAT   why   helped-you
          Why did you help who?   (Data from Kiss 1994)

Therefore, even in languages that possess a similar strategy for generating simple content questions, there are subtle differences in the creation of multiple interrogatives. The question of why these differences arise is currently an area of intense research (see Rudin 1988).

4.0. Summary

Language structures evolve to accommodate the communicative needs of speakers. It is not surprising, then, that languages universally develop mechanisms to carry out three very basic functions of communication: asking questions, making assertions, and issuing commands. As testimony to the genius of language, these habitualized structures can be employed for purposes other than what their form suggests: For example, interrogatives can be used to make statements, and declaratives can in turn be used to make requests.

Although languages universally develop declarative, imperative, and interrogative sentence types, the particulars of these structures vary to as great a degree as most other aspects of language. There are differences in morphology, word order, and intonation. Within the variety, however, emerges common patterns. Many were noted previously, such as the tendency to remove tense distinctions in imperative sentences and the frequency of sentence final intonation patterns that mark interrogatives.

To this point in the book, I have been concerned primarily with simple sentences—that is, sentences containing a single clause. The review of basic sentence types in this chapter has provided a convenient conclusion to that narrow focus. In the final two chapters, I explore the basics of how languages form more complex sentences.

5.0. Key Terms

Content interrogatives	Inversion
Declarative	Polar interrogative
Imperative	Prohibitives
In situ	Speech act

Indirect speech act   Tag question
Interrogative   Yes-no question

Notes

1. The description of Hungarian question word placement is slightly simplified in that the preverbal focus position is not a strictly linear notion. Therefore, there are some additional constraints that I am ignoring. See Kiss (1994) for a complete discussion.

2. Double interrogatives are perhaps most commonly employed when the bulk of the information present in the question is already known to the speaker. For example, (19b) might naturally occur in the following scenario: A little boy runs in the house in a state of agitation. Out of breath, he blurts out to his father, "A snake bit Paul on the hand!" The father, who had been engrossed in reading the paper when his son arrived on the scene, does not comprehend the statement in its entirety. He knows that his son has just told him that some person has been bit by a snake and that his son specified what part of the person's anatomy has been bitten. In this scenario, the father presupposes that "a snake bit someone somewhere" when he asks the question in (19b).

3. I have ignored many details of the Hungarian data here for simplicity, but it is worth noting that the language does not perfectly mirror the English situation as is sometimes intimated (e.g., see Haegeman 1994). First, the question words in Hungarian can be preceded by a subject so they are not necessarily in sentence-initial position. Second, it is not the case that all question words have to be fronted in multiple interrogatives (Kiss 1994 identifies some of the pragmatic considerations that determine whether movement is obligatory).

Complex Clauses

15

Subordination

To this point in our typological overview of language, I have focused almost exclusively on simple sentences—that is, sentences containing a single clause. In the remaining chapters, I shift the attention to complex sentences—that is, sentences that contain two or more clauses. Given two clauses, A and B, that occur together in a sentence, there are three potential structural relations that might hold between them: A and B might be assigned equal status, A might be dependent on B, or B might be dependent on A. The latter two options are types of **subordination.**

1.0. Principal Types of Subordinate Clauses

Traditional grammar has posited three basic types of subordinate clauses: adverbial, complement, and relative. **Adverbial clauses** are employed to provide the situational context for the event or state that is described in a main clause (1).

(1) a. The boy was very sick **after the snake bit him.**

      b. He screamed **because the snake bit him.**

The adverbial clause is much like an adverb both in the types of meanings it conveys and in the fact that it is an adjunct (not syntactically required by the verb in any way).

    Complement clauses are arguments of (and therefore syntactically essential to) the clause in which they are embedded (2).

(2) a. Everyone knew **the snake bit the boy.**

      b. **That the snake bit the boy** upset me.

Complement clauses are much like nouns because they often bear grammatical relations, such as subject and object, that are typically fulfilled by noun phrases. Furthermore, it is possible to replace complement clauses with pronouns (as in *It upset me* in (2b)).

    Relative clauses function much like adjectives because they are usually modifiers of a noun phrase.

(3) a. I saw the snake **that bit the boy.**

      b. The boy **who was bitten** died last night.

In many languages, certain manipulations of these clause types can render them as phrases. For instance, participle phrases can generally replace adverbial clauses depicting time ("After I go to the store" → "After going to the store").

■ 1.1. Characteristics of Subordinate Clauses

Subordination can differ quite substantially from language to language. It is possible, however, to find some characteristics of subordinate clauses that are fairly typical. Some of these properties will be examined in this section. Keep in mind that none of the characteristics is a "necessary and sufficient" condition for subordination; therefore, structural dependency must be determined for each language in its own right.

In terms of prosody, there is often no intonation break in between subordinate and main clauses. That is, there is no pause or no falling pitch or both. Although this generalization is meant to hold for all three types of subordinate clauses, it does not hold equally well. In general, the tighter the dependence between the main and subordinate clauses, the less likely it is to find intonation breaks. This means complement clauses, which are actually arguments of the clause, are rarely set off from the main clause by pauses or a special intonation. Adverbial clauses, on the other hand, are more amenable to such prosodic disruption because they are adjuncts.

Subordinate structures in the languages of the world are typically morphologically marked by some kind of subordinating particle or affix. This subordinator may carry lexical content—that is, contribute substantial semantic information to the clause (4), or it may be semantically empty (5).

(4) I eat beets **if/when/because** they are in season.

(5) I hope **that** I can go.

When the subordinator is primarily a signal of syntactic dependence and does not carry meaning, it can be omitted in certain constructions in many languages. This is true of example (5) where *that* may be omitted from the complement clause without changing the meaning of the sentence or rendering it ungrammatical.

In some languages, certain subordinate structures regularly use a nonfinite form of the verb. Indeed, this is the dominate strategy in natural language. This pattern is found in the complements of some English verbs (6a) and adverbial participle constructions (6b).

(6) a. I wanted **to go** to Buffalo yesterday.
    b. **Running** up the hill full speed, John became winded.

The verbs in these subordinate structures are considered nonfinite because they are tenseless and carry no agreement.

It is also common to find that languages produce subordinate structures through **nominalization.** In this case, the verb is transformed into a nominal by use of derivational morphology. Commonly, the subject of the nominalized verb is treated as a possessor (7).

(7) u-kima-na   nɨɨ   su=panaʔi-ti=
    his-come-NOML   I   know-ASP
    I know that he has come.   (Data from Charney 1993)

This Comanche (Uto-Aztecan: United States) sentence presents a typical case of subordination formed through nominalization. The verb is made nonfinite by the addition of the suffix -*na*. The notional subject of this verb is the possessive *u*- ("his").

Another feature that can distinguish subordinate structures from main clauses is that they use fewer constituents or possibly a different order of constituents. A familiar instance of the latter kind is found in German (Germanic: Germany). Main clauses generally employ a subject-verb-object (SVO) order (8a), whereas subordinate clauses use SOV (8b).

(8)   *S*   *V*   *O*
   a. Der   König   liebt   den   Hund
      The   king   loves   the   dog.
                                   S   *O*   *V*
   b. Ich   weiß,   [daß   der   König   den   Hund   liebt]
      I   know   [that   the   king   the   dog   loves]
      I know that the king loves the dog.

One final way in which subordinate constructions differ in their behavior from main clauses is that their discourse function is usually one of backgrounding, explanation, or description, even in action-oriented narratives. This in particular is true of adverbial and relative clauses. Although main clauses may also contain information about setting or context, their primary function is to encode the main events or propositions of the discourse.

2.0. Adverbial Clauses

Perhaps the major issue that arises in the description of adverbial clauses and other adverbial structures is the meaning, or range of meanings, they can contribute to a sentence. Recall that adverbial constructions are considered "adjuncts" because they typically supplement the information contained by a proposition (i.e., the main clause) rather than serving as arguments of this proposition. Within this broad characterization, there is room for adverbials with many different types of meaning. In this section, I simply list some of the more common uses of adverbial clauses, interjecting typologically based comments when appropriate. Before doing so, it should be noted that many languages do not use adverbial clauses at all or use them infrequently. This is particularly true in languages that have complex tense and aspect systems or sets of verbal affixes that carry out the same function as adverbial phrases and clauses in languages such as English.

■ **2.1. Time**

Adverbial structures can function to provide information about the relative temporal ordering of two events (9).

(9) [ate   abeuka   nu-kása-ka]   nu-khawendya   beke   kuhú
    [until   when   1S-come-SEQ]   1S-pay   FUT   she
    As soon as I come, I shall pay her.   (Data from Aikhenwald 1995)

The Bare (Equatorial-Tucanoan: Columbia) adverbial clause is marked in two ways: by the sequence of **subordinating conjunctions**, *ate abeuka* ("as soon as"), and the sequential suffix *-ka* on the verb of the subordinate clause. Note further that the tense of the adverbial construction is only determinable by its relation to the main clause. It carries no independent marking for tense.

This kind of tense and aspect dependency is common with adverbial clauses. Even in English, which does have tense and aspect marked on the finite verbs of adverbial clauses, the choice of tense is constrained by the tense of the main clause. For example, one can say "we'll leave when Sonny gets here" but not "we'll leave when Sonny got/will get here."

Although English and many other languages are replete with subordinators expressing time, this is by no means typical in the languages of the world. Some languages, such as Otomi (Oto-Manguean: Mexico), tend to let the tense and aspect markers of the verbs determine the relative temporality of the main and subordinate clauses (10).

(10)

Mi-zøni   ya   kam-ta   bi-?yɔni   kha   ši-pati   kar-hmę
PST-arrive(IMPF) now   my-father   PST-ask   QUES   PST-heated(STAT)   the-tortilla
(When) My father had arrived, he asked if the tortillas were heated.

(Data from Thompson and Longacre 1985)

■ **2.2. Location**

Another frequent meaning expressed by adverbial structures is location.

(11) The police were digging **where Jeffrey had planted a garden.**

Unlike time adverbials, it is rare for a language to have a robust set of location subordinators. Instead, languages are more likely to employ other structures such as adpositional phrases (e.g., *in Jeffrey's newly planted garden*) or relative clauses.

■ **2.3. Cause**

In structuring discourse, it is often desirable to indicate the causes or motivations behind the occurrence of some event (12).

(12) **Because John won the lottery,** he gave his professor a generous gift **to say thanks.**

The sentence in (12) employs two unique structures to provide information about the cause of the main action. Notice that these structures indicate different types of causation. The clause introduced by *because* describes an enabling event, but the infinitive phrase reveals John's personal motivation. By using different constructions, English can easily distinguish between these major types of causation.

Other languages signal the difference between enablement and purpose not in the type of construction but with mood—for example, Ngizim (West Chadic: Nigeria):

(13) a. Ata   abən   gáaɗà   aci   ngaa
        eat(PRFV)   food   SUB   he   well
        He ate food because he was well.
     b. Vəru   gàaɗà   dà   ši   səma
        go.out(PRFV) SUB   SBJV   drink   beer
        He went out to drink beer.

                              (Data from Schuh as cited in Thompson and Longacre 1985)

As can be seen in (13), Ngizim employs the same subordinator in the two types of causation but distinguishes between motivation and enablement by use of the subjunctive marker *dà* (13b). Thompson and Longacre (1985, 185) point out that the use of the subjunctive, which standardly·encodes hypothetical or unrealized events, is motivated by the fact that the intention of the act in (13b) is yet to be realized at the time that the main clause event occurs.

■ 2.4. Conditional

Most languages allow formation of special conditional structures. Generally, tense, aspect, and mood are used to give the conditional construction different meanings (14).

(14) a. **If you can't beat 'em,** join 'em.
　　b. **If Bill is still at the office,** he can finish the report.
　　c. **If the Smiths drove quickly,** they are home by now.

(15) a. **If I were a rich man,** I would fiddle all day long.
　　b. **If Ted had been more responsible,** they would have arrived safely.

The basic semantic parameter for conditional sentences is **real** versus **unreal** conditions. Real conditions are those that potentially could be fulfilled (14). They may be general truths as in (14a), present situations (14b), or past situations (14c). Unreal conditions are those that cannot be fulfilled. They can either be hypothetical statements (15a) or counterfactuals (15b).

In English, as in most languages, the various types of conditional statements are indicated by choices of tense, aspect, and mood in the **protasis** (the "if clause") and the **apodosis** (the "then clause"). For example, the apodosis of real conditions is generally declarative or imperative and in the present or future tense. The set of conditional structures can become quite complex in languages that make multiple distinctions between mood, aspect, and tense. To get a sense for this, examine the following sentences from ancient Greek (Hellenic):

(16) a. ean　　eip-ēi　　　　　ti　　　　autou　　akou-s-ometha
　　　　if　　say-3S.AOR.SBJV　anything　him　　hear-FUT-1P.IND
　　　　If he says anything, we will hear him.

b. ei   hoi   polemoi   elth-oien   polem-oite
   if   the   enemy   come-3P.AOR.OPT   fight-2P.PRES.OPT
   If the enemy should come, you would fight.

c. ei   erch-etai   kalōs   poi-ei
   if   come-3S.PRES.IND   well   do-3S.PRES.IND
   If he is coming, he is doing the right thing.

The data exhibit that Greek uses three unique moods in conditional statements: indicative, subjunctive, and optative. The conditionals can be built on
various combinations (far more than in (3)) of moods in the two clauses, and
both clauses can be marked for several tense and aspect distinctions. The end
result is numerous possibilities for the expression of conditions, all of which
vary, sometimes subtly, in meaning.

■ 2.5. Concessive Clauses

One final type of adverbial meaning deserves mention: **concessives.**
These are clauses that reflect a contrast of some sort between the main and
subordinate clauses. The following is an example from Malayalam
(Dravidian: India):

(17) **maṛa   peyyuka-āṇe-enkil-um**   J.   purattu   pokunnu
     rain   fall.INF-AUX-if-even   John   out   go
     Even though it is raining, John is going out.   (Data from König 1988)

All languages appear to have some way to indicate contrast between propositions, although not all do so by use of a subordinate structure. In those that
do, however, the use of a subordinating particle appears to be the dominate
way to create the contrast.

■ 2.6. Unspecified Relationship

In the preceding sections, I have examined some of the primary adverbial
meanings for which languages develop special morphosyntactic devices. The
kinds of information that adverbials provide, however, are often predictable
from the linguistic or extralinguistic context. For this reason, it is common to
leave the logical connection between two clauses unspecified and permit the

reader or listener to draw his or her own conclusions as to the precise nature of the relationship.

(18) a. **Having told a few jokes,** Harvey proceeded to introduce the speaker.
    b. **Having abducted the puppy,** the kidnappers wrote out the ransom note.

The likely interpretation for the adverbial expression in (18a) is temporal priority. The adverbial structure in (18b) also indicates temporal priority, but here there is the added meaning of enablement. Without first carrying out an abduction, the kidnappers would have no grounds to draft a ransom note.

3.0. Complement Clauses

A complement clause is a clause that is an argument of a predicate, typically as a subject (19a) or direct object (19b).

(19) a. **When you leave** makes no difference to me.
    b. I cannot believe **that you ate the whole thing.**

The clause that the complement is embedded within is commonly referred to as the **matrix** clause.

Complements do not always occur as full clauses but instead may arise as phrases headed by nonfinite verb forms such as infinitives (20a) and participles (20b).

(20) a. **Knowing the answers** makes taking the exam easier.
    b. I want him **to leave.**

It is a controversial matter whether a pronoun such as *him* in (20b) is part of the matrix clause or part of the complement. The decision on how to analyze it often depends on one's theoretical assumptions. I set the issue aside here.

It is also possible to have multiple embedding of complements.

(21) I want [to believe [that you are right]].

In this example, there are two complements and two matrix clauses. The most deeply embedded clause, *that you are right,* is the complement of the verb *to believe.* Simultaneously, the complex structure *to believe that you are right* is the complement of the clause headed by *want.*

Two primary mechanisms for signaling the dependency of the complement are noticeable from the examples in (19) through (21): use of a **complementizer** (19) (i.e., a subordinating particle) and a nonfinite verb form (20 and 21). Indeed, both these mechanisms are common cross-linguistically.

The placement of the complementizer appears to derive from the basic constituent order of a language. In VO languages, complementizers nearly always, or perhaps even always, occur at the beginning of the complement clause. Both complement-initial and complement-final subordinating particles are found in OV languages. Less commonly, complementizers are found at some point in the middle of the complement. This is true of Mparntwe Arrernte (Pama Nyungan: Australia), in which the complementizer is a clitic that is attached to the first constituent in a complement clause (22).

(22)	Re	itelare-me	John-**rle**	petye-ke
	3S.SBJ	know-nonPST(PROG)	John-that	come-PST(CMPLT)
	He knows that John came.			

(Data from Van Valin and Wilkins 1993)

In other languages, such as Kanuri (Western Saharan: Nigeria), the complementizer is a verbal affix.

(23)	Sáva-nyi	íshin-**rò**	tśmăŋśnà
	friend-my	come-3S(DAT)	thought.1S(PFV)
	I thought my friend would come.		

(Data from Lukas as cited in Noonan 1985)

In (23), the complementizer is a clitic that also is employed in the language as a dative case marker.

■ 3.1. The Complexity Continuum

At the outset of the previous section, it was noted that complements can occur in different forms, either as clauses or phrases headed by a nonfinite verb form. Givón (1980) has argued that the choice of which complement type

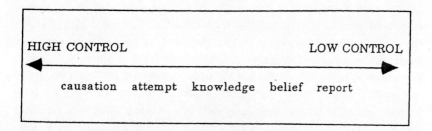

Figure 15.1. Degree of Verb's Control Over Complements

is used reflects its semantic relationship to the matrix clause verb. He proposes a set of semantic criteria by which to rank verbs in terms of the semantic influence they hold over their complements. On the one extreme are verbs such as *report*. In a sentence such as "The store owner reported that vandals had soaped his windows," the store owner has no control over the event described in the complement. The event exists totally independently from the act of reporting it. At the other extreme are verbs such as *force* (e.g., "The store owner forced them to clean up the window"). In this case, the store owner is largely in control of the genesis and successful completion of the event of cleaning described in its complements. A rough breakdown of some verb types by degree of control is provided in Figure 15.1.

Givón (1980) then notes that the degree of structural integration between a complement and a matrix verb roughly correlates to the semantic integration. Consider the two examples just described. In the first, the complement has all the properties of an independent clause: the verb is in finite form (*had soaped*), the verb exhibits typical subject agreement, and there is a nominal with subject properties. In the second sentence, in which there is a greater degree of semantic integration, the complement is headed by a nonfinite form (*to clean up*), the verb has lost its subject agreement marking, and the agent of the complement is arguably grammatically connected to the main clause—that is, it has direct object properties. For example, it receives accusative case, and it can become the subject of the matrix clause through passivization ("They were forced to clean up").

Crucially, Givón (1980) is careful not to make the easily falsifiable claim that there is a one-to-one mapping between structure and meaning. He is not suggesting that every time an infinitive clause is employed in languages it will reflect a high degree of control, or that every time a finite clause is used as a complement it indicates a low degree of control. Such claims are clearly erroneous. Rather, he proposes that if a point along the scale in Figure 15.1 is associated with a certain syntactic structure, then a point to the left cannot be associated with a less integrated structure. Rather, the two will be treated in the same way or the point to the left will be marked by a more highly integrated structure. For example, a language might use infinitives to encode the complements of belief verbs (equivalent to "I believed him to be happy"). Then one would not expect to find verbs of causation always taking complements with finite verbs.

Even understood in its weaker form, Givón's (1980) proposal cannot be taken as anything other than a general tendency in language. Even in English, one occasionally encounters specific verbs that violate expectations. The verb *want,* for example, can only take an infinitival complement. Thus, one can say "Hanni wants Tony to attend the conference" but not "Hanni wants that Tony attends the conference." One would have to rate the verb *want* fairly low on the scale of control and thus would not expect verbs that presumably are at the same point or fall to the left of *want* on the scale in Figure 15.1 to take full clausal complements, but they do—for example, "Hanni convinced Tony that he should attend the conference." By Givón's criteria, the complement of *convince* is more conceptually integrated than a complement of *want.* It is using a device, however, that reflects less structural integration.

Nevertheless, the intuition behind Givón's (1980) proposal seems right. Certainly, a number of languages do appear to restrict the choice of complements along the basis of his proposal. For example, in Futunu-Aniwa (Austronesian: Vanuatu), object complements can either be built on infinitives (24a) or finite verbs (24a and 24b).

(24) a. avau   no   kanieni   (i)   ta   kaukau
         I   TNS   want   INF   swim
         I want to swim.

     b. akimau   no   kanieni   pe   ka   go
         we.two   TNS   want   that   TNS   go
         We want to go. (Lit: We want that (we) go)

     c. kivea   kono   mentua   pe   maka   let
         they   TNS   think   that   TNS   late
         They think that they might be late.

                                                    (Data from Dougherty 1983)

The option of using a finite clause such as that in (24c) is restricted to verbs reporting speech and verbs of mental activity. Verbs such as *kanieni* ("want"), which imply a higher degree of control over the action expressed in the complement, use both infinitives and finite clausal complements.

Because of the empirical support, the idea that the degree of conceptual integration between verb and complement is signaled by the structural integration of the two has arisen in several different guises in the literature, although in somewhat different forms than Givón's (1980) proposal (see Foley and Van Valin 1984; Haiman 1985; Noonan 1985).

4.0. Relative Clauses

Relative clauses, also referred to as adjective clauses, are typically found as modifiers of a noun, as in Ewe (Niger-Congo: Ghana):

(25) a. amɛ   si   [_____   fiɛ   agbalɛ̃-a]
       person   REL   buy   book-DEF
       the person that bought the book

     b. agbalɛ   si   [Kofi   fiɛ   _____]
       book   REL   Kofi   buy
       the book Kofi bought

     c. amɛ   si   [Kofi   fi   agbalɛ̃-a   na _____]
       person   REL   Kofi   buy   book-DEF   for
       the person whom Kofi bought the book for   (Data from Lewis 1984)

The entity being modified by the relative clause, "person" in (25a and 25c) and "book" in (25b), is referred to as the **head noun** or **relativized noun**. Often, relative clauses are introduced by a particle or word, such as *si* in (25). Such words are called **relativizers** or **relative pronouns**. The latter label is typically reserved for cases in which the relative pronoun specifies nominal properties such as case, animacy, person, and so on. In English, for example, *that* is a relativizer (see the gloss of (25a)), whereas *who, whom, which,* and *whose* are relative pronouns. The choice of which pronoun is selected depends on the relationship of the relativized noun to the adjective clause.

(26) a. dziewczyna   [**która**   Janek   lubi _____]
              girl   who(ACC)   Janek   likes
              the girl who Janek likes

   b. devuška   [**kotoroj**   Vanja   daval   den'gi _____]
              girl   who(DAT)   Vanja   gave   money
              the girl whom Vanja gave the money to   (Data adapted from Dyła 1984)

In (26a), the Polish (Balto-Slavic: Poland) relative clause is modifying the head noun *dziewczyna* ("girl"). The choice of an accusative relative pronoun is determined by the fact that it is understood as the object of the verb in the adjective clause, and objects of this verb are put in the accusative. Likewise, the dative pronoun *kotoroj* ("whom") is appropriate in (26b) because it is understood as the indirect object of the relative clause. Relative pronouns tend to be identical to the interrogative or demonstrative pronoun set that languages have.

■ 4.1. Restrictive Versus Nonrestrictive Relative Clauses

In addition to variations in the form that relative clauses can take (an issue I return to later), there is potential variation in the semantic relationship that a relative clause has to the noun it modifies. Compare the following sentences in (27a) and (27b):

(27) a. My brother **who lives in Chicago** is visiting.

   b. My brother, **who lives in Chicago,** is visiting.

A felicitous use of (27a) requires that the speaker have more than one brother. The adjective clause functions to specify the referent of *brother* from among a set of possibilities (e.g., the brother from Boston, the brother from Los Angeles, the brother from London, and the brother from Chicago). Conversely, if used properly, (27b) necessitates that the speaker has a single brother or that the listener already knows the precise referent of *my brother.* In this case, the adjective clause is not identificational (the task of identification has been fully accomplished via the head noun) but purely descriptive, providing additional information about the speaker's sibling. The former type of relative clause is called **restrictive** and the latter **nonrestrictive.**

In English, the two types of relative clauses not only differ orthographically but also in terms of formal properties. Most notably, (27b) is set off intonationally from the sentence in which it is embedded, whereas (27a) is not. It is additionally true that the relative pronoun *who* may be replaced with the relativizer *that* in (27a) but not in (27b).

A formal distinction between these two types of relative clauses is not found in all languages. The restrictive use is apparently more basic because all languages that have nonrestrictive relative clauses also have restrictive counterparts but not vice versa.

■ 4.2. Typological Variation in Relative Clauses

Not surprisingly, languages vary in the relativization strategies that they employ. In this section, attention is drawn to many areas of divergence. It was noted previously that the presence of a relativizer is characteristic of relative clauses. The presence of a relativizer, however, is not necessary for relativization to occur (cf. "the guy you told me about"). Certain languages never utilize a relativizer or a relative pronoun. This is true of Japanese (Japanese-Ryukyuan: Japan):

(28) [watasi ga hon o ataeta] kodomo
    I   SBJ   book   OBJ   give.PRV   child
    the child I gave a book to

The relative clause (in brackets) contains no word or particle equivalent to the English *that* and no relative pronoun.

The Japanese example reveals another cross-linguistic disparity in relative clauses—their position with respect to the noun that they modify. In Ewe, Polish, and English, the relative clause is found after the noun. Japanese demonstrates the opposite pattern. The relative positions of a noun and its modifying adjective clause are clearly related to the basic constituent order of the language. VO languages almost without exception use the noun + relative clause order.[1] OV languages, on the other hand, exhibit both orders with a weak preference for noun + relative clause ordering (Dryer 1992).

There are other less common patterns of word order relationships between a head noun and a relative clause. In some languages, such as Bambara

(Niger-Congo: Mali), a head noun may be located within the relative clause (29).

(29) tyε   ye   [ne   ye   so   mìn   ye]   san
     man   PST   I   PST   horse REL   see   buy
     The man bought the horse (that) I saw.

                              (Data from Bird as cited in Keenan and Comrie 1977)

Some languages also appear to allow **headless relative clauses** (30).

(30) hos   ou   lambanei   ton   stauron   autou . . .
     REL.NOM.MSC   not   take-3S   ART   cross   his
     (The person) who does not take his cross . . .

In Greek (30), it is possible to use a relative clause without a head noun. The effect is to signify indefinite reference very much like the English use of indefinite relatives that begin with *whoever, whatever,* and so on. Notice that these, too, are headless.

Another major difference in how languages carry out relativization is their treatment of the relativized noun. In many languages, the strategy is to leave a gap at the position in the adjective clause where the relativized noun normally would occur in an independent clause (29). This was indicated previously in the Ewe and Polish data. Gapping of this sort is an extremely common phenomenon, and it may be the only strategy that is ever used in languages that employ prenominal relative clauses.

Another option available in language, however, is to indicate the relativized noun by including a personal pronoun in the relative clause, as in Persian (Indic: Iran):

(31)
Man   zan-i   ra   [ke   John be   u   sibe zamini   dad   mishenasam]
I   woman-the DO   that John to   her   potato   gave   know
I know the woman that John gave the potato to (her).

                                        (Data cited in Keenan 1985b)

In (31), there is no gapped constituent within the relative clause. Rather, the pronoun *u* ("her"), by virtue of being co-indexed with the head noun, indicates which constituent is being relativized.

Both gapping and marking the relativized noun with a pronoun can be utilized by the same language. In English, the gapping strategy is overwhelmingly dominant, but even so pronouns are occasionally used in complex structures. For example, some speakers of English accept "I am looking for those documents which I can never remember where I put them" (see Sells 1984). In other languages, the use of the two strategies is more equally acceptable.

One final parameter over which languages vary in their formation of relative clauses is what nominals they allow to be relativized. English is somewhat unusual in the broad range of constituents that are relativized (32).

(32) Subject: the woman that _____ likes Mary
     Direct object: the woman (that) Mary likes _____
     Oblique: the woman (that) Mary spoke with _____
     Possessor: the woman whose family Mary knows _____
     Comparative: the woman that Mary is taller than _____
     Clause: Mary got good grades, which surprised my parents.

In a 50-language sample, Keenan and Comrie (1977) found that many languages permit relativization of only a subset of these options. For example, Malagasy (Austronesian: Madagascar) relativizes only subjects.

(33) ny   mpianatra [izay   nahita   ny   vehivavy]
     the   student   that   saw   the   woman
     the student who saw the woman

Although Comrie and Keenan found that there are differences in what individual languages relativize, the variation is not random but follows a clear pattern.

To capture this pattern, they proposed the **Noun Phrase Accessibility Hierarchy** (Figure 15.2). The hierarchy operates in the usual manner. If a language can relativize a position on the hierarchy, then it can also relativize all positions to the left. In addition, all languages with relative clauses allow relativization of the subject. As a general tendency, the accessibility hierarchy works well. It does have some exceptions, however, and several modifications have been proposed to render it more accurate (see Keenan and Comrie 1977, 1979; see also Fox 1987; Lehmann 1986). Two of the more significant modifications are noted here.

Subject > Direct Object > Oblique > Possessor

Figure 15.2. The Noun Phrase Accessibility Hierarchy

First, some exceptions to the hierarchy arise because a given language employs more than one strategy for relative clause formation. Persian, for example, uses both a pronoun retention strategy, see (31), and gapping (34).

(34) Mardi   [ke   _____   bolandqadd   bud]
     man   that   tall   was
     the man that was tall

The two relative clause structures in Persian are not equally applicable in all circumstances. The relativization of subjects is almost always carried out through gapping, the relativization of direct objects uses both gapping and pronouns, and for other nominal types pronoun retention is used. If one examined only the pronoun retention strategy, Persian would be an anomaly for the accessibility hierarchy because pronoun retention is not used for subjects. Therefore, Keenan and Comrie propose that the universal nature of the hierarchy can be salvaged if one interprets it as making two claims: (a) The subject will always be relativizable, and (b) a given relativization strategy will cover a contiguous portion of the hierarchy.

The second modification that has been suggested for the accessibility hierarchy is that the left-most position be defined as absolutive rather than subject. Whether this alteration can be universally applied (Fox 1987) or used only when dealing with languages that are organized on an ergative-absolutive basis remains an open question.

■ **4.3. Additional Considerations**

Two additional parameters of variation in the structure of relative clauses are examined in this section. The first is the phenomenon of **preposition stranding.** In English, when relativization of obliques occurs, the preposition associated with the relativized noun may appear in its conventional position within the adjective clause (35a) or it may be placed before the relative pronoun (35b). This latter option is called **pied-piping.**

(35) a. the man whom/that I spoke **to**

    b. the man **to** whom I spoke

Languages with prepositions that allow relativization of nouns governed by these prepositions do not always allow both options. Indeed, it is unusual to permit the stranding of prepositions as in (35a).

Another consideration in an overview of relative clauses is how to classify constructions in languages that are similar to relativization but do not share many of the typical properties. For example, many languages use a participle phrase instead of any of the canonical strategies described previously.

(36) [_____ buju-m maa-ča] etiken
            reindeer-ACC kill-PART old.man

    the old man, who killed the reindeer   (Data from Malchukov 1995)

As a nominal modifier, this participle construction from Even (Manchu-Tungusic: Russia) is quite similar to a relative clause. It could be described as a relative clause built on a gapping strategy that employs no relativizer. In general, if a language tends toward using nonfinite verbs for other embedded structures (such as adverbials and complements) then there is sufficient grounds to consider constructions such as that in (36) as a relative clause. In a language in which there is abundant use of finite clauses in embedded structures, then participial modifiers are best treated independent of relative clauses. On this basis, English nominal modifiers such as *going into to the store* in (37) would not be considered a type of relative clause.

(37) the woman [going into the store] looks like Sharon Stone.

5.0. Summary

The ability to embed clauses within other structures is one of the hallmarks of human language. By virtue of this ability, which is shared by all languages, speakers can, in principle, generate infinitely long sentences. Consider the combination of a noun + a relative clause, such as "the firefighter who saved the police officer." The relative clause itself contains the nominal *police officer,* which can also be modified by a relative clause as in "the firefighter who saved the policeman who arrested the teenager." The noun *teenager* might also be modified by a relative clause, thereby extending the initial structure to "the firefighter who saved the police officer who arrested the teenager who frustrates his parents." I could go on using such recursion to create larger and larger structures ad infinitum. Clearly, such subordination enhances the productive capacity of language in an impressive way.

In addition to noting the structural importance of subordination, it is also useful to recognize that the grammatical functions of subordinate clauses can differ. In this chapter, I have examined three of the fundamental types of subordinate clauses: complement clauses, adverbial clauses, and relative clauses. In addition to describing the difference between them, I suggested several important parameters over which these various clause types differ from language to language.

In Chapter 16, I continue to examine complex sentences. There, two further ways in which languages combine clauses, coordination and cosubordination, are discussed.

6.0. Key Terms

Adverbial clauses	Noun Phrase Accessibility Hierarchy
Apodosis	Protasis
Complement clauses	Real condition
Complementizer	Relative pronouns
Head noun	Relativized noun
Headless relative clauses	Relativizers
Matrix clause	Subordinating conjunctions
Nominalization	Subordination
(Non)restrictive relative clause	Unreal condition

Note

1. Chinese is a potential counterexample to this putative absolute universal. There is some controversy, however, as to whether Chinese should be analyzed as SVO or SOV.

16

Coordination and Cosubordination

In Chapter 15, the traditional distinction between subordination and coordination was briefly introduced. In short, subordination occurs when two clauses are combined and one of the clauses is grammatically dependent on the other. **Coordination,** on the other hand, arises when the two clauses (or other elements) are combined but neither one is embedded in or dependent on the other (Dik 1968). An example is provided in (1).

(1) Yoruba is spoken in Nigeria, and Wolof is spoken in Senegal.

The conjunction *and* signals that the two clauses are a linguistic unit, but there is no grammatical dependence between them. Indeed, they could both occur independently of one another. This is not true in the case of subordination.

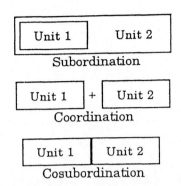

Figure 16.1. Types of Complex Sentences

   The difference between coordination and subordination has been an
integral part of linguistic theory for a long time, but it does not exhaustively
capture the range of associations that may hold between clauses. There are
also instances of complex structures that do not readily fit into either of these
categories (see C. Lehmann 1988 for an overview). Consider the following
data from Barai (Trans-New Guinea: New Guinea):

(2) Fu   fi   fase   isoe
     3S   sit   letter   write
     He sat (down) and wrote a letter.   (Data from Olson 1981)

The sentence in (2) contains two verbs, *fi* ("sit") and *isoe* ("write"). Neither
of the verbs is a semantic argument of the other. Therefore, there is no semantic
dependency nor is there embedding. Both these properties are typical of
coordination. The two verbs, however, share the same subject and are understood to have the same tense and mood. In these ways, there seems to be
dependency between them of the kind normally associated with subordination. Borrowing a term from Olson (1981), the relationship in (2) can be
described as **cosubordination.** The three-way distinction between subordination, coordination, and cosubordination has been conveniently depicted by
Foley and Van Valin (1984) in Figure 16.1.[1]
   In this chapter, I examine coordination and two kinds of cosubordinate
constructions: serial verbs (as in (2)) and switch reference.

1.0. Coordination

Coordination arises when two linguistic units are combined but there is no grammatical dependence between them. Note that this independence is structural but not necessarily semantic.

(3) Burger King opened a new restaurant on Main Street, and the traffic became unbearable.

When one interprets this sentence, a causal role is assigned to the first clause. This semantic relationship could easily be made explicit by subordinating one of the two clauses (e.g., "Because Burger King . . ."), but the use of the conjunction *and* leaves the nature of the semantic connection to inference. Some conjunctions do specify some kind of semantic relationship, such as the English words *but* and *or*. Languages differ with regard to how many conjunctions they possess and what the precise semantic range is of these conjunctions. The most common forms, however, are those that are meaningless (such as *and*), express contrast (such as *but*), and express disjunction (such as *or*).

All languages have some way to combine clauses in a manner similar to English. The details of these constructions differ, however. In the following section, some of the parameters of variation are explored. Then, attention is turned to the coordination of linguistic units that are smaller than the clause.

■ 1.1. Forms of Coordination

The two basic strategies for coordination are juxtaposition and linking devices. **Juxtaposition** consists merely of placing clauses in sequence (4 and 5).

(4) Veni, vidi, vici. [Latin (Italic)]
   I came, I saw, I conquered.

(5) John loved Jane; Jane hated John. This was a big problem for a married couple.

As the data reveal, juxtaposition is not restricted to the combination of two clauses. A comparison of (5) with the English examples in (1) and (3) also makes it clear that languages may employ more than one coordination strategy. There are languages, however, that exclusively use juxtaposition as a means of coordination. Kawaiisu (Uto-Aztecan: United States) is one such case:

(6) iga-ki-na=ina   kakari-na=ina
     enter-DIR-COMP-3S   sit-COMP-3S
     He came in and (he) sat down.

                    (Adapted from Zigmond, Booth, and Munro 1990)

As with juxtaposition, the use of **linking** devices (typically called **conjunctions**) generally requires the clauses to be contiguous. However, there is an overt morpheme signaling the coordination (7 and 8).

(7) Anoin nun   ben   **awane** mo   dabá   niar toen
     go   we   with and   you   will   he   see
     Go with us and you will see him.

                                      [Guaymi (Chibchan: Panama)]
                                        (Data from Alphonse 1956)

(8) ale   nya   thsibe thyea asa   **xe**   atha   de-a
     Ale   TOP   banjo   play   Asa   and.TOP   knife forge
     Ale was playing the banjo and Asa was forging a knife.

                                   [Lisu (Tibeto-Burman: China)]
                                        (Data from Hope 1974)

As these examples show, the linking morphemes can be quite diverse. In Guaymi (7), the conjunction appears between the two constituents it coordinates. In Lisu (8), the linker does double duty as a topic marker; if the two sentences were not conjoined, a different topic marker would be employed. Rather than being placed between the clauses, it appears after the topic of the second clause.

Because linkers can serve multiple functions, it becomes difficult to make generalizations about their typical placement relative to the clauses that they combine. It seems to be the case that when a conjunction plays no other role than to indicate coordination, it will usually fall in between the two clauses. If the linker plays an additional role, then its position is usually determined by its nonconjoining role (as in (8)).

Linkers are not always used uniquely for the task of coordination. Not uncommonly, they also serve as adpositions or case markers indicating instrumental or comitative functions.

(9) a. mɔ **nɛ** éyibí ɲwé mi
he with stick hit me
He hit me with the stick.

b. mɔ **nɛ** aní ódéfee ca
he with our chief.DEF quarreled
He quarreled with our chief.

c. ńša koáni bansrá mɔ **nɛ** amɔ nɛ ńta tumpáɲ komé ba
some people visited him and they with bottle of liquor brought
Some people came to visit him and they brought a bottle of liquor.

(Data from Frajzyngier 1974)

These data from Awutu (Niger-Congo: Ghana) each contain the morpheme *nɛ,* which is glossed either as a preposition (9a) and (9b) or a conjunction (9c). In (9a), *nɛ* indicates the tool by which the act of hitting is accomplished. That is, it flags the instrumental nominal. In (9b), the same morpheme marks a comitative nominal—the person with which the quarreling occurs. The use of *nɛ* in (9c) is an instance of coordination. The utilization of the same morpheme for these three functions has an intuitive semantic basis. In each case, the morpheme is signaling joint participation in an event.

Languages often have several conjunctions or several coordination strategies or both. As J. Payne (1985a) argues, however, it is possible to distinguish between unmarked and marked forms.[2] The unmarked form is the one that is semantically most neutral. It permits an array of interpretations depending on the context. In English, the unmarked form is *and* (10).

(10) a. John walked in the door and threw his books on the table.
b. Mary lifted John up, and he made it over the wall.
c. John cooked, and Mary cleaned.

One finds in (10) that *and* can hold different meanings, including temporal sequencing (10a), cause (10b), and contrast (10c). This is typical for unmarked conjunctions. In many languages, the linking devices are all marked forms, and juxtaposition is the unmarked strategy that can carry a range of meanings.

Marked forms, on the other hand, are more restricted in their interpretation. Consequently, they also have a more limited distribution. In English, *but* is contrastive, for example, and is not employed for temporal sequencing or causation.

In some instances, marked conjunctions can have complex form. This is true of the so-called **correlative conjunctions** in English (11).

(11) a. Mary sent **both** cookies **and** flowers to gain John's affection.

   b. **Either** John will do the dishes **or** Mary will leave the house.

The function of correlatives is to emphasize the significance of the conjuncts as individual entities while still maintaining their similarity. Thus, in (11a) the appearance of the correlative conjunction *both . . . and* highlights the fact that more than one gift was presented by Mary to accomplish her goals.

■ 1.2. Range of Constituents in Coordination

As many of the previous examples reveal, coordination is not restricted to the clause level. Smaller linguistic units can be combined, although languages vary as to which units can be combined and how they are combined. For example, Fijian (Austronesian: Fiji) uses one linker, *kei,* to combine noun phrases and a different linker, *ka,* for the coordination of other units (Dixon 1988; Payne 1985a); Hausa (West Chadic: Nigeria) has an overt linker *da* for the coordination of noun phrases but no linker for clauses (Abraham 1941).

In his review of coordination, J. Payne (1985a) discovered that when languages employ different coordination strategies depending on the type of units to be combined, the choice of strategy operates according to the following hierarchy:

Clause > verb phrase > adjective phrase > adpositional phrase > noun phrase

The tendency is for any given strategy to cover a continuous segment of the hierarchy. To better understand the claim of this hierarchy, consider a hypothetical language that possesses two strategies for coordination: (a) juxtaposition and (b) a linker that appears in between the items to be coordinated. Furthermore, these strategies cannot be applied in all situations; indeed, they are mutually exclusive. Juxtaposition arises when one wishes to combine clauses or noun phrases. The linker is employed in all other cases. Such a language violates the hierarchy because "clause" and "noun phrase," the two structures that are coordinated by juxtaposition, are not next to each other on the hierarchy.

■ 1.3. Clause Reduction

When clauses are coordinated, a particular phrase often occurs in both of the conjoined clauses (12).

(12) John is **laughing hard,** and Mary is **laughing hard** too.

Rather than repeating the phrase, it is often times possible to omit one of its occurrences (13).

(13) John is laughing hard, and Mary is too.

This process is called **clause reduction** or **ellipsis.** Whether ellipsis is allowable at all (or even which constituents can be elided) depends on the particular language under study.

(14) a. John bought a car and _____ left town.
  b. John chose a Buick and Mary _____ a Chevrolet.
  c. John likes ____ but Mary hates hatchbacks.

(15) a. Sumie wa inu o nadete _____ neko o tataita
    Sumie TOP dog ACC pat   cat ACC hit
    Sumie patted the dog and hit the cat.
  b. Sumie wa inu o nadete Taro wa _____ tataita
    Sumie TOP dog ACC pat Taro TOP   hit
    Sumie patted and Taro hit the dog.
  c. Sumie wa inu o _____ Norio wa ki o mita
    Sumie TOP dog ACC   Norio TOP tree ACC saw
    Sumie saw the dog and Norio the tree.

(Data from Mallinson and Blake 1981)

In these data, the point in the sentence at which an item has been elided is marked by a blank. In both (14a) and (14b), the gapped constituent is in the second clause, although it is a subject nominal in the former and a verb in the latter. In (14c), the ellipsis occurs in the first clause in which the direct object nominal has been gapped.

The Japanese (Japanese-Ryukyuan: Japan) data in (15) are similar. They show, respectively, the gapping of a subject, a verb, and an object. Japanese differs from English, however, in that English elides the verb of the second clause and the object of the first, whereas Japanese omits the first verb and the second object. This suggests that the direction of the reduction is based on the linear position of the particular constituent to be elided. Initial and medial constituents are omitted from the second clause. The final constituent is omitted from the first clause.

Several further typological statements about clause reduction should be noted: No language has backward (first clause) reduction only; a language will allow omissions of both objects and verbs, or neither; and languages avoid the omission of constituents either from the very beginning or from the very end of conjoined structures.

2.0. Cosubordination

Having examined the basics of coordination, I now turn to cosubordination. Recall that cosubordination occurs when two units are combined and there is dependency between them but neither structure is embedded in the other. Because of these properties, cosubordinate structures cannot easily be considered coordination or subordination. Two of the most common examples of cosubordination are serial verb constructions and switch reference. Both of these constructions are examined briefly in this section.

■ 2.1. Serial Verbs

A **serial verb construction** is composed of multiple finite verbs that are not conjoined, as in (16).

(16) ó   mú   ìwé   wá
      he   took   book   came

He brought the book.   (Data from Bamgboṣe 1974)

For present purposes, assume that the Yoruba (Niger-Congo: Nigeria) sentence in (16) contains two clauses, one headed by the verb *mú* ("took") and one headed by the verb *wá* ("came"). The example displays a common feature of serial verb constructions—namely, that the two clauses share a subject. They do not, however, share all arguments. In (16), *ìwé* ("book") is the object of *mú,* but it finds no place in the argument structure of the intransitive verb *wá*. Thus, the constituency of (16) can be represented as follows:

(17) [ó [mú ìwé] [wá]]

It is also common to find serial sentences in which there is no overt subject in the second clause because this subject is coreferent with an object of the first clause.

(18) **Olú   tèlé**   *Ayo   lo   oja*
     Olu   followed   Ayo   went   market
     Olu accompanied Ayo to the market.   (Data from Lawal 1983)

In (18), Ayo can be taken as the object of *tèlé,* in which case it appears to form a unit with the first clause (in bold type), or it can be taken as the subject of *lo,* in which case it appears to form a unit with the second clause (in italics).

Although in (16) the clauses shared a subject, and in (18) the object of the first clause was essentially acting as the subject of the second clause, it is also possible for two transitive verbs to share multiple arguments, as in (19).

(19) Olú   gún   íyan   je
     Olu   pounded   yam   ate
     Olu made and ate pounded yam.

In this sentence, *Olú* acts as the semantic subject of both verbs and *íyan* acts as the semantic object.

In each of these serial verb constructions, it is as if the two clauses have been compressed rather than coordinated, which is typical of this kind of cosubordination.

Serialization often puts restrictions on the distribution of certain verbal categories. One common pattern is that verbs in noninitial clauses receive no person marking. In some languages, verbs in serial sentences must have the same tense and aspect throughout. One such example is Akan (Niger-Congo: Ghana):

(20) a. mekɔɔ   mebaae
        I.went   I.came
        I went and came back.
     b. *mekɔɔ   maba
        I.went   I.have.come.
        I went and have come back.   (Data from Schacter 1974)

The restriction that serial verbs carry the same tense-aspect renders (20a) grammatical but (20b) ungrammatical. Like the sharing of arguments, the requirement on parallel use of verbal categories is indicative of the mutual dependence of the clauses in cosubordination. Note that no such constraint on tense and aspect holds in coordinate structures in Akan.

(21) mekɔɔ   na   maba
     I.went   and   I.have.come
     I went and have come back.

■ 2.2. Switch Reference

Switch-reference systems track whether the subject of a given clause is carried over into a second clause (22a) or whether a new subject is used in the second clause (22b).

(22) a. Artwe   alyelhe-me-**le**   petye-me
        man-NOM   sing-(non)PST.PROG-SS   come-(non)PST.PROG
        The man is coming singing.
     b. Artwe   alyelhe-(me)-**rlenge**   ayenge   petye-me
        man-NOM   sing-((non)PST.PROG)-DS   1S.NOM   come-(non)PST.PROG
        I'm coming while the man is singing.   (Data from Wilkins 1988)

The Arrernte (Pama-Nyungan: Australia) sentence in (22a) exemplifies same-subject marking (glossed as SS). The suffix -le appears on the first verb, indicating that the subject of the second verb is identical. Alternatively, the suffix -*rlenge* marks a change of subject between the two clauses in the second sentence.

In some ways, switch reference seems simply to be a special case of coordination. Two clauses are combined, and the linker stipulates information in addition to the coordination. There is often, however, a restriction placed on the use of verbal categories very much like what was shown for serial constructions in the preceding section. In the Arrernte data, for example, both the verbs appear marked for tense. The absolute tense for the entire sentence, however, is determined by the tense affix on the second verb. Rather than being taken absolutely, the tense of the first verb is taken relative to that of the second. Thus, if one wants to indicate that the event of the first verb occurs prior to that of the second verb, a different tense suffix is employed.

(23) Nhenhe-le   re   arlkwe-ke-le   inte-ke-rlke
     here-LOC   3S.ERG   eat-PST.COMPLT-SS lie-PST.COMPLT-too
     This is where it ate and then slept as well.

The fact that the eating and sleeping happened in the past is revealed by the past completive suffix on the second verb, *inte-* ("lie"). The use of the past completive on the first verb indicates that the act of eating was prior to sleeping. Such interaction between tense markers, which is absent in coordination, is indicative that the switch-reference sentence is an example of cosubordination.

The markers for same-subject and different-subject marking are almost always associated with the verb in switch-reference systems. Some instances of sentential particles used for switch reference, however, have been found. For example, the language Daga (Trans-New Guinea: New Guinea) employs the suffix -*wa* at the end of a noun phrase to signal different subjects (Murane 1974).

Unlike the Arrernte data in (22), there is not always a pair of morphemes dedicated to the switch-reference system but rather a single marker for different subjects. In these cases, unmarked clauses are typically used as an indication of same subject.

Switch-reference languages tend to be subject-object-verb (SOV), although some are verb initial. The constituent order (OV or VO) determines which clause contains the morpheme signaling same or different subjects.

Example (24):
a. tommeke   ma   ʔyomasi
   it.wasn't.warm DS I.didn't.drink.it
   Since it (beverage) wasn't warm, I didn't drink it.
b. ʔap kiʔ toXi ma yopaʔit
   deer the it.died DS it.was.eaten
   Whenever a deer died, it was eaten.   (Data from Marlett 1984)

Example (25):
a. [Oky ramo] ava-ve rei nd-o-o-i
   rain DS   man-none badly NEG-3-go-NEG
   Since it was raining, no one went.
b. Yvytu [oky vy e'ỹ]
   wind   rain SS NEG
   The wind blew, but not because of rain   (Data from Dooley 1989)

Typically, in SOV languages, the earlier clause is so marked, and vice versa in VO languages (see Haiman and Munro 1983 and papers therein).

There are two issues in particular that can complicate what seems to be a fairly straightforward switch-reference construction. First, languages do not always use switch reference to encode subject (dis)continuation. Sometimes, instead, the marking indicates whether an overall topic, rather than the local subject, continues to be the same or is different. On a similar note, some languages seem to be sensitive to the notion subject but at an abstract level. This is the case in Seri (Hokan: Mexico):

(24) a. tommeke   ma   ʔyomasi
        it.wasn't.warm   DS   I.didn't.drink.it
        Since it (beverage) wasn't warm, I didn't drink it.
     b. ʔap   kiʔ   toXi   ma   yopaʔit
        deer   the   it.died   DS   it.was.eaten
        Whenever a deer died, it was eaten.   (Data from Marlett 1984)

In (24a), we see the expected marking to indicate a different subject. In (24b), however, where the two surface subjects are coreferent, there is still different-subject marking. According to Marlett (1984), this is because at an abstract level the subject of the second clause is something other than "deer."

An additional complicating variable that can enter into switch-reference systems is how they treat subjects that are not fully coreferent but are semantically associated in some way. For instance, the "empty" subject of meteorological verbs in Guarani (Equatorial-Tucanoan: Brazil) can trigger unexpected marking (25).

(25) a. [Oky   ramo]   ava-ve   rei   nd-o-o-i
        rain   DS   man-none   badly   NEG-3-go-NEG
        Since it was raining, no one went.
     b. Yvytu   [oky   vy   e'ỹ]
        wind   rain   SS   NEG
        The wind blew, but not because of rain   (Data from Dooley 1989)

In (25a), because there is clearly no coreference between the subjects of the two clauses, different-subject marking is found. In (25b), however, the dummy subjects of the two clauses trigger same-subject agreement!

Similarly, languages differ with respect to how they mark clauses with subjects that are partially coreferent. Guarani represents one possibility:

(26) a. [Pe-ro-via   e'ỹ   rã]   ja-je'oi-pa   tema
        2S-COM-believe NEG   DS   1+2-go-P-all   persistently
        If you don't believe it, let's go [and see].

   b. [jo-guer-aa ma   t-ape   rupi   ramo] ka'i   jagua pe   aipo-e-'i . . .
      RCP-COM-go already NPOSSD-path along DS   monkey dog   DAT ATTN-3-say
      As they [the dog and the monkey] were going along with each other
         along the road, the monkey said to the dog . . .

In the first sentence (26a), the subject referent ("you") of the first clause is included within the subject referent of the second ("we"), but different-subject marking is used. The same is true of (26b), in which the second referent is included in the first.

3.0. Summary

In this chapter, I have offered general comments on two methods of combining clauses—coordination and cosubordination. The former is the familiar process whereby two (or more) constituents are combined into a single larger unit in which neither constituent is grammatically dominant. Several fascinating properties of coordination emerge when examined from a cross-linguistic perspective. Among other properties, languages vary as to which constituents they allow to be coordinated, and they vary in the types of mechanisms they dedicate to coordination.

Cosubordination constitutes a kind of middle ground between coordination and subordination (which was discussed in Chapter 15). In cosubordination, two elements are combined, neither one fully dependent on the other but having a mutual grammatical dependence. Two linguistic phenomena, serial verbs and switch reference, were examined that exemplify cosubordination, but they do not exhaust the full range of structures that fall under this rubric (see Foley and Van Valin 1984; Van Valin 1993b).

4.0. Key Terms

Clause reduction	Ellipsis
Conjunctions	Juxtaposition
Coordination	Linking
Correlative conjunctions	Serial verb construction
Cosubordination	Switch reference

Notes

1. Foley and Van Valin (1984) and Van Valin (1993b) use the features of dependency and embedding to define the three types: subordination is [+dependent, +embedded], coordination is [–dependent, –embedded], and cosubordination is [+dependent, –embedded]. The fourth possible combination of features apparently does not exist (although see Watters 1993). Note that I have not followed them fully in recounting the various complex clause types. In particular, I included adverbial clauses in the discussion on subordination in Chapter 15. Adverbial clauses, however, are not embedded structures, and for this reason they would be an instance of cosubordination or coordination (depending on the kind of adverbial clause under consideration) in the scheme depicted by Diagram 15.1. I depart from Foley and Van Valin entirely for convenience because adverbial clauses have traditionally been treated under the rubric of subordination.

2. The terms *marked* and *unmarked* are used here because they are found in J. Payne (1985a). It is clear, however, that Payne is not using them in the traditional sense, but rather to mean something akin to semantically "non-neutral" and "neutral," respectively.

GLOSSARY

Absolute Tense. Temporal reference established on the basis of the tense marking within a single clause—for example, "Rupert coughed" is an instance of absolute tense because the past time reference can be determined without reference to any tense marking that occurs outside the clause. Absolute tense contrasts with relative tense.

Absolute Universal. A property of linguistic structure that is not counterexemplified in any language.

Absolutive. A grammatical relation that subsumes S and P, where S is equivalent to the subject of an intransitive clause, and P is equivalent to the direct object of a transitive clause.

Accomplishment. A type of predicate that is characterized by causative semantics—for example, *bury* ("cause to be buried") and *kill* ("cause to die").

Accusative-Focus. A case system in which P, the sole verbal argument in an intransitive clause, is treated distinctly from the two arguments of a transitive clause.

Achievement. A type of predicate that indicates a change of state or dynamic circumstances such as *die* or *learn.*

Activity. A type of predicate that indicates a dynamic event in which there is no change of state such as *sing* and *run.*

Adverbial Clause. A subordinate clause which provides a situational context for the event or state that is described in a main clause. An adverbial clause is dependent on a main clause, but it is not embedded within it.

Affixal Language. A language that permits a series of morphemes to be affixed to a lexical head (i.e., a verb, noun, or adjective). Affixal languages (also called synthetic languages) contrast with isolating languages.

Agent. A semantic role for an entity that is instigating an action. *Smokey* is the agent in the sentence "Smokey lit the fire."

Agglutinative Language. A language in which strings of morphemes occurring within a word are easily segmentable. Agglutinative languages contrast with fusional languages.

Agreement. A morphological relationship between two or more constituents in which the syntactically dependent constituents are placed in a form that corresponds to that of the head.

Aktionsart. An inherent or lexical aspect of verbs. See also **achievement, activity, accomplishment,** and **state.**

Anterior. An aspect that signifies a past event with present relevance. It is also referred to as "perfect." Because of the deictic nature of anterior aspect, many linguists treat it as a tense instead.

Anticausative. A valence-decreasing device which detransitivizes a transitive verb that has causal semantics.

Antipassive. A valence-decreasing device which demotes the object of a transitive verb, thereby detransitivizing it.

Apodosis. The "then clause" of an "If . . . then . . ." conditional sentence. The "if clause" is referred to as the **protasis.**

Applicative. A valence-increasing device that encodes an oblique nominal as an object of the verb. The resultant construction is often referred to as an applied construction.

Applied Constructions. See **applicative.**

Arguments. Elements that play a central role in the proposition laid forth by a verb. In the sentence, "Heather lost the money," the nominals *Heather* and *the money* are both arguments because the verb *lose* requires expression of both an entity that does the losing and an entity that is being lost.

Aspect. A grammatical category used to depict the internal temporal structure of a situation.

Atelic. A term used to describe the aspect of events that have no inherent end point—for example, *read* and *swim*. Atelic contrasts with telic.

Bound Morpheme. A morpheme that cannot stand alone but rather must co-occur within a word with another morpheme.

Case. Morphological marking that establishes the grammatical relation and or semantic role that a nominal bears to the clause in which it occurs.

Causative Construction. A linguistic device by which the relationship between two events is explicitly captured within a single clause. For example, "The professor made her students cry" is a causative construction involving (a) the students' crying and (b) the professor's acting to bring about the crying.

Causative constructions differ in whether they depict "direct causation" (situations in which the actions of the causer have immediate impact on the actions of the causee) or "indirect causation."

Circumfixes. Morphemes consisting of two or more parts that are separated by intervening material (affixes or roots).

Clause Reduction. See **ellipsis.**

Closed Class. A lexical class in which membership is basically fixed. In English, for instance, prepositions are a closed class because novel prepositions cannot be created except in extremely limited circumstances. Closed class contrasts with open class.

Complement Clause. A clause that functions as an argument of the clause in which it is embedded.

Complementizer. A formal element that marks the subordinate relationship that a complement clause holds to a main clause.

Completive. An aspectual notion used to describe an event that has a clear terminal point—for example, *shatter* or *explode.*

Complex Implicational Universal. See **implicational universal.**

Concessive Clause. A subordinate clause that reflects contrast of some kind with the main clause. For example, the adverbial clause in "Although Blake is five years old, he can drive a car" is a concessive clause.

Conjunction. A formal item or process that functions to coordinate like constituents.

Content Interrogative. A question that requests a particular piece of information rather than the truth value of a proposition. Content interrogatives employ question words (such as *who, how,* and *why*) to elicit information—for example, "Who won the Kentucky Derby?" Content interrogatives contrast with polar interrogatives.

Continuous Aspect. See **imperfective.**

Coordination. The creation of a structure that combines two or more clauses (or other elements), neither of which is embedded in or dependent on the other.

Correlative Conjunction. A coordination strategy that involves two (or more) conjunctive elements operating together—for example, *neither . . . nor* or *both . . . and.*

Cosubordination. The combination of two formal elements that creates a dependency relationship between them but with neither element dependent on the other. Serial verb structures often exemplify cosubordination.

Dative Shift. A realignment of the grammatical relations of a ditransitive verb without altering its valency. Dative shift has occurred in the sentence "Christine sent her husband a box of chocolates," in which both postverbal nominals appear to be direct objects. In the corresponding sentence, "Christine sent a box of chocolates to her husband," the distinct grammatical relationship of *her husband* is indicated by the preposition *to.*

Declarative Sentence. A sentence that expresses a statement. Because the verbs of declarative sentences often have a distinct form from those in other sentence types (such as imperatives), declarative is also considered a mood.

Definiteness. A semantic property of nominals that indicates reference to a specific identifiable entity.

Deixis. The anchoring of a sentence to its immediate context. Deictic words, such as *here, now,* and *he,* do not have a set reference but vary in meaning depending on the context in which they arise.

Deontic Modality. That realm of meaning concerned with obligation and permission. Deontic modality contrasts with epistemic modality. Deontic modality is often signaled through mood affixes or modal auxiliaries.

Dependent. An intuitive term used in linguistic analysis to identify those elements in a construction that are licensed by a head or modify a head.

Dependent Marking. The morphological marking of a head-dependent relationship in which the marking occurs on the dependent element. Dependent marking contrasts with head marking. See also **double marking** and **split marking.**

Derivational Morpheme. A bound morpheme that alters the lexical class of the stem to which it attaches or otherwise modifies the semantics of the stem in a significant manner. For example, *-al* can be suffixed to a noun to derive a verb as in *nation-national.* Derivational morphology contrasts with inflectional morphology.

Diachronic. Looking at how language changes over the course of time. Diachronic contrasts with synchronic.

Discontinuous Constituents. Elements of the same phrase that do not appear adjacent to each other because material from a different phrase (or phrases) intervenes. In the sentence, "I met a guy yesterday at school who said he had never been to the library," the noun *guy* and the relative clause *who said he had never been to the library* are discontinuous constituents. Intuitively, they are both members of the same noun phrase, but they are separated by *yesterday at school.*

Ditransitive. A clause in which the verb has both an indirect object and a direct object.

Double Marking. The morphological marking of a head-dependent relationship in which the marking occurs on both the dependent element and the head element. See also **dependent marking** and **split marking.**

Dummy Subject. A pronominal subject that has no actual reference, such as *It* in "It is raining."

Durative. An aspectual notion used to describe events that continue for a certain period of time—for example, the verb *to sail* necessarily refers to an event that is extended in time. It cannot occur instantaneously. Durative contrasts with punctual.

Ellipsis. The omission of part of a structure that is recoverable from the context. Ellipsis is often employed in the coordination of clauses. In the sentence, "I like to wash and Mary likes to break dishes," the direct object of the verb *wash* has undergone ellipsis.

Epistemic Modality. That realm of meaning concerned with the degrees of possibility that a proposition is true or false. Epistemic modality contrasts with deontic modality. It is often marked in language with mood affixes or with modal auxiliaries.

Ergative. A grammatical relation that subsumes A, where A is equivalent to the subject of a transitive clause. The term is also used for case markers that mark A. Ergative contrasts with nominative.

Ergative-Absolutive. A case system in which S and P are marked in the same way, but differently from A, where S is the sole argument of an intransitive predicate, A is equivalent to the subject of a transitive predicate, and P is equivalent to the object of a transitive predicate.

Evidentials. A set of verbal markers that convey the quality of information on which an assertion is based.

External Explanation. An explanation of linguistic structure that draws on considerations outside the language system.

Free Morpheme. A morpheme that is not phonologically dependent on any other morpheme. Free morphemes contrast with bound morphemes.

Fusional Language. A language in which the boundaries between morphemes are hard to determine. A fusional language contrasts with an agglutinative language.

Gender. A semantic property of a nominal used to indicate the real-world gender of its referent. The term gender can also be used more broadly to refer to a nominal class that has little or nothing to do with the actual gender of its referent.

Genus. Very roughly, a language family in which the genetic affiliations between members can be fairly loose. The plural is "genera."

Government. A syntactic relationship between two constituents in which one constituent (the head) determines the morphological marking that occurs on the second (the dependent). The marking does not encode any semantic information about the head.

Grammatical Relation. The morphosyntactically signaled function a constituent plays in the grammar of a clause.

Grammaticalization. A process of language change by which a free lexical morpheme becomes semantically generalized and phonologically reduced.

Head. An intuitive notion in linguistic analysis used to describe the central element in a construction. The head is usually an obligatory element.

Head Marking. The morphological marking of a head-dependent relationship in which the marking occurs on the head element. Head marking contrasts with dependent marking.

Headless Relative Clause. A relative clause that does not appear to modify any noun.

Heavy Constituent Principle. The functional principle that heavy constituents (those that contain a large number of grammatical elements) tend to be placed after the head that they modify.

Highly Informative. A textual entity that bears a significant amount of semantic content relative to other entities in the surrounding discourse context. Highly informative elements tend to be placed toward the beginning of the clauses in which they occur.

Holistic Typology. The classification of languages as wholes on the basis of a significant linguistic feature (or features).

Imperative Sentence. A sentence that expresses a command. Because the verbs of imperative sentences often have a distinct form from those in other sentence types (such as declaratives), imperative is also considered a mood.

Imperfective. An aspectual category that is employed to make reference to the internal structure of an event. Imperfective contrasts with perfective. Imperfective aspect is also commonly referred to as **continuous** or **progressive,** although there have been recent attempts to distinguish between these three labels.

Implicational Universal. A universal that relates two properties of language by using one property as a precondition for the other. Such universals can be put in the form "if X, then Y." More than one precondition can be used (If X, then if Y, then Z), in which case the statement is called a **complex implicational universal.**

In Situ. A term used to refer to the location of question words that do not move to the front of the sentence but remain in their "normal" structural position—for example, the word *what* in the question "John put his signature on what?" remains **in situ.**

Inceptive. An aspectual notion used to highlight the beginning of an event.

Independent Language Sample. A sample which contains languages that bear only very distant or no genetic relationship and are not from the same geographic region.

Index of Fusion. A measure of the ease with which individual morphemes can be segmented from others in a language.

Index of Synthesis. A measure for the amount of affixation that occurs in an individual language.

Indicative Sentence. A sentence that asserts the truth of some proposition. Traditionally, the term *indicative* has been used to capture the similarity of interrogative and declarative sentences so that they can be set off against other sentence types, such as imperatives. Because the verbs of indicative sentences often have a distinct form from those in other sentence types (such as imperatives), indicative is also considered a mood.

Indirect Speech Act. A sentence which is used in a manner that does not directly follow from its form. For instance, when one frames a sentence in the form of a question (such as "Can you take out the garbage?") to modify the behavior of an interlocutor and not to elicit information, one has just engaged in an indirect speech act.

Infix. A morpheme that is affixed by placing it entirely within a root.

Inflectional Language. A language that permits a great deal of affixation but without a one-to-one correspondence between affixes and the semantic information being indicated. Generally, the term **inflectional language** is used in the same way as **fusional language.**

Inflectional Morpheme. Affixes that indicate grammatical relationships. Inflectional morphology contrasts with derivational morphology.

Internal Explanation. An explanation of universals based on properties of language systems themselves.

Interrogative Sentence. A sentence that is designed to elicit information. Interrogative is also considered a mood in some cases. In English, interrogatives are marked by **inversion**—the rearrangement of auxiliary verbs and subjects. For example, "Does everyone know what time it is?" has the auxiliary *does* placed before the subject. This order is a departure from what one finds in other sentence types.

Intransitive. A clause in which the verb does not have a direct object.

Inversion. See **interrogative.**

Irrealis. A term used to depict situations that are not or not yet a reality, only possibilities.

Isolating Language. A language that does not generally combine more than one morpheme into a word.

Iterative. An aspectual term that refers to an event that takes place repeatedly—for example, "I was coughing all night" (the act of coughing occurs repeatedly).

Juxtaposition. A strategy for coordination of clauses that consists of simply placing the clauses in sequence.

Left-Branching Structure. A consituent in which a structurally complex element occurs to the left of a noncomplex element. For example, the construction "my friend's parents" is left branching because the unit *my friend's,* which has internal structure, is to the left of *parents.* Right-branching represents the opposite scenario—the structurally more complex unit appears to the right of the less complex unit—for example, "Parents of my friend" is right branching because the unit with internal structure, *of my friend,* is to the right of *parents.*

Lexical Aspect. See **Aktionsart.**

Lexical Class. A category of words, such as nouns or verbs, that share certain semantic, morphological, or syntactic properties, or all three. Lexical classes are also called **parts of speech.**

Lexical Semantics. The meaning of words and units smaller than words.

Linguistic Areas. Regions where languages share linguistic features due to sustained contact for long periods of time.

Marked. A comparative term that indicates the unit that bears greater formal substance. For example, in the pair *cat-cats* the plural is the marked element because it has an extra morpheme. Conversely, *cat* is unmarked. These terms are also utilized more broadly to refer to a default structure (unmarked) versus a structure that appears in limited circumstances (marked). In this broader sense, markedness is often based on pragmatic considerations.

Matrix Clause. A main clause. Matrix clauses contrast with embedded clauses.

Modality. The semantic realm concerned with attitudes toward events—that is, their necessity, likelihood, actuality, and so on. See also **mood.**

Mood. A grammatical category that expresses speakers' assertions about propositions—for example, whether the propositions can, do, or should occur. Mood is usually indicated by affixes or modal auxiliaries. Typical inflectional categories of mood are **optative** and **subjunctive.**

Morpheme. The minimal unit bearing meaning in language.

Negative. A grammatical category employed to deny the actuality of a proposition or some portion thereof.

Neutral System. A case system in which there is no morphosyntactic differentiation between S, A, and P, where S is the sole argument of an intransitive clause, A is equivalent to the subject of a transitive clause, and P is equivalent to an object of a transitive clause.

No Structure Language. Languages in which very little, if any, affixation is used. The term *no structure language* is equivalent to *isolating language.*

Nominal. A term used for a category that contains nouns, pronouns, and noun phrases.

Nominalization. The transformation of a stem into a nominal from some other lexical class.

Nominative-Accusative. A case system in which S and A are encoded the same way, where S is the single argument of an intransitive clause and A is equivalent to the subject of a transitive clause.

Nonabsolute Universal. A property of languages that usually holds true and, therefore, represents a significant tendency for languages generally.

Nonrestrictive Relative Clause. See **restrictive relative clause.**

Noun Classifier. A morpheme that functions to indicate the semantic class of a noun.

Noun Incorporation. The affixation of a noun root to a verbal stem.

Noun Phrase Accessibility Hierarchy. A proposal that there is an implicational relationship among grammatical relations in terms of whether they can be relativized or not. The implicational relationship is set up as a hierarchy: subject < direct object < indirect object < oblique.

Open Class. A lexical class in which membership is in principle unlimited. Nouns and verbs are probably open classes in all languages.

Optative. A mood category that is typically used to express desires and hopes.

Parameters. The principled differences that exist among languages.

Part of Speech. See **lexical class.**

Partial Typology. Classification of specific features of languages rather than languages as wholes.

Patient. A semantic role that indicates the entity being directly affected by the action of the verb.

Perfect. See **anterior.**

Perfective. An aspectual category that is employed to express an event as a bounded point in time. Perfective contrasts with imperfective.

Periphrastic Construction. A construction in which multiple verb forms are used to express what can commonly be expressed by a single verb in conjunction with affixes.

Pied-Piping. The phenomenon in which adpositions are fronted together with a question word in interrogative sentences and relative clauses. For example, pied-piping occurs in "To whom did you speak?" The construction contrasts with preposition stranding, which leaves the preposition in situ: "Whom did you speak to?"

Polar Interrogative. A question that is framed such that the minimally expected answer is "yes" or "no." As such, polar interrogatives do not involve question words. Polar interrogatives contrast with content interrogatives.

Portmanteau Morpheme. A single formal unit that signals two (or more) distinct semantic categories.

Pragmatically Marked. See **marked.**

Predication. A semantic function that involves describing the behavior or properties of objects. Verbs are generally thought to be involved in predication as are adjectives.

Prefix. A bound morpheme that is affixed to the front of a root.

Preposition Stranding. See **pied-piping.**

Pro-Drop. Dropping the pronominal subject of a language because the information can be determined by agreement morphology on the verb.

Progressive. See **imperfective.**

Prohibitive. A negative command—for example, "Don't take candy from a baby!"

Prosody. A phonological term that refers to pitch and intonation.

Protasis. See **apodosis.**

Prototype. An ideal example of a category.

Punctual. An aspectual term used to describe an event that happens instantaneously rather than being extended in time: *blink, snap,* and so on.

Purposive. A semantic role which describes the element that provides the reason why an event occurs.

Real Condition. A condition that could potentially be fulfilled—"If Bill sees you tomorrow . . ."

Realis. A term used to depict situations that a speaker judges to be or to have been actual events.

Reduplication. A type of morphological marking in which the form of the affix is determined by repetition of part or all of the root.

Reference. The semantic function of naming objects in the real world.

Relative Clause. A clause that modifies a noun, much in the same way that an adjective does. For example, "the woman *whom I love.*"

Relative Tense. Temporal reference of a clause established on the basis of tense marking that occurs outside of the clause. For example, the participle *running* is not directly marked for tense, but when it occurs as part of an adverbial expression, "Running down the street, we saw several drug dealers," it is immediately recognized that the running took place in the past. We know this because the main verb is in past tense.

Relativizer. A formal element that serves to signal the dependency of a relative clause. The word *that* can be used as a relativizer in English, as in "the hamburger that Ronald ate."

Restrictive Relative Clause. A relative clause that serves to restrict the possible reference of the noun it modifies—for example, with respect to the noun phrase *the man*, there is a massive number of people in the world that the noun *man* might refer to. The addition of a relative clause ("the man who is from Arkansas") narrows these possibilities significantly. Hence, it is restrictive. **Nonrestrictive relative clauses** are those that provide supplementary information about a nominal but do not narrow the potential reference, as in "President Clinton, who is from Arkansas."

Right-Branching Structure. See **left-branching structure.**

Root. The core element of a word. It carries the heaviest semantic load and places restrictions on what kinds of morphemes, if any, may be affixed to it.

Sample. The set of languages used for a particular research project.

Scope. A term that indicates the part of a sentence affected by the meaning of a particular form, such as a negative.

Semantic Role. The semantic relationship that a nominal bears to the rest of the clause. Common semantic roles include agent, patient, locative, and benefactive.

Serial Verb Construction. Multiple finite verbs that are used in sequence and are not conjoined.

Sociocentric Orientation. The notion that speakers and writers tend to place most importance on themselves and those listening to them.

Speech Act. An act of communication defined in terms of the functions its speaker intends for it.

Split Ergativity. A morphosyntactic system that operates either on a nominative-accusative basis or an ergative-absolutive basis. The split between the two systems can occur across components in the grammar (e.g., pronouns being treated in one way and nouns in another), on the basis of tense, or in other ways.

Split Intransitivity. A morphosyntactic system that encodes the single argument of an intransitive clause either as a subject or as an absolutive depending on the verb that heads the clause.

Split Marking. A language that contains roughly equal numbers of dependent-marking and head-marking constructions.

Sprachbund. A geographic area in which languages from different language families share a linguistic feature (or features) that is not found in all of the language families represented.

State. A type of predicate that denotes properties or nondynamic circumstances— for example, *be sad, perceive,* and so on.

Stative. An aspectual term used to describe states of existence or mental processes.

Subjunctive. A mood category used to express an attitude of uncertainty on the part of the speaker or a hypothetical situation.

Subordinating Conjunctions. An overt marker that signals the subordinate status of adverbial clauses or phrases.

Subordination. The combination of units such that one is dependent on the other.

Suffix. A bound morpheme that is affixed to the end of a root.

Suppletion. A morphological term used to describe a situation in which two morphemes have obvious semantic affinity but no formal connection—for example, *go-went.*

Suprafix. The use of suprasegmental elements, such as tone or stress, to manipulate the meaning of a root. For example, *cónvict* is a noun, but with stress on the second syllable (*convíct*) it is a verb.

Switch Reference. A system of clause combining that includes an indication of whether the clauses share the same subject or whether there has been a switch in subject from one clause to the next.

Synchronic. Looking at a language at a single stage in its development. Synchronic contrasts with diachronic.

Synthetic Language. A language in which there is abundant use of affixation. Synthetic languages contrast with isolating languages.

Tag Question. A specialized form of a question that is added to the end of a statement and that typically involves an auxiliary verb and a pronoun. For example, "Sally Ride was a great astronaut, wasn't she?" A tag question generally presupposes the answer.

Telic. A term used to describe the aspect of events that have an inherent end point—for example, *cough, snap,* and so on. Telic contrasts with atelic.

Temporal. A semantic role describing nominals that establish when an event occurred.

Tense. A grammatical category which is used to express the temporal relationship that a proposition has to the moment of speech or some other time.

Time Stability. A proposal that concepts tend to be lexicalized according to their likelihood to persist through time. Temporally stable concepts (*mountain*) are lexicalized as nouns, whereas temporally unstable concepts (*weep*) are lexicalized as verbs.

Transitive. A clause in which the verb has a direct object.

Tripartite. A morphosyntactic system in which S, A, and P all receive unique treatment, where S is the sole argument of an intransitive verb, A is equivalent to the subject of a transitive verb, and P is equivalent to the object of a transitive verb. See also **nominative-accusative** and **ergative-absolutive.**

Unmarked. See **marked.**

Unreal Condition. A condition that cannot be fulfilled. It is either hypothetical or counterfactual—for example, the "if clause" in "If I were the President, I would declare it National Typology Week."

Yes-No Questions. See **polar interrogatives.**

REFERENCES

Abraham, Roy Clive. 1941. *A Modern Grammar of Spoken Hausa.* London: Crown Agents for the Colonies.

Aikhenwald, Alexandra. 1995. *Bare.* Languages of the World 100. München-Newcastle: Lincom Europa.

Allan, Keith. 1977. "Classifiers." *Language* 53: 284-310.

Allen, Barbara J., Donna B. Gardiner, and Donald G. Frantz. 1984. "Noun Incorporation in Southern Tiwa." *International Journal of American Linguistics* 50: 292-311.

Allen, Barbara J., Donald G. Frantz, Donna B. Gardiner, and David M. Perlmutter. 1990. "Possessor Ascension and Syntactic Levels in Southern Tiwa." *Studies in Relational Grammar 3.* Eds. P. M. Postal and B. D. Joseph. Chicago: U Chicago P. 321-83.

Allen, W. Sidney. 1956. "Structure and System in the Abaza Verbal Complex." *Transactions of the Philological Society* 1956: 127-76.

Alphonse, Ephraim S. 1956. *Guaymi Grammar and Dictionary.* Washington, DC: GPO.

Anderson, Stephen R. 1992. *A-Morphous Morphology.* Cambridge Studies in Linguistics 62. Cambridge, UK: Cambridge UP.

Baker, Mark C. 1988. *Incorporation: A Theory of Grammatical Function Changing.* Chicago: U Chicago P.

Bamgboṣe, Ayo. 1974. "On Serial Verbs and Verbal Status." *Journal of West African Languages* 9: 17-48.

Barnes, Janet. 1984. "Evidentials in the Tuyuca Verb." *International Journal of American Linguistics* 50: 255-71.

Bell, Alan. 1978. "Language Samples." Greenberg, Ferguson, and Moravcsik vol. 4, 123-56.

Berinstein, Ava. 1990. "On Distinguishing Surface Datives in K'ekchi." Postal and Joseph 3-48.

Berlin, Brent, and Paul Kay. 1969. *Basic Color Terms: Their Universality and Evolution.* Berkeley: U of California P.

Bhat, D. N. S. 1991. *Grammatical Relations: The Evidence Against Their Necessity and Universality.* New York: Routledge.

293

————. 1994. *The Adjectival Category.* Studies in Language Companion Series 24. Philadelphia: Benjamins.

Bickford, J. Albert. 1988. "The Semantics and Morphology of Mixtec Mood and Aspect." *Work Papers of the Summer Institute of Linguistics.* Vol. 32. North Dakota: Summer Institute of Linguistics. 1-39.

Binnick, Robert I. 1979. *Modern Mongolian: A Transformational Syntax.* Toronto: U of Toronto P.

Bird, Charles. 1968. "Relative Clauses in Bambara." *Journal of West African Languages* 5: 35-47.

Björkhagen, Im. 1962. *Modern Swedish Grammar.* Norstedts: Svenska Bokförlaget.

Blake, Barry. 1990. *Relational Grammar.* New York: Routledge.

————. 1994. *Case.* Cambridge Textbooks in Linguistics. Cambridge, UK: Cambridge UP.

Bloomfield, Leonard. 1933. *Language.* New York: Holt, Rinehart & Winston. Chicago: U of Chicago P, 1984.

Boas, Franz, and Ella Deloria. 1941. *Dakhota Grammar.* Memoirs of the National Academy of Sciences XXIII. Washington, DC: National Academy of Sciences.

Brown, Roger Langham. 1967. *Wilhelm von Humboldt's Conception of Linguistic Relativity.* Janua Linguarum, Series Minor 65. The Hague: Mouton.

Butterworth, Brian, Bernard Comrie, and Östen Dahl, eds. 1984. *Explanations for Language Universals.* Berlin: Mouton. (Published simultaneously as vol. 21-1 of *Linguistics*)

Bybee, Joan. 1985. *Morphology.* Amsterdam: Benjamins.

Bybee, Joan, William Pagliuca, and Revere Perkins. 1990. "On the Asymmetries in the Affixation of Grammatical Material." Croft, Denning, and Kemmer 1-42.

Bybee, Joan, Revere Perkins, and William Pagliuca. 1994. *The Evolution of Grammar: Tense, Aspect and Modality in the Languages of the World.* Chicago: U of Chicago P.

Bynon, Theodora. 1977. *Historical Linguistics.* Cambridge Textbooks in Linguistics. Cambridge, UK: Cambridge UP.

Campbell, Lyle, Vit Bubenik, and Leslie Saxon. 1988. "Word Order Universals: Refinements and Clarifications." *Canadian Journal of Linguistics* 33: 209-30.

Chafe, Wallace L. 1976. "Givenness, Contrastiveness, Definiteness, Subjects, Topics, and Point of View." Li 25-56.

————. 1987. "Cognitive Constraints on Information Flow." Tomlin 21-51.

————. 1994. *Discourse, Consciousness, and Time.* Chicago: U of Chicago P.

Charney, Jean Ormsbee. 1993. *A Grammar of Comanche.* Lincoln: U of Nebraska.

Chomsky, Noam. 1957. *Syntactic Structures.* Janua Linguarum, Series Minor 4. The Hague: Mouton.

————. 1965. *Aspects of the Theory of Syntax.* Cambridge, MA: MIT P.

————. 1970. "Remarks on Nominalisation." *English Transformational Grammar.* Eds. R. A. Jacobs and P. S. Rosenbaum. Waltham, MA: Ginn. 184-221.

————. 1981. *Lectures on Government and Binding.* Dordrecht: Foris.

————. 1988. *Language and Problems of Knowledge: The Managua Lectures.* Cambridge, MA: MIT P.

————. 1991. "Linguistics and Cognitive Science: Problems and Mysteries." *The Chomskyan Turn.* Ed. A. Kasher. Cambridge, MA: Blackwell.

————. 1992. *A Minimalist Program for Linguistic Theory.* Occasional Papers in Linguistics. Cambridge, MA: MIT P.

Chung, Sandra. 1976. "On the Subject of Two Passives in Indonesian." Li 57-98.

Chung, Sandra, and Alan Timberlake. 1985. "Tense, Aspect, and Mood." Shopen vol. 3, 202-58.

Cole, Peter. 1982. *Imbabura Quechua.* Lingua Descriptive 5. Amsterdam: North-Holland.

Comrie, Bernard. 1976a. *Aspect.* Cambridge Textbooks in Linguistics. Cambridge, UK: Cambridge UP.

———. 1976b. "The Syntax of Causative Constructions: Cross-Linguistic Similarities and Divergences." Shibatani 261-312.

———. 1981. *The Languages of the Soviet Union.* Cambridge, UK: Cambridge UP.

———. 1984. "Form and Function in Explaining Language Universals." Butterworth, Comrie, and Dahl 87-103.

———. 1985a. "Causative Verb Formation and Other Verb-Deriving Morphology." Shopen vol. 3, 309-48.

———. 1985b. *Tense.* Cambridge Textbooks in Linguistics. Cambridge, UK: Cambridge UP.

———, ed. 1987. *The World's Major Languages.* Oxford, UK: Oxford UP.

———. 1989. *Language Universals and Linguistic Typology.* 2nd ed. Chicago: U of Chicago P. (First edition published 1981)

Constable, Peter G. 1989. "Reflexives in Vera Cruz Haustec." *Work Papers of the Summer Institute of Linguistics.* Vol. 33. North Dakota: Summer Institute of Linguistics. 31-66.

Cooke, Joseph R. 1968. *Pronominal Reference in Thai, Burmese, and Vietnamese.* University of California Publications in Linguistics 52. Berkeley: U of California P.

Cooreman, Ann. 1994. "A Functional Typology of Antipassives." Fox and Hopper 49-88.

Corbett, Greville. 1991. *Gender.* Cambridge, UK: Cambridge UP.

Corbett, Greville G., Norman M. Fraser, and Scott McGlashan, eds. 1993. *Heads in Grammatical Theory.* Cambridge, UK: Cambridge UP.

Croft, William. 1990. *Typology and Universals.* Cambridge Textbooks in Linguistics. Cambridge, UK: Cambridge UP.

———. 1995. "Autonomy and Functional Linguistics." *Language* 71: 490-532.

Croft, William, Keith Denning, and Suzanne Kemmerer, eds. 1990. *Studies in Typology and Diachrony: Papers Presented to Joseph H. Greenberg on His 75th Birthday.* Amsterdam: Benjamins.

Crowley, Terry. 1992. *An Introduction to Historical Linguistics.* 2nd ed. Aukland: Oxford UP.

Cutler, Anne, John A. Hawkins, and Gary Gilligan. 1985. "The Suffixing Preference: A Processing Explanation." *Linguistics* 23: 723-58.

Dahl, Östen. 1979. "Typology of Sentence Negation." *Linguistics* 17: 79-106.

———. 1985. *Tense and Aspect Systems.* Oxford, UK: Blackwell.

Davies, John. 1981. *Kobon.* Lingua Descriptive Studies 3. Amsterdam: North-Holland.

Davies, William D. 1986. *Choctaw Verb Agreement and Universal Grammar.* Dordrecht: Reidel.

Dayley, John P. 1989. *Tümpisa (Panamint) Shoshone Grammar.* University of California Publications in Linguistics 115. Berkeley: U of California P.

DeLancey, Scott. 1981. "An Interpretation of Split Ergativity and Related Patterns." *Language* 57: 626-57.

Derbyshire, Desmond C. 1977. "Word Order Universals and the Existence of OVS Languages." *Linguistic Inquiry* 8: 590-99.

———. 1985. *Hixkaryana and Linguistic Typology.* Dallas: Summer Institute of Linguistics.

Derbyshire, Desmond C., and Geoffrey K. Pullum. 1981. "Object Initial Languages." *International Journal of American Linguistics* 47: 192-214.

Dik, Simon. 1968. *Coordination: Its Implications for the Theory of General Linguistics.* Amsterdam: North-Holland.

———. 1978. *Functional Grammar.* Amsterdam: North-Holland.

Dixon, R. M. W. 1972. *The Dyirbal Language of North Queensland.* Cambridge, UK: Cambridge UP.

———. 1979. "Ergativity." *Language* 55: 59-138.

———. 1982. *Where Have All the Adjectives Gone?* Ed. T. Givón. Amsterdam: Mouton.

———. 1988. *A Grammar of Boumaa Fijian.* Chicago: U of Chicago P.

Dooley, Robert A. 1989. "Switch Reference in Mbya Guarani: A Fair-Weather Phenomenon." *Work Papers of the Summer Institute of Linguistics.* Vol. 33. North Dakota: Summer Institute of Linguistics. 93-120.

———. 1993. *Combining Functional and Formal Approaches to Language* (photocopied material). Grand Forks, ND: Summer Institute of Linguistics.

Dougherty, Janet W. D. 1983. *West Futunu-Aniwa: An Introduction to a Polynesian Outlier Language.* University of California Publications in Linguistics 102. Berkeley: U of California P.

Downing, Pamela, and Michael Noonan, eds. 1995. *Word Order in Discourse.* Typological Studies in Language 30. Amsterdam: Benjamins.

Dowty, David. 1979. *Word Meaning and Montague Grammar.* Dordrecht: Reidel.

———. 1991. "Thematic Proto-Roles and Argument Selection." *Language* 67: 547-619.

Dryer, Matthew S. 1988a. "Object-Verb Order and Adjective-Noun Order: Dispelling a Myth." *Lingua* 74: 185-217.

———. 1988b. "Universals of Negative Position." Hammond, Moravcsik, and Wirth 93-124.

———. 1989a. "Discourse-Governed Word Order and Word Order Typology." *Universals of Language.* Belgian Journal of Linguistics 4. Eds. M. Kefer and J. van der Auwera. 69-90.

———. 1989b. "Large Linguistic Areas and Language Sampling." *Studies in Language* 13: 257-92.

———. 1991. "SVO Languages and the OV:VO Typology." *Journal of Linguistics* 27: 443-82.

———. 1992. "The Greenbergian Word Order Correlations." *Language* 68: 81-138.

———. 1994. "The Discourse Function of the Kutenai Inverse." *Voice and Inversion.* Ed. T. Givón. Amsterdam: Benjamins. 65-99.

———. 1995. "Frequency and Pragmatically Unmarked Word Order." Downing and Noonan 105-35.

Dubinsky, Stanley. 1990. "Japanese Direct Object to Indirect Object Demotion." Postal and Joseph 49-86.

Dyła, Stefan. 1984. "Across the Board Dependencies and Case in Polish." *Linguistic Inquiry* 15: 701-05.

Ebeling, C. L. 1966. "Review of Chikobava and Cercvadze's *The Grammar of Literary Avar.*" *Studia Caucasica* 2: 58-100.

Elson, Benjamin F. 1956. "Sierra Popoluca Morphology." Diss. Cornell U.

Everett, Daniel L. 1989. "Clitic Doubling, Reflexives, and Word Order Alternations in Yagua." *Language* 65: 339-72.

———. 1994. "The Sentential Divide in Language and Cognition. *Pragmatics & Cognition* 2: 131-66.

Fanning, Buist M. 1990. *Verbal Aspect in New Testament Greek.* Oxford, UK: Clarendon.

Farrell, Patrick. 1994. *Thematic Relations and Relational Grammar.* Outstanding Dissertations in Linguistics. New York: Garland.

Foley, William A., and Robert D. Van Valin, Jr. 1984. *Functional Syntax and Universal Grammar.* Cambridge, UK: Cambridge UP.

———. 1985. "Information Packaging in the Clause." Shopen vol. 1, 282-364.

Forchheimer, Paul. 1953. *The Category of Person in Language.* Berlin: de Gruyter.

Foster, Joseph F., and Charles A. Hofling. 1987. "Word Order, Case, and Agreement." *Linguistics* 25: 475-99.

Fox, Barbara A. 1987. "The Noun Phrase Accessibility Hierarchy Revisited." *Language* 63: 856-70.

Fox, Barbara A., and Paul J. Hopper, eds. 1994. *Voice: Beyond Form and Function.* Typological Studies in Language 27. Amsterdam: Benjamins.

Frajzyngier, Zygmunt. 1974. "NP nɛ (NP) in Awutu: A Problem in Case Grammar." *Language Sciences,* 8-14.

Freedland, L. S. 1951. *Language of the Sierra Miwok.* Indiana University Publications in Anthropology and Linguistics VI. Bloomington: Indiana U.

Fukui, Naoki. 1995. "The Principles-and-Parameters Approach: A Comparative Syntax of English and Japanese." Shibatani and Bynon 327-72.

Gedney, William J. 1991. *The Yay Language.* Michigan Papers on South and Southeast Asia. Ed. T. J. Hudak. Ann Arbor: U of Michigan, Center for South and South East Asian Studies.

Gerdts, Donna B. 1989. "Relational Parameters of Reflexives." *Theoretical Perspectives on Native American Languages.* Eds. D. B. Gerdts and K. Michelson. Albany: State U of New York. 259-80.

———. 1990. "Relational Visibility." *Grammatical Relations: A Cross-Theoretical Perspective.* Eds. K. Dziwirek, P. Farrell, and E. Mejias-Bikandi. Stanford, CA: CSLI. 199-214.

———. 1991. "Case, Chomage, and Multipredicate Domains in Korean." *Proc. of the Harvard Workshop on Korean Linguistics 4.*

———. 1992. "Morphologically-Mediated Relational Profiles." *Proc. of the Eighteenth Annual Meeting of the Berkeley Linguistics Society.* 322-37.

Gerdts, Donna B., and Lindsay J. Whaley. 1992. "Kinyarwanda Multiple Applicatives and the 2-AEX." *Paper from the Twenty-Eighth Regional Meeting of the Chicago Linguistic Society.* 186-205.

Gibson, Jeanne D. 1980. "Clause Union in Chamorro and in Universal Grammar." Diss. U of California at San Diego.

Gill, H. S., and Henry A. Gleason. 1963. *A Reference Grammar of Punjabi.* Hartford: Hartford Seminary Foundation.

Givón, Talmy. 1971. "Historical Syntax and Synchronic Morphology: An Archaeologist's Field Trip." *Proc. of the Seventh Regional Meeting of the Chicago Linguistics Society.* 394-415.

———. 1973. "The Time-Axis Phenomenon." *Language* 49: 890-925.

———. 1976. "Topic, Pronoun and Grammatical Agreement." Li 149-88.

———. 1979. *On Understanding Grammar.* New York: Academic Press.

———. 1980. "The Binding Hierarchy and the Typology of Complements." *Studies in Language* 4: 333-77.

———. 1984/1990. *Syntax: A Functional-Typological Introduction.* Amsterdam: Benjamins. 2 vols.

Glover, Warren. 1974. *Semantic and Grammatical Structures in Gurung (Nepal).* Norman, OK: Summer Institute of Linguistics.

Greenberg, Joseph H. 1954. "A Quantitative Approach to the Morphological Typology of Language." *Method and Perspective in Anthropology.* Ed. R. F. Spencer. Minneapolis: U of Minnesota. 192-220. (Reprinted in the *International Journal of American Linguistics* 26: 178-94. 1960)

———. ed. 1963. *Universals of Language.* Cambridge, MA: MIT P.

———. 1966. "Some Universals of Language With Particular Reference to the Order of Meaningful Elements." Greenberg 73-113.

———. 1974. *Language Typology: A Historical and Analytical Overview.* Janua Linguarum, Series Minor 184. The Hague: Mouton.

———. 1978. "Diachrony, Synchrony, and Language Universals." Greenberg, Ferguson, and Moravcsik vol. 1, 61-92.

Greenberg, Joseph H., C. A. Ferguson, and E. A. Moravcsik. Eds. 1978. *Universals of Human Language.* Stanford, CA: Stanford UP. 4 vols.

Gregores, Emma, and Jorge A. Suarez. 1967. *A Description of Colloquial Guarani.* The Hague: Mouton.

Haegeman, Liliane. 1994. *Introduction to Government and Binding Theory.* 2nd ed. Oxford, UK: Blackwell.

Haiman, John. 1980. "The Iconicity of Grammar: Isomorphism and Motivation. *Language* 54: 565-89.

———. 1983. "Iconic and Economic Motivation." *Language* 59: 781-819.

———. 1985. *Natural Syntax: Iconicity and Erosion.* Cambridge, UK: Cambridge UP.

Haiman, John, and Pamela Munro, eds. 1983. *Switch Reference and Universal Grammar.* Amsterdam: Benjamins.

Hale, Ken. 1983. "Warlpiri and the Grammar of Non-Configurational Languages." *Natural Language and Linguistic Theory* 1: 5-47.

———. 1992. "Basic Word Order in Two 'Free Word Order' Languages." Payne 63-82.

Hall, Christopher J. 1988. "Integrating Diachronic and Processing Principles in Explaining the Suffixing Preference." Hawkins 321-49.

Hammond, Michael, Edith A. Moravcsik, and Jessica R. Wirth, Eds. 1988. *Studies in Syntactic Typology.* Typological Studies in Language 17. Amsterdam: Benjamins.

Hanks, William. 1990. *Referential Practice: Language and Lived Space Among the Maya.* Chicago: U of Chicago P.

Harris, Alice. 1982. "Georgian and the Unaccusative Hypothesis." *Language* 58: 290-306.

Haspelmath, Martin. 1990. "The Grammaticization of Passive Morphology." *Studies in Language* 14: 25-72.

———. 1994. "Passive Participles Across Languages." Fox and Hopper 151-77.

Haugen, Einar. 1987. "Danish, Norwegian, and Swedish." Comrie 157-79.

Hawkins, John A. 1979. "Implicational Universals as Predicators of Word Order Change." *Language* 55: 618-48.

———. 1983. *Word Order Universals.* New York: Academic Press.

———, ed. 1988a. *Explaining Language Universals.* Oxford: Blackwell.

———. 1988b. "On Explaining Some Left-Right Asymmetries in Syntactic and Morphological Universals." Hammond, Moravcsik, and Wirth 321-57.

———. 1990. "A Parsing Theory of Word Order Universals." *Linguistic Inquiry* 21: 223-62.

———. 1994. *A Performance Theory of Order and Constituency.* Cambridge, UK: Cambridge UP.

Hawkins, John A., and Anne Cutler. 1988. "Psycholinguistic Factors in Morphological Asymmetry." Hawkins 280-317.

Heath, Jeff. 1976. "Antipassivization: A Functional Typology." *Proc. of the Second Annual Meeting of the Berkeley Linguistics Society.* 202-11.

Hetzron, Robert. 1972. *Ethiopian Semitic.* Manchester: Manchester UP.

———. 1976. "On the Hungarian Causative Verb and Its Syntax." Shibatani 371-98.

Hope, Reginald R. 1974. *The Deep Syntax of Lisu Sentences.* Canberra: Australian National U.

Hopper, Paul J., and Sandra Thompson. 1984. "The Discourse Basis for Lexical Categories in Universal Grammar." *Language* 60: 703-52.

Hubbard, Philip L. 1980. "The Syntax of the Albanian Verb Complex." Diss. U of California at San Diego.

Hu, Z. Y. 1986. *Elunchunyu jianzhi.* Beijing: Minzu Chubanshe.

Huang, C.-T. J. 1982. "Logical Relations in Chinese and a Theory of Grammar." Diss. MIT.

Hudson, Richard A. 1987. "Zwicky on Heads." *Journal of Linguistics* 23: 109-32.

von Humboldt, Wilhelm. 1971. *Linguistic Variability & Intellectual Development.* Trans. G. Beck and F. Raven. Philadelphia: U of Pennsylvania P. (Originally published in 1836 by the Royal

Academy of Sciences in Berlin under the title *Über die Verschiedenheit des menschlichen Sprachbaues und ihren Einfluss auf die geistige Entwickelung des Menschengeschlechts*)

Hyman, Larry M. 1984. "Form and Substance in Language Universals." Butterworth, Comrie, and Dahl 67-85.

Ingram, David. 1978. "Typology and Universals of Personal Pronouns." Greenberg, Ferguson, and Moravcsik vol. 3, 213-48.

Jackendoff, Ray S. 1987. "The Status of Thematic Relations in Linguistic Theory." *Linguistic Inquiry* 18: 369-411.

Jacobsen, W. H. 1979. "Noun and Verb in Nootkan." *The Victoria Conference on Northwestern Languages*. Ed. B. S. Erfat. Victoria, BC: British Columbia Provincial Museum. 83-153.

Jakobson, Roman. 1929. "Remarques sur l'Évolution Phonologique du Russe Comparée à Celle des Autres Langues Slave." *Travaux du Cercle Linguistique de Prague* 2: 7-116.

———. 1963. "Implications of Language Universals for Linguistics." Greenberg 263-98.

Josephs, Lewis S. 1975. *Palauan Reference Grammar.* Honolulu: U of Hawaii P.

Kakumasu, J. Y. 1976. "Gramática Generativa Preliminar da língua Urubú. *Série Lingüística* 5: 267-300.

Kay, Paul, and Chad K. McDaniel. 1978. "The Linguistic Significance of the Meanings of Basic Color Terms." *Language* 54: 610-46.

Kayne, Richard S. 1994. *The Antisymmetry of Syntax.* Linguistic Inquiry Monographs 25. Cambridge, MA: MIT P.

Keating, Patricia, Wendy Linker, and Marie Huffman. 1983. "Patterns in Allophone Distribution for Voiced and Voiceless Stops." *UCLA Working Papers in Phonetics* 57: 61-78.

Keenan, Edward L. 1976. "Towards a Universal Definition of 'subject.' " Li 303-33.

———. 1985a. "Passive in the World's Languages." Shopen vol. 1, 243-81.

———. 1985b. "Relative Clauses." Shopen vol. 2, 141-70.

Keenan, Edward L., and Bernard Comrie. 1977. "Noun Phrase Accessibility and Universal Grammar." *Linguistic Inquiry* 8: 63-99.

———. 1979. "Data on the Noun Phrase Accessibility Hierarchy." *Language* 55: 333-51.

Kibrik, Alexandr E. 1985. "Toward a Typology of Ergativity." *Grammar Inside and Outside the Clause*. Nichols and Woodbury 268-323.

———. 1991. "Semantically Ergative Languages in Typological Perspective." *Work Papers of the Summer Institute of Linguistics*. Vol. 35. North Dakota: Summer Institute of Linguistics. 67-90.

Kimenyi, Alexandre. 1980. *A Relational Grammar of Kinyarwanda.* Berkeley: U of California P.

Kiss, Katalin É. 1994. "Sentence Structure and Word Order." *The Syntactic Structure of Hungarian*. Syntax and Semantics 27. Eds. F. Kiefer and K. Kiss. New York: Academic Press. 1-90.

Klein-Andreu, Flora, ed. 1983. *Discourse Perspectives on Syntax.* New York: Academic Press.

König, Ekkehard. 1988. "Concessive Connectives and Concessive Sentences: Cross-Linguistic Regularities and Pragmatic Principles." Hawkins 145-66.

Kornfilt, Jaklin. 1987. "Turkish and the Turkic Languages." Comrie 619-44.

Kouwenberg, Silvia, and Eric Murray. 1994. *Papiamentu.* Languages of the World 83. München-Newcastle: Lincom Europa.

Kozintseva, Natalia. 1995. *Modern Eastern Armenian.* Languages of the World/Materials 22. München-Newcastle: Lincom Europa.

Kuno, Susumo. 1973. *The Structure of the Japanese Language.* Cambridge, MA: MIT P.

———. 1974. "The Position of Relative Clauses and Conjunctions." *Linguistic Inquiry* 5: 117-36.

———. 1987. *Functional Syntax.* Chicago: U of Chicago P.

Language Files. 1992. 5th ed. Columbus: Ohio State U, Department of Linguistics.

Lawal, S. Adenike. 1983. "On Defining Complex Sentences in Yoruba." Diss. U of Essex.

Lee, Michael. 1988. "Language, Perception, and the World." Hawkins 211-46.

Lehmann, Christian. 1988. "Towards a Typology of Clause Linkage." *Clause Combining in Grammar and Discourse.* Eds. J. Haiman and S. Thompson. Amsterdam: Benjamins. 181-225.

Lehmann, Winfred P. 1973. "A Structural Principle of Language and Its Implications." *Language* 49: 47-66.

——. 1978a. "Conclusion: Toward an Understanding of the Profound Unity Underlying Languages." Lehmann 395-432.

——, ed. 1978b. *Syntactic Typology.* Austin: U of Texas P.

——. 1986. "On the Typology of Relative Clauses." *Linguistics* 24: 663-80.

Lewis, Marshall. 1984. "Relative Clauses in Aŋlɔ Ewe." *Studies in African Linguistics* suppl. 9, 196-202.

Li, Charles N., ed. 1975. *Word Order and Word Order Change.* Austin: U of Texas P.

——, ed. 1976. *Subject and Topic.* New York: Academic Press.

Li, Charles N., and Sandra A. Thompson. 1981. *Mandarin Chinese: A Functional Reference Grammar.* Berkeley: U of California P.

Lorimer, David L. R. 1935. *The Burushaski Language.* 3 vols. Cambridge, MA: Harvard UP.

Lukas, J. 1967. *Study of the Kanuri Language.* International African Institute.

Lyon, S. 1967. "Tlahuitoltepec Mixe Clause Structure." *International Journal of American Linguistics* 33: 25-45.

Lyons, John. 1991. *Chomsky.* 3rd ed. Cambridge, UK: Cambridge UP.

Mace, John. 1962. *Modern Persian.* London: English Universities P.

Maddieson, Ian. 1984. *Patterns of Sounds.* Cambridge, UK: Cambridge UP.

Malchukov, Andrei L. 1995. *Even.* Languages of the World 12. München-Newcastle: Lincom Europa.

Mallinson, Graham, and Barry J. Blake. 1981. *Language Typology.* Amsterdam: North-Holland.

Marchese, Lynell. 1986. *Tense/Aspect and the Development of Auxiliaries in Kru Languages.* Dallas: Summer Institute of Linguistics and U of Texas at Arlington.

Marcus, David. 1978. *A Manual of Akkadian.* New York: UP of America.

Marlett, Stephen A. 1984. "Switch-Reference and Subject Raising in Seri." *The Syntax of Native American Languages.* Syntax and Semantics 16. Eds. E. D. Cook and D. B. Gerdts. New York: Academic Press. 247-68.

Marslen-Wilson, William D., and Lorraine K. Tyler. 1980. "The Temporal Structure of Spoken Language Understanding." *Cognition* 8: 1-71.

McLendon, Sally. 1978. "Ergativity, Case and Transitivity in Eastern Pomo." *International Journal of American Linguistics* 44: 1-9.

Merlan, Francesca. 1981. "Some Functional Relations Among Subordination, Mood, Aspect, and Focus in Australian Languages." *Australian Journal of Linguistics* 1: 175-210.

Merrifield, William R., Constance M. Naish, Calvin R. Rensch, and Gillian Story. 1982. *Laboratory Manual for Morphology and Syntax.* 5th ed. (third impression). Dallas: Summer Institute of Linguistics.

Micelli, Gabriele, and Alfonso Caramazza. 1988. "Dissociation of Inflectional and Derivational Morphology." *Brain and Language* 35: 24-65.

Michelson, Karin. 1991. "Semantic Features of Agent and Patient Core Case Marking in Oneida." *Buffalo Papers in Linguistics* 91-01: 114-46.

Mithun, Marianne. 1986. "On the Nature of Noun Incorporation." *Language* 62: 32-38.

——. 1992. "Is Basic Word Order Universal?" Payne 15-61.

Mondloch, James. 1978. *Basic Quiche Grammar.* Albany: State U of New York Institute for Mesoamerican Studies.

Mohanan, K. P. 1982. "Grammatical Relations and Clause Structure in Malayalam." *The Mental Representation of Grammatical Relations.* Ed. J. Bresnan. Cambridge, MA: MIT P. 504-89.
Moravcsik, Edith A. 1978. "Agreement." Greenberg, Ferguson, and Moravcsik vol. 4, 331-74.
Morgan, David. 1994. "Semantic Constraints on Relevance in Lobala Discourse." *Discourse Features of Ten Languages of West-Central Africa.* Ed. S. Levinsohn. Dallas: The Summer Institute of Linguistics and U of Texas at Arlington. 125-49.
Morolong, Malillo, and Larry M. Hyman. 1977. "Animacy, Objects and Clitics in Sesotho." *Studies in African Linguistics* 8: 199-218.
Moshi, Lioba. 1994. "Time Reference Markers in KiVunjo-Chaga." *Journal of African Languages and Linguistics* 15: 127-59.
Murane, Elizabeth. 1974. *Daga Grammar.* Norman, OK: Summer Institute of Linguistics.
Myers-Scotton, Carol. 1993. *Dueling Languages: Grammatical Structure in Code-Switching.* Oxford, UK: Clarendon.
Myhill, John. 1992a. *Typological Discourse Analysis.* Oxford, UK: Blackwell.
———. 1992b. "Word Order and Temporal Sequencing." Payne 265-78.
Neidle, Carol. 1988. *The Role of Case in Russian Syntax.* Dordrecht: Kluwer.
Newmeyer, Frederick J. 1983. *Grammatical Theory: Its Limits and Its Possibilities.* Chicago: U of Chicago P.
Nichols, Johanna. 1986. "Head-Marking and Dependent-Marking Grammar." *Language* 62: 56-119.
———. 1992. *Linguistic Diversity in Space and Time.* Chicago: U of Chicago P.
Nichols, Johanna, and Anthony C. Woodbury, eds. 1985. *Grammar Inside and Outside the Clause.* Cambridge, UK: Cambridge UP.
Noonan, Michael. 1985. "Complementation." Shopen vol. 2, 42-140.
Okell, John. 1969. *A Reference Grammar of Colloquial Burmese.* 2 vols. London: Oxford UP.
Olson, Mike. 1981. "Barai Clause Junctures: Toward a Functional Theory of Interclausal Relations." Diss. Australian National U.
Palmer, F. R. 1986. *Mood and Modality.* Cambridge Textbooks in Linguistics. Cambridge, UK: Cambridge UP.
———. 1994. *Grammatical Roles and Relations.* Cambridge Textbooks in Linguistics. Cambridge, UK: Cambridge UP.
Payne, Doris L. 1985. "Aspects of the Grammar of Yagua: A Typological Perspective." Diss. U of California at Los Angeles.
———. 1987. "Information Structuring in Papago Narrative Discourse." *Language* 63: 783-804.
———. 1992a. "Nonidentifiable Information and Pragmatic Order Rules in 'O'odham." Payne 137-66.
———, ed. 1992b. *Pragmatics of Word Order Flexibility.* Amsterdam: Benjamins.
Payne, John R. 1985a. "Complex Phrases and Complex Sentences." Shopen vol. 2, 3-41.
———. 1985b. "Negation." Shopen vol. 1, 197-242.
Perkins, Revere. 1980. "The Coevolution of Grammar and Culture." Diss. State U of New York at Buffalo.
———. 1989. "Statistical Techniques for Determining Language Sample Size." *Studies in Language* 13: 293-315.
Postal, Paul M., and Brian D. Joseph, eds. 1990. *Studies in Relational Grammar 3.* Chicago: U of Chicago P.
Pullum, Geoffrey. 1979. "Rev. of *Universals of Human Language,*" eds. J. H. Greenberg, C. A. Ferguson, and E. A. Moravcsik. *Linguistics* 17: 925-44.
Quakenbush, J. Stephen. 1992. "Word Order and Discourse: An Austronesian Example." Payne 279-303.

Ramat, Paolo. 1987. *Linguistic Typology.* Berlin: de Gruyter.

––––––. 1995. "Typological Comparison: Towards a Historical Perspective." Shibatani and Bynon 27-48.

Raz, Shlomo. 1983. *Tigre Grammar and Texts.* Malibu: Undena.

Rijkhoff, Jan, Dik Bakker, Kees Hengeveld, and Peter Kahrel. 1993. "A Method of Language Sampling." *Studies in Language* 17: 169-203.

Rijksbaron, Albert. 1984. *The Syntax and Semantics of the Verb in Classical Greek.* Amsterdam: Gieben.

Rosen, Carol. 1984. "The Interface Between Semantic Roles and Initial Grammatical Relations." *Studies in Relational Grammar 2.* Eds. D. Perlmutter and C. Rosen. Chicago: U of Chicago P.

Rudin, Catherine. 1988. "On Multiple Questions and Multiple wh-Fronting." *Natural Language and Linguistic Theory* 6: 445-501.

Ruhlen, Merritt. 1987. *A Guide to the World's Languages, Vol. 1: Classification.* Stanford, CA: Stanford UP.

Russell, Bertrand. 1948. *Human Knowledge: Its Scope and Limits.* New York: Simon & Schuster.

Sabimana, Firmard. 1986. "The Relational Structure of the Kirundi Verb." Diss. Indiana U.

Sadock, Jerrold M., and Arnold M. Zwicky. 1985. "Speech Act Distinctions in Syntax." Shopen vol. 1, 155-96.

Salkie, Raphael. 1990. *The Chomsky Update.* London: Unwin Hyman.

Sapir, Edward. 1921. *Language.* New York: Harcourt, Brace and World.

Saxton, Dean. 1982. "Papago." *Uto-Aztecan Grammar, Vol. 3.* Ed. R. Langacker. Dallas: Summer Institute of Linguistics. 93-266.

Schacter, Paul. 1974. "A Transformational Account of Serial Verbs." *Studies in African Linguistics* suppl. 5, 253-70.

––––––. 1985. "Parts-of-Speech Systems." Shopen vol. 1, 3-61.

Schuh, Russell G. 1972. "Aspects of Ngizim Syntax." Diss. U of California at Los Angeles.

Searle, John. 1969. *Speech Acts: An Essay in the Philosophy of Language.* Cambridge, UK: Cambridge UP.

Seiler, Wolf. 1978. "The Modalis Case in Iñupiaq." *Work Papers of the Summer Institute of Linguistics.* Vol. 22. 71-85. North Dakota: Summer Institute of Linguistics.

Sells, Peter. 1984. "Syntax and Semantics of Resumptive Pronouns." Diss. U of Massachusetts at Amherst.

Senn, Alfred. 1966. *Handbuch der Litauischen Sprache, I: Grammatik.* Heidelberg: Winter.

Sgall, Petr. 1995. "Prague School Typology." Shibatani and Bynon 49-84.

Shibatani, Masayoshi. 1973. "Lexical Versus Periphrastic Causatives in Korean." *Journal of Linguistics* 9: 281-97.

––––––, ed. 1976. *The Grammar of Causative Constructions.* Syntax and Semantics 6. New York: Academic Press.

Shibatani, Masayoshi, and Theodora Bynon, eds. 1995. *Approaches to Language Typology.* Oxford, UK: Clarendon.

Shopen, Timothy, ed. 1985. *Language Typology and Syntactic Description.* 3 vols. Cambridge, UK: Cambridge UP.

Silverstein, Michael. 1976. "Hierarchy of Features and Ergativity." *Grammatical Categories in Australian Languages.* Ed. R. M. W. Dixon. Canberra: Australian Institute of Aboriginal Studies. 112-71.

Skalička, Vladamir. 1935. *Zur ungarischen Grammatik.* Prague.

––––––. 1979. *Typologische Studien.* Braunschweig/Wiesbadden: Vieweg.

Song, Jae Jung. 1991a. "Causatives and Universal Grammar: An Alternative Explanation." *Transaction of the Philological Society* 89: 65-94.

————. 1991b. "On Tomlin, and Manning and Parker on Basic Word Order." *Language Sciences* 13: 89-97.

Steever, Sanford B. 1987. "Tamil and the Dravidian Languages." Comrie 725-46.

Swadesh, Morris. 1938. "Nootka Internal Syntax." *International Journal of American Linguistics* 9: 77-102.

Talmy, Leonard. 1976. "Semantic Causative Types." Shibatani 43-116.

————. 1985. "Lexicalization Patterns: Semantic Structure in Lexical Forms." Shopen vol. 3, 57-149.

————. 1987. "The Relation of Grammar to Cognition." *Topics in Cognitive Linguistics*. Ed. B. Rudzka-Ostyn. Amsterdam: Benjamins.

Tesnière, Lucien. 1959. *Elements de Syntaxe Structurale*. Paris: Klincksieck.

Thompson, Sandra A. 1978. "Modern English From a Typological Point of View: Some Implications of the Function of Word Order." *Linguistische Berichte* 54: 19-35.

————. 1988. "A Discourse Approach to the Cross-Linguistic Category 'Adjective.' " Hawkins 167-85.

Thompson, Sandra A., and Robert E. Longacre. 1985. "Adverbial Clauses." Shopen vol. 2, 171-234.

Tomlin, Russell S. 1986. *Basic Word Order: Functional Principles*. London: Croom Helm.

————, ed. 1987. *Coherence and Grounding in Discourse*. Amsterdam: Benjamins.

Trubetzkoy, Nikolai S. 1931. "Die Phonologischen Systeme." *Travaux du cercle Linguistique de Prague* 4: 96-116.

————. 1939. *Grundzüge der Phonologie*. Prague: Cercle Linguistique de Prague.

Tucker, A. N., and J. T. Mpaayei. 1955. *A Maasai Grammar*. London: Longmans.

Van Valin, Robert D., Jr. 1985. "Case Marking and the Structure of the Lakhota Clause." Nichols and Woodbury 363-413.

————, ed. 1993a. *Advances in Role and Reference Grammar*. Amsterdam: Benjamins.

————. 1993b. "A Synopsis of 'Role and Reference Grammar.' " Van Valin 1-164.

Van Valin, Robert D., Jr., and David P. Wilkins. 1993. "Predicting Syntactic Structure From Semantic Representation: *Remember* in English and Its Equivalents in Mparntwe Arrernte." Van Valin 499-534.

Vendler, Zeno. 1967. *Linguistics in Philosophy*. Ithaca, NY: Cornell UP.

Venneman, Theo. 1973. "Explanation in Syntax." *Syntax and Semantics 2*. Ed. J. Kimball. New York: Academic Press. 1-50.

————. 1974a. "Analogy in Generative Grammar: The Origin of Word Order." *Proceedings of the Eleventh International Congress of Linguists*. Ed. L. Heilmann. Bologna: Il Mulino. 79-83.

————. 1974b. "Theoretical Word Order Studies: Results and Problems." *Papiere zur Linguistik* 7: 5-25.

————. 1976. "Categorial Grammar and the Order of Meaningful Elements." *Linguistic Studies Offered to Joseph Greenberg on the Occasion of His Sixtieth Birthday*. Ed. A. Juilland. Saratoga, CA: Anma Libri. 615-34.

Wald, Benji. 1987. "Swahili and the Bantu Languages." Comrie 991-1014.

Watters, James K. 1988. "Topics in Tepehua Grammar." Diss. U of California at Berkeley.

————. 1993. "An Investigation of Turkish Clause Linkage." Van Valin 535-60.

Weber, David J. 1981. "A Note on Valence: Quechua vs. Quichean." *Notes on Linguistics* 20: 25-29.

————. 1983. *Relativization and Nominalized Clauses in Huallaga Quechua*. Berkeley: U of California P.

Whaley, Lindsay J. 1993. "The Status of Obliques in Linguistic Theory." Diss. State University of New York at Buffalo.

White, Lydia, Lisa Travis, and Anna MacLachlan. 1992. "The Acquisition of Wh-Question Formation by Malagasy Learners of English: Evidence for Universal Grammar." *Canadian Journal of Linguistics* 37: 341-68.

Wilkins, David P. 1988. "Switch-Reference in Mparntwe Arrernte (Aranda): Form, Function, and Problems of Identity." Complex Sentence Constructions in Australian Languages. Ed. P. Austin. Amsterdam: Benjamins. 141-76.

Witherspoon, Gary. 1977. *Language and Art in the Navajo Universe*. Ann Arbor: U of Michigan P.

Zhang, Yan Chang, Bing Li, and Xi Zhang. 1989. *The Oroqen Language*. Beijing: Jilin UP.

Zigmond, Maurice L., Curtis G. Booth, and Pamela Munro. 1990. *Kawaiisu*. University of California Publications in Linguistics 119. Berkeley: U of California P.

Zwicky, Arnold. 1985. "Heads." *Journal of Linguistics* 21: 1-29.

INDEX

Abaza language, xxi, 165, 166
Abkhaz language, xxi, 166, 179
Abraham, R. C., 272
Absolute tense, 217
    definition of, 281
    versus relative tense, 209-210, 281
Absolute universal(s), 32, 52, 54
    definition of, 281
    See also Language universals
Absolutive nominal, 72, 73, 73, 291
    definition of, 281
Accomplishment(s), 216, 217, 282
    definition of, 215, 281
Accusative-focus system, 158, 169
    definition of, 281
Achenese language, xxii, 71
Achievement(s), 216, 217, 282
    definition of, 215, 281
Active sentences, 43-45
Activities, 216, 217, 282
    definition of, 215, 281
Adpositions, 289
Adverbial clauses, 247-248, 249, 250-255,
    266, 283, 291
    cause and, 252-253
    concessives and, 254, 283
    conditional, 253-254
    definition of, 281

    location and, 252
    time and, 251
    unspecified relationships in, 254-
        255
Affix, 283, 287, 290
    bound, 115, 116
    nominalizing, 187
Affixal language(s), 20, 28, 282
    definition of, 282
    versus isolating languages, 282
    See also Synthetic languages
Affixal morpheme, 119
Affixation, 114, 287, 288
    circumfixing, 117, 119
    extensive use of, 131
    infixing, 117, 119
    mapping, 133
    measure, 286
    reduplicating, 117, 119
    suprafixing, 119, 126
    See also Index of Fusion; Index of Synthe-
        sis; Prefixation; Suffixation
Affix ordering, 114, 124-125
Afro-Asiatic languages, xxi, 11, 38. *See also*
       specific Afro-Asiatic languages
Agent, 66, 67, 73, 161
    as semantic role, 56, 65, 290
    definition of, 282

ABOUT THE AUTHOR

Lindsay Whaley earned a Ph.D. in linguistics at the State University of New York at Buffalo. He currently holds a joint appointment in classics and linguistics at Dartmouth College in Hanover, New Hampshire.